Basic Algebra: First S

cK-12 *flexbooK*
next generation textbooks

To access a customizable version of this book, as well as other interactive content, visit www.ck12.org

CONTRIBUTORS
Cover photo by Dansk: Dedikeret til matematik
Cover Source: commons.wikimedia.org/

Contents

CHAPTER  Real Number System

Chapter Outline

1.1 Real Numbers

Categorize rational numbers and know that real numbers that are not rational are irrational. Convert a decimal expansion to a rational number.By the end of this lesson, you should be able to define and give an example of the following vocabulary words:

- **Rational Number** - a number that can be written as a quotient $\frac{a}{b}$, where a and b are integers and $b \neq 0$. The decimal form of a rational number either terminates or repeats.
- **Irrational Number** - a real number that cannot be written as a quotient of two integers. The decimal form of an irrational number is non-terminating and non-repeating.
- **Natural/Counting Number** - the numbers...1, 2, 3, 4...consisting of the counting numbers.
- **Whole Number** - the numbers...0, 1, 2, 3, 4...consisting of the natural numbers including zero.
- **Integers** - the numbers...-4, -3, -2, -1, 0, 1, 2, 3..., consisting of the negative integers, zero, and the positive integers.

Example 1

All of the numbers you have learned about so far in math belong to the real number system. Positives, negatives, fractions, and decimals are all part of the real number system. The diagram below shows how all of the numbers in the real number system are grouped.

Real Numbers

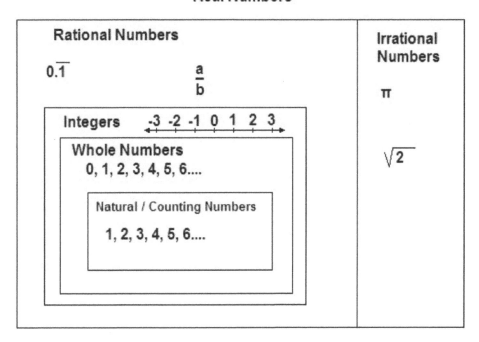

If a real number can be expressed as a **rational number**, it falls into one of two categories.

- If the denominator of its simplest form is one, then it is an **integer** (i.e. -2, -1, 0, 1, etc..). Integers can be broken down further into**:**
    - **whole** numbers (counting numbers plus 0)
    - **natural** numbers (just counting numbers, leave out the 0).

- If not, it is a **fraction** (this term also includes decimals, since they can be written as fractions.)

If the number <u>cannot</u> be expressed as the ratio of two integers (i.e. as a fraction), it is **irrational**. Irrational numbers have decimals that do not terminate or repeat (more on that later).

Can you think of any famous irrational numbers? By now, you should know at least one. Remember, an irrational number keeps going on and on (nonterminating) and does not have a repeating pattern, so it can't be written as a fraction. Watch this video to check out some famous irrational numbers.

Watch This

MEDIA
Click image to the left or use the URL below.
URL: https://www.ck12.org/flx/render/embeddedobject/52886

CK-12 Foundation: 0210S Irrational Numbers (H264)

Example 2

Write $-0.\overline{37}$ as a rational number $\left(\frac{a}{b}\right)$.

To convert a decimal expansion to a rational number, first set-up an equivalent equation and solve for x.

$x = 0.\overline{37}$ or $0.373737...$

To write an equivalent equation, move one repeating section to left of the decimal by multiplying both sides by 10^n, where n is the number of repeating digits. In this case the repeating section contains 2 digits, so multiply both sides by 100 or 10^2.

$100x = 37.\overline{37}$

Now subtract x from 100x, then solve for x and simplify to find the rational number.

$$100x = 37.\overline{37}$$
$$- \quad x = 0.\overline{37}$$

$$99x = 37$$
$$x = \frac{37}{99}$$

Tips & Tricks

- Rational Numbers can belong to more than one group, so the number 2 is classified as a natural number, whole number, integer, rational number, and a real number.
- Rational Numbers can be written as a terminating or repeating decimal.
- Irrational Numbers in the decimal form are non-terminating and non-repeating.
- When converting decimal expansion to rational numbers, set-up an equivalent equation by multiplying each side by 10^n, where n is the number of repeating digits. Then, subtract x from both sides and simplify.

Practice

1. Classify each of the following numbers as a rational, integer, whole and/or natural number. Some numbers will have more than one classification.

    a. 3.45

    b. -9

    c. 1,270

    d. 0

    e. $1.\overline{23}$

2. Identify which of the following are rational numbers and which are irrational numbers.

    a. 23.7

    b. $-3.\overline{3}$

    c. π

    d. 2.8956

    e. - 0.4682749302......

    f. -9

3. Classify each of the following numbers as irrational, rational, integer, whole and/or natural number. Some numbers will have more than one classification.

    a. $\frac{4}{5}$

    b. -232,323

    c. 98

    d. 2.38048303851...

    e. 3.567567

    f. $\frac{22}{43}$

4. Express the following decimals as fractions.

    a. 0.439

    b. $0.\overline{7}$

    c. $0.\overline{24}$

    d. $-0.\overline{12}$

    e. $1.\overline{45}$

5. Is the number 0.303003030003.... a rational number? Why or Why not?

Bobcat Review

1. Express the following fractions as decimals.

    a. $\frac{1}{2}$

    b. $-\frac{1}{3}$

    c. $\frac{28}{64}$

    d. $-3\frac{5}{11}$

    e. $-\frac{17}{22}$

2. Order the following students by height from the tallest to shortest. Betsy is $5\frac{7}{8}'$, Andrew is $5\frac{11}{12}'$, Lisa is $5.65'$, and George is $5.2'$.

3. Complete the following statements with either >, <, or =.

    a. $\frac{6}{7}$ _____ $\frac{8}{9}$

    b. 0.2878 _____ $\frac{7}{24}$

    c. $-\frac{1}{5}$ _____ -0.21

    d. $-\frac{7}{9}$ _____ $-\frac{21}{29}$

    e. $\frac{5}{6}$ _____ $0.8\overline{3}$

Bobcat Stretch

1. Convert the following decimals to a fractions.

      a. $1.\overline{327}$

      b. $-0.\overline{4857}$

      c. $0.25\overline{38}$

      d. $-5.4839\overline{22}$

Further Review

For more videos and practice problems,

- click here to go to Khan Academy.
- search for "converting 1-digit repeating decimals to fractions" on Khan Academy (www.khanacademy.org).
- click here for more practice problems to review how to convert a fraction to a repeating decimal.
- go to Khan Academy's Common Core page standard 8.NS.A.1 (www.khanacademy.org/commoncore/grade -8-NS).

Watch this video to review converting decimal expansions to rational numbers.

MEDIA
Click image to the left or use the URL below.
URL: https://www.ck12.org/flx/render/embeddedobject/104632

Answers

1.a. Rational

  b. Rational, Integer

  c. Rational, Integer, Whole, Natural

  d. Rational, Integer, Whole

  e. Rational

2.a. Rational

  b. Rational

  c. Irrational

  d. Rational

  e. Irrational

  f. Rational

3.a. Rational

  b. Rational, Integer

  c. Rational, Integer, Whole, Natural

  d. Irrational

  e. Rational

  f. Rational

4.a. 0.439 can be expressed as $\frac{4}{10} + \frac{3}{100} + \frac{9}{1000}$, or just $\frac{439}{1000}$.

  b. $\frac{7}{9}$

  c. $\frac{8}{33}$

  d. $-\frac{4}{33}$

  e. $\frac{144}{99} = \frac{16}{11}$

5. Irrational

Bobcat Review

1.a. 0.5

  b. $-0.\overline{3}$

  c. 0.4375

  d. $-3.\overline{45}$

  e. $-0.77\overline{27}$ or $-0.7\overline{72}$

2. Andrew, Betsy, Lisa and George

3.a. <

  b. <

  c. >

  d. <

  e. =

Bobcat Stretch

1. a. $\frac{442}{333}$ or $1\frac{109}{333}$

  b. $-\frac{4857}{9999}$

  c. $0.25\overline{38}$ can be expressed as $\frac{25}{100} + \frac{38}{9900}$, which is equivalent to $\frac{2513}{9900}$.

  d. $-\frac{5429083}{990000}$ or $-5\frac{479083}{990000}$

1.2 Rational and Irrational Numbers

Estimate values of square roots. Compare size of irrational numbers and plot real numbers on a number line.

By the end of this lesson, you should be able to define and give an example of the following vocabulary words:

- **Terminating Decimal** - a decimal that has a final digit. If the quotient of two numbers has a remainder of zero.
- **Repeating Decimal** - a decimal that has one or more digits that repeat without end.
- **Non-terminating/Non-repeating Decimal** - a decimal that does not terminate or repeat - it goes on forever.
- **Radical** - the symbol $\sqrt{\ }$ is called a radical sign. It is used to represent the positive square root. The symbol $-\sqrt{\ }$ represents the negative square root.
- **Perfect Square** - any number that has integer square roots.

Example 1

When the square root of a number is a whole number, this number is called a perfect square. 9 is a perfect square because $\sqrt{9} = 3$.

Not all square roots are whole numbers. Many square roots are irrational numbers, meaning there is no rational number equivalent. For example, what is the square root of 5? There is no whole number multiplied by itself that equals five, so to find the value of $\sqrt{5}$, we can use estimation.

Estimate $\sqrt{5}$.

The perfect square below 5 is 4, and the perfect square above 5 is 9.

Therefore, $4 < 5 < 9$, so $\sqrt{5}$ is between $\sqrt{4}$ and $\sqrt{9}$ or $2 < \sqrt{5} < 3$

Because 5 is closer to 4 than 9, the decimal is a low value:

$\sqrt{5} \approx 2.2$

Now let's approximate $\sqrt{5}$ even closer. We can evaluate 2.2^2 and 2.3^2, which equals 4.84 and 5.29 respectively.

$2.2 < \sqrt{5} < 2.3$

Because 5 is closer to 4.84 than 5.29, we can further approximate that:

$\sqrt{5} \approx 2.24$

Let's check our approximation, $2.24^2 = 5.0176$. If you wanted to, you could keep repeating this process to approximate an even closer square root.

Example 2

Real numbers can be listed in order even if they are different types of real numbers. The easiest way to do this is to convert all the real numbers into decimals. Compare the following numbers and list them from least to greatest.

$\frac{3}{4}, 1.23, \sqrt{2}, \frac{2}{3}, 1$ and $\frac{8}{7}$

First, write each number as a decimal.

$\frac{3}{4} = 0.75, 1.23, \sqrt{2} \approx 1.4142, \frac{2}{3} = 0.\overline{66}, 1, \frac{8}{7} = 1.\overline{142857}$.

Now compare the numbers and write the decimals, in order, starting with the smallest and ending with the largest:

$0.\overline{66}, 0.75, 1, 1.\overline{142857}, 1.23, 1.4142$

Finally, exchange the decimals with the original numbers: $\frac{2}{3}, \frac{3}{4}, 1, \frac{8}{7}, 1.23, \sqrt{2}$

Example 3

One way to compare numbers is to use a number line. Plot $1.25, \frac{7}{2}$, and $2\sqrt{6}$ on a number line.

To plot these numbers, convert them all to decimals. $1.25, \frac{7}{2} = 3.5$, and $2\sqrt{6} \approx 4.899$ (The symbol $\approx$ means *approximately*.) Draw your number line and plot the points. Recall that 0 is called the origin.

Depending on your scale, you can have hash marks at half-values or only even values. The placement of each number on the number line is an approximate representation of each number.

Tips & Tricks

TABLE 1.1:

Real Numbers	Any number that can be plotted on a number line.	*Examples:* $8, 4.67, -\frac{1}{3}, \pi$
Rational Numbers	Any number that can be written as a fraction, including repeating decimals.	*Examples:* $-\frac{5}{9}, \frac{1}{8}, 1.\overline{3}, \frac{16}{4}$
Irrational Numbers	Real numbers that are not rational. When written as a decimal, these numbers do not end nor repeat.	*Exampe,* $\pi, -\sqrt{2}, \sqrt[3]{5}$

Practice

1. Identify the following decimals as either terminating, repeating and/or irrational.

     a. $0.\overline{33}$

     b. 3.56789.....

     c. 3.456789

     d. $-1.\overline{2879}$

     e. -0.4592

2. Estimate the following square roots to the nearest tenth.

     a. $\sqrt{6}$

     b. $\sqrt{3}$

     c. $\sqrt{27}$

     d. $\sqrt{109}$

     e. $\sqrt{60}$

3. Compare the following numbers. Complete each sentence with <, >, or =.

     a. $\sqrt{7}$ _____ 2.716382...

     b. $-0.27392...$ _____ $-0.274892....$

     c. 2.95 _____ $\sqrt{8}$

     d. $\frac{3}{5}$ _____ $-\sqrt{1}$

     e. $\sqrt{100}$ _____ 10

4. List $-\frac{1}{4}, \frac{3}{2}, -\sqrt{3}, \frac{3}{5}$, and 2 in order from greatest to least.

5. Plot the following numbers on a number line. Use an appropriate scale.

  a. $-1, 0.3, \sqrt{2}$

  b. $-\frac{1}{4}, -2\frac{1}{2}, 3.15$

  c. $1.4, \frac{5}{6}, \sqrt{9}$

  d. $-\sqrt{6}, \frac{4}{3}, \pi$

6. Order the following set of numbers from least to greatest: $-4, -\frac{9}{2}, -\frac{1}{3}, -\frac{1}{4}, -\pi$

7. Mr. Anderson wants to plant a new school garden in the shape of a square. There is space enough to plant a 150 square foot garden. Estimate the length of each side of the garden to the nearest tenth.

Bobcat Review

1. Write down one example of each of the following: a fraction, a decimal, an integer, a natural number, and a whole number.

2. What is the most specific subset of real numbers that the following numbers belong in?

  a. 5.67
  b. $-\sqrt{6}$
  c. $\frac{9}{5}$
  d. 0
  e. -75
  f. $\sqrt{16}$

3. List ALL the subsets that the following numbers are a part of.

  a. 4
  b. $\frac{6}{9}$
  c. π

Bobcat Stretch

1. Estimate to $\sqrt{208}$ to the nearest hundredth.

2. Compare each pair of numbers using $<$, $>$, and $=$.

    a. $-2\frac{8}{9}$ ___ -2.75
    b. $\frac{10}{15}$ ___ $\frac{8}{12}$
    c. $-\sqrt{50}$ ___ $-5\sqrt{2}$
    d. $1\frac{5}{6}$ ___ 1.95

3. Plot the following number set on a number line:

$$-\sqrt{\frac{1}{4}}, \ -0.25, \ \sqrt{\frac{2}{3}}, \ \frac{2}{3}, \ 0.13$$

Further Review

For more videos and practice problems,

- click here to go to Khan Academy.
- search for "recognizing rational and irrational numbers" on Khan Academy (www.khanacademy.org).
- click here to go to Khan Academy for more estimating square root practice problems.
- search for "approximating irrational numbers" on Khan Academy (www.khanacademy.org).
- go to Khan Academy's Common Core page standard 8.NS.A.2 (www.khanacademy.org/commoncore/grade -8-NS).

Watch this video for further review on how to estimate square roots.

 Multimedia

MEDIA

Click image to the left or use the URL below.
URL: https://www.ck12.org/flx/render/embeddedobject/104633

Answers

1.a. Repeating

  b. Irrational

  c. Terminating

  d. Repeating

  e. Terminating

2.a. ≈ 2.4

  b. ≈ 1.7

  c. ≈ 5.2

  d. ≈ 10.4

  e. ≈ 7.7

3. a. $<$

  b. $>$

  c. $>$

  d. $>$

  e. $=$

4. $2, \frac{3}{2}, \frac{3}{5}, -\frac{1}{4}, -\sqrt{3}$

5.

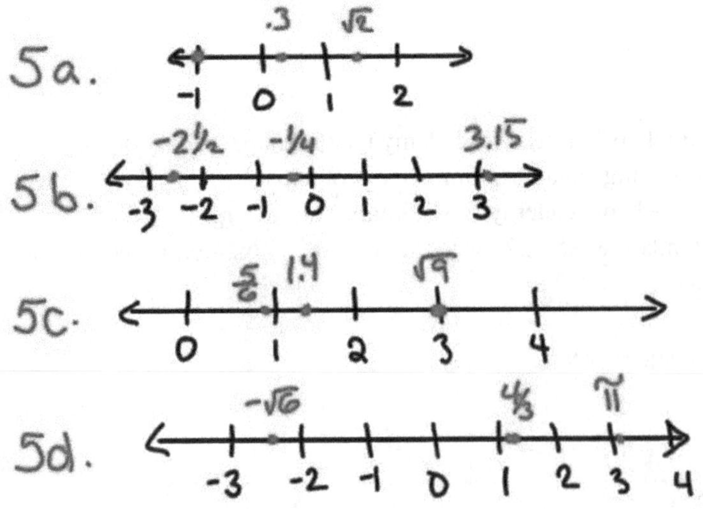

FIGURE 1.1

6. $-\frac{9}{2}, -4, -\pi, -\frac{1}{3}, -\frac{1}{4}$

7. 12.2 feet

Bobcat Review

1. Variable, for example: $\frac{2}{3}$, 0.33, −3, 3, 0

2.a. Rational

b. Irrational

c. Rational

d. Whole

e. Integer

f. Natural

3. a. Rational, Integer, Whole, Natural

b. Rational

c. Irrational

Bobcat Stretch

1. 14.42

2. a. <

b. =

c. =

d. <

3. $-\sqrt{\dfrac{1}{4}}$, −0.25, 0.13, $\frac{2}{3}$, $\sqrt{\dfrac{2}{3}}$ on a number line in order.

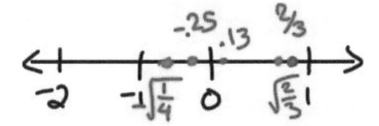

FIGURE 1.2

1.3 Factors and Prime Factorization of Mono-mials

Factor a monomial in expanded and exponent form. Determine whether a number is prime or composite

By the end of this lesson, you should be able to define and give an example of the following vocabulary words:

- **Factor** - A number or expression that is multiplied by another number or expression to get a product.
- **Monomial** - A number, a variable, or a product of a number and one or more variables with whole-number exponenets.
- **Prime** - a whole number greater than 1 whose only positive factors are 1 and itself.
- **Composite** - a whole number greater than 1 that has positive factors other than 1 and itself.
- **Expanded Form** - a form of prime factorization.
- **Exponent Form** - a form of prime factorization.

Example 1

What are the factors of twelve?

To do this systematically, we should first start with the number 1 and then move on to 2, then 3, etc... These are all of the factors for 12.

$$1 \times 12$$
$$2 \times 6$$
$$3 \times 4$$

5, 7, 8 etc are not factors of 12 because we can't multiply them by another number to get 12.

Example 2

A composite number is a number that has more than two factors like the number 12 from the previous example. 12 has 6 factors. Most numbers are composite numbers.

Prime numbers are special numbers as they only have two factors. You can only multiply one and the number itself to get a prime number.

Is 13 a prime or composite number?

Prime, since you can only get thirteen if you multiply 1 and 13.

Example 3

We can combine factoring and prime numbers together too. This is called ***prime factorization.***

Factor 108.

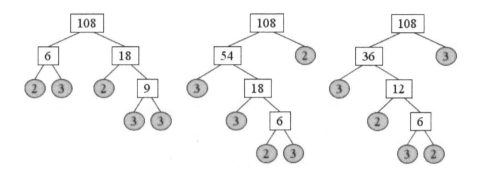

Notice each factor tree is different, but still produces the same prime factorization.

So, $108 = 2 \cdot 2 \cdot 3 \cdot 3 \cdot 3$ (expanded form) or $108 = 2^2 \cdot 3^2$ (exponent form).

Example 4

You can also factor monomials. Just prime factorize the number as the variables are already in exponent form.

Factor $136a^3b^6$

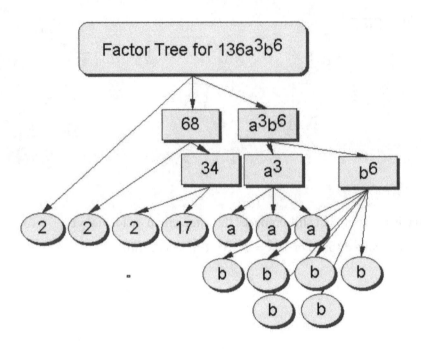

So, $136a^3b^6 = 2 \cdot 2 \cdot 2 \cdot 17 \cdot a \cdot a \cdot a \cdot b \cdot b \cdot b \cdot b \cdot b \cdot b$ (expanded form) or $136a^3b^6 = 2^3 \cdot 17 \cdot a^3 \cdot b^6$ (exponent form)

Tips & Tricks

- To factor a negative monomial, factor out the (-1) and then factor as usual. Write (-1) as one of the factors in the final answer. For example: $-16m^2n^2 = -1 \cdot 2 \cdot 2 \cdot 2 \cdot 2 \cdot m \cdot m \cdot n \cdot n$
- Here are the prime numbers from 1 - 100.

1	2	3	4	5	6	7	8	9	10
11	12	13	14	15	16	17	18	19	20
21	22	23	24	25	26	27	28	29	30
31	32	33	34	35	36	37	38	39	40
41	42	43	44	45	46	47	48	49	50
51	52	53	54	55	56	57	58	59	60
61	62	63	64	65	66	67	68	69	70
71	72	73	74	75	76	77	78	79	80
81	82	83	84	85	86	87	88	89	90
91	92	93	94	95	96	97	98	99	100

Practice

1. List all of the factors for the following numbers.

    a. 45

    b. 16

    c. 60

    d. 124

    e. 308

    f. 59

2. Are any of the numbers in problem 1 prime? Why or Why not?

3. List the prime factors for each of the following numbers - in both expanded and exponent form.

    a. 15

    b. 16

    c. 56

    d. 47

    e. 124

    f. 375

4. The EGJH is having a game night in two weeks - 48 seventh graders and 44 eighth graders have signed up. The last time that EGJH had a social, it was a little unorganized and the teachers weren't happy. This time, Allison (President of Student Council) and Hector (the Vice President) have promised to organize it and have a plan for all of the students. They have four different activities planned and want to organize students in rotating groups; they think that having enough options will keep things less chaotic. They are struggling with how best to arrange the students to visit each of the four activities and intermingle the 7th and 8th graders. They want the groups to not be too large and to have around the same number of students per group. How should Allison and Hector organize the groups, so no one activity gets over-crowded?

5. Factor the following monomials and write the answer is both expanded and exponent form.

    a. $72x^2y^2$

    b. $50a^4b^3$

    c. $232c^3m^3$

    d. $-24xy^4$

6. Ryan wants to build a rectangular pool that is 160 square feet.

    a. What are all the possible dimensions of the pool he could build (using only whole numbers)?

    b. Which pool design has the least perimeter?

    c. After speaking with his contractor, he was told he can actually fit a pool that is 170 square feet. What are the possible dimensions of the pool he could build now with this new information (using only whole numbers)?

    d. Which new pool design has the least perimeter?

    e. Which dimension would you recommend building? Explain?

    f. What if the contractor came back and said he can only fit a pool that is 135 square feet due to building restrictions. Can you predict which possible pool design would result in the least perimeter for a 135 square feet rectangular pool (using only whole numbers)? Explain?

Bobcat Review

1. Estimate $\sqrt{22}$ to the tenth.

2. Plot the following numbers on a number line: $-\sqrt{2}, 2.34, \frac{10}{6}, -2.563, \frac{8}{3}$

3. Write the numbers from problem 2 from greatest to least.

Bobcat Stretch

1. List all of the factors for 623.

2. What are the prime factors for the following numbers in both expanded and exponent form.

    a. 1924

    b. 30,784

    c. 424,242

3. Your class is packing fresh fruit baskets for a nursing home. Over the week your class collected 260 bananas, 208 oranges, and 324 apples. Your class wants to make as many baskets as possible with a nice variety of fruit (2 or more pieces of each fruit in each basket). All the baskets need to be the same and you want to use as much of the fruit as possible. How would you suggest packing the baskets? Explain (How many baskets would your plan create? What fruit is contained in each basket? How much fruit would be left over?).

4. Factor $32x^3y^{-2}$. Write your answer in both expanded and exponent form. (Hint: $\frac{1}{y} = y^{-1}$)

Further Review

For more videos and practice problems,

- click here to go to Khan Academy.
- search for "prime factorization" on Khan Academy (www.khanacademy.org).

Watch this video for a review of Prime Factorization (1st video) and Divisibility Rules (2nd video).

MEDIA
Click image to the left or use the URL below.
URL: https://www.ck12.org/flx/render/embeddedobject/105399

MEDIA
Click image to the left or use the URL below.
URL: https://www.ck12.org/flx/render/embeddedobject/105400

Answers

1. a. 1 X 45, 3 X 15, 5 X 9

   b. 1 X 16, 2 X 8, 4 X 4

   c. 1 X 60, 2 X 30, 3 X 20, 4 X 15, 5 X 12, 6 X 10

   d. 1 X 124, 2 X 62, 4 X 31

   e. 1 X 308, 2 X 154, 4 X 77, 7 X 44, 11 X 28, 14 X 22

   f. 1 x 59

2. Yes, 59. It is only divisible by 1 and 59, thus prime.

3.a. $3 \cdot 5$

   b. $2^4, 2 \cdot 2 \cdot 2 \cdot 2$

   c. $2 \cdot 2 \cdot 2 \cdot 7, 2^3 \cdot 7$

   d. $1, 47$

   e. $2 \cdot 2 \cdot 31, 2^2 \cdot 31$

   f. $3 \cdot 5 \cdot 5 \cdot 5, 3 \cdot 5^3$

4. Hector and Allison need to organize the students into four groups to go with the four different activities. They can start by writing out all of the factors for 7th grade. The factors will give them the combinations of students that can be sent in groups.

$$48$$
$$1 \times 48$$
$$2 \times 24$$
$$3 \times 16$$
$$\left. \begin{array}{l} 4 \times 12 \\ 6 \times 8 \end{array} \right\}$$ These are the two groups that make the most sense

Now let's find the factors of eighth grade.

$$1 \times 44$$
$$2 \times 22$$
$$4 \times 11 -$$ This is the group that makes the most sense.

If Hector and Allison arrange 7th graders into 4 groups of 12 and eight graders into 4 groups of 11, then the groups will be about the same size. There will be 23 students at each activity at one time. This definitely seems like a manageable number.

5. a. $2 \cdot 2 \cdot 2 \cdot 3 \cdot 3 \cdot x \cdot x \cdot y \cdot y, \ 2^3 \cdot 3^2 \cdot x^2 \cdot y^2$

   b. $2 \cdot 5 \cdot 5 \cdot a \cdot a \cdot a \cdot a \cdot b \cdot b \cdot b, \ 2 \cdot 5^2 \cdot a^4 \cdot b^3$

   c. $2 \cdot 2 \cdot 2 \cdot 29 \cdot c \cdot c \cdot c \cdot m \cdot m \cdot m, \ 2^3 \cdot 29 \cdot c^3 \cdot m^3$

   d. $-1 \cdot 2 \cdot 2 \cdot 2 \cdot 3 \cdot x \cdot y \cdot y \cdot y \cdot y, \ -1 \cdot 2^3 \cdot 3 \cdot x \cdot y^4$

6. a. 1 X 160, 2 X 80, 4 X 40, 5 X 32, 8 X 20, 10 X 16

   b. 10 X 16

   c. 1 X 170, 2 X 85, 5 X 34, 10 X 17

   d. 10 X 17

   e. Variable answers

   f. 9 X 15

Bobcat Review

1. 4.7

2.

3. $\frac{8}{3}, 2.34, \frac{10}{6}, -\sqrt{2}, -2.563$

Bobcat Stretch

1. 1 X 623, 7 X 89

2. a. $2 \cdot 2 \cdot 13 \cdot 37, \ 2^2 \cdot 13 \cdot 37$

   b. $2 \cdot 2 \cdot 2 \cdot 2 \cdot 2 \cdot 2 \cdot 13 \cdot 37, \ 2^6 \cdot 13 \cdot 37$

   c. $2 \cdot 3 \cdot 3 \cdot 7 \cdot 7 \cdot 13 \cdot 37, \ 2 \cdot 3^2 \cdot 7^2 \cdot 13 \cdot 37$

3. Variable answers.

   Factors 260: (130,2)(65,4)(52,5)(26,10)(20,13)

   Factors 208: (104,2)(52,4)(26,8)(16,13)

   Factors 324: (162,2)(108,3)(81,4)(54,6)(36,9)(27,12)

4. $2^5 \cdot x^3 \cdot y^{-2}, \ 2 \cdot 2 \cdot 2 \cdot 2 \cdot 2 \cdot x \cdot x \cdot x \cdot \frac{1}{y} \cdot \frac{1}{y}$

1.4 Greatest Common Factor (GCF) of Monomials

Find the greatest common factor (GCF) of two or more monomials.

By the end of this lesson, you should be able to define and give an example of the following vocabulary words:

- **Common Factor** - A whole number or variable that is a factor of two or more monomials.
- **GCF** - The greatest whole number or variable that is a factor of two or more monomials.
- **Relatively Prime** - Two or more monomials whose GCF is 1.

Example 1

Find the GCF of 20 and 30.

To solve, first list all the factors for each number.

   Factors of 20: 1, 2, 4, 5, 10, 20

   Factors of 30: 1, 2, 3, 5, 6, 10, 15, 30

Then, select the largest factor they both have in common, which is 10.

So, the GCF of 20 and 30 is 10.

Example 2

Find the GCF of 20 and 30 using a factor tree.

Make a prime factor tree for each number.

$$
\begin{array}{cc}
20 & 30 \\
/\ \backslash & /\ \backslash \\
4\quad 5 & 5\quad 6 \\
/\ \backslash & /\ \backslash \\
2\ \ 2 & 3\ \ 2 \\
2^2 \times 5 & 5 \times 3 \times 2
\end{array}
$$

To find the greatest common factor (GCF), find the product of the common prime factors.

In this case, 5 and 2 are the common prime factors, so the **GCF is 10 ($2 \times 5 = 10$).**

Example 3

Find the GCF of $27p^2qr^5$ **and** $15p^3r^3$**.**

First, find the prime factorization of each monomial, including all variables (and a -1 factor if necessary).

$$-27p^2qr^5 = -1 \cdot 3 \cdot 3 \cdot 3 \cdot p \cdot p \cdot q \cdot r \cdot r \cdot r \cdot r \cdot r$$

$$15p^3r^3 = 3 \cdot 5 \cdot p \cdot p \cdot p \cdot r \cdot r \cdot r$$

Then, take the product of all common factors (highlighted in red). Their product is:

$$3 \cdot p \cdot p \cdot r \cdot r \cdot r$$

So, the GCF is $3p^2r^3$**.**

Tips & Tricks

- For the variable portion of a monomial, find only the variable(s) in common and select the variable with the smallest exponent.
- If the GCF is 1, then it is relatively prime.

Practice

1. Explain why selecting the variable with the smallest exponent works when determining the GCF for monomials.

2. Find the GCF for the following numbers using the list method (from example 1).

    a. 14 and 28

    b. 14 and 30

    c. 16 and 36

    d. 24 and 60

    e. 72 and 108

    f. 17 and 43

    g. 36 and 21 and 78

3. Find the GCF for the following numbers using prime factorization (from example 2).

    a. 18 and 81

    b. 80 and 200

    c. 132 and 99

    d. 135 and 117

    e. 504 and 126

    f. 26 and 65 and 91

    g. 13 and 34 and 41

4. EGJH's basketball coach has decided to host a big basketball tournament between seventh and eight graders. 48 seventh graders signed up and 44 eighth graders signed up for the tournament.

    a. The biggest question is how many teams to divide the students from each grade into. The coach wants to have the same number of teams, otherwise it will be difficult to have even games for a tournament. How many teams should the coach form for each grade?

    b. How many students will be on each 7th grade team?

    c. How many students will be on each 8th grade team?

5. Find the GCF of the following monomials.

     a. $6x^3y^2$ and $6x^2y$

     b. $16a^5b^3$ and $40ab$

     c. $88p^4q^6$ and $178p^3q^3$

     d. $-54m^3n^5$ and $-96mn^2$

     e. $34c^5d^7$ and $-378c^6d^8$

     f. $42x^4y^2$ and $189xy$ and $105x^5y^2$

     g. $54a^4b^3c^2$ and $162a^2b^2c$ and $126a^2b^2$

6. Write a factoring problem where the answer is relatively prime.

7. Lincoln Park has decided to add a dog park. They want a 1,504 square feet fenced-in area for large dogs right next to a 1,024 square feet fenced-in area for small dogs. The areas will share a side to cut down on fencing material. What dimensions should the city build so the shared sides are exactly the same keeping in mind that the fencing material comes in 1 foot segments (and they don't want to cut any segments)? How much fencing material should the contractor buy?

8. Your last class service project for the nursing home was such a success that your class has decided to do another one. This time you've collected 138 bananas, 184 oranges, and 230 apples. What is the maximum number of baskets you can create with no fruit leftover? What does each basket contain?

Bobcat Review

1. Write $0.\overline{46}$ as a rational number (hint: $\frac{a}{b}$ format).

2. Write $1.\overline{21}$ as a fraction.

3. Write $-2.\overline{3}$ as a fraction.

Bobcat Stretch

1. What is the GCF for the monomials?

    a. 425 and 255 and 595 and 1190

    b. $-68m^6n^2o^5$ and $136m^3n^3o^3$ and $204m^4n^3$ and $102m^2np^2$ and $51n^3p^2$

    c. $81a^2b^2c^2$ and $-135a^5b^2c^4$ and $216a^2b^2c^-2$ and $-54a^2b^4$

2. You inspired another class to do a service project. They chose to collect canned goods for the county food bank. The food bank specifically requested them to collect soup, beans, vegetables, fruit and tuna and have them pre-boxed and ready for distribution. After a month, the class collected 212 cans of tuna, 159 cans of vegetables, 265 cans of beans, 106 cans of fruit, and 318 cans of soup. How many boxes can they make? They want each box to have the same variety of cans and have no cans leftover. What does each box contain?

Further Review

For more videos and practice problems,

- click here to go to Khan Academy.
- search for "greatest common divisor" on Khan Academy (www.khanacademy.org).

Watch this video for a review of finding the GCF.

 Multimedia

MEDIA
Click image to the left or use the URL below.
URL: https://www.ck12.org/flx/render/embeddedobject/105519

Answers

1. The GCF includes common factors between the numbers and variables in a monomial.

2.a. 14

  b. 2

  c. 4

  d. 12

  e. 36

  f. 1 - Relatively Prime

  g. 3

3.a. 9

  b. 40

  c. 33

  d. 9

  e. 126

  f. 13

  g. 1 - Relatively prime

4. a. 4

  b. 12

  c. 11

5. a. $6x^2y$

  b. $8ab$

  c. $2p^3q^3$

  d. $-6mn^2$

  e. $2c^5d^7$

  f. 21xy

  g. $18a^2b^2$

6. Variable answers where the GCF is 1 (relatively prime)

7. Large dog park: 32sqft X 47sqft, small dog park: 32sqft X 32 sqft, 254 feet of fencing.

8. 46 baskets, each basket contains 3 bananas, 4 oranges and 5 apples.

Bobcat Review

1. $\frac{46}{99}$

2. $\frac{40}{33}$

3. $\frac{-21}{9} = \frac{-7}{3} or - 2\frac{1}{3}$

Bobcat Stretch

1. a. 85

 b. 17n

 c. $27a^2b^2$

2. 53 boxes with each containing 4 cans of tuna, 3 cans of vegetables, 5 cans of beans, 2 cans of fruit, and 6 cans of soup.

1.5 Simplifying and Evaluating Variable Expressions

Simplify and evaluate variable expressions that involve division.

By the end of this lesson, you should be able to define and give an example of the following vocabulary words:

- **Equivalent Fractions** - Fractions that represent the same part-to-whole relationship. Equivalent fractions have the same simplest form.
- **Simplest Form** - An expression whose numerator and denominator have only a common factor of 1 (relatively prime). This can be achieved by dividing out (canceling) all common factors between the numerator and denominator.

Example 1

Simplify the expression $\frac{-12x}{-3xy}$.

First, factor the numerator and denominator.

$\frac{-1 \cdot 2 \cdot 2 \cdot 3 \cdot x}{-1 \cdot 3 \cdot x \cdot y}$

Second, divide out common factors. For example, $\frac{-1}{-1} = 1$, $\frac{3}{3} = 1$, and $\frac{x}{x} = 1$, so those factors "cancel out".

Finally, simplify the leftover terms and write the expression in its simplest form.

$\frac{4}{y}$

Example 2

Evaluate the expression $\frac{8y^3}{-2y}$, when y = 3.

First, factor the numerator and denominator.

$$\frac{2 \cdot 2 \cdot 2 \cdot 2 \cdot y \cdot y \cdot y}{-1 \cdot 2 \cdot y}$$

Second, divide out the common factors. For example, $\frac{2}{2} = 1$ and $\frac{y}{y} = 1$.

Then, simplify the leftover terms and write the expression in its simplest form.

$-6y^2$

Finally, substitute 3 for y, evaluate the powers (remember your order of operations) and simplify. For example, $-6 \cdot (3^2)$.

-54

Tips & Tricks

- Always simplify expressions if possible before evaluating.
- Evaluate expressions following the order of operations guidelines: parentheses, exponents, multiplication & division, addition & subtraction.

Practice

1. Simplify the following expressions.

   a. $\frac{-18x}{-2}$

   b. $\frac{-24y}{2y}$

   c. $\frac{28ab}{-7b}$

   d. $\frac{-18b}{-9ab}$

2. Find the error(s) and then correct the mistakes to find the correct answer.

   $\frac{-21a^2b^3}{14ab} = \frac{3ab}{2}$

3. Simplify the following expressions.

   a. $\frac{32x^2}{14x^4}$

   b. $\frac{28xyz}{-16abc}$

   c. $\frac{-44x^2y^3}{-56x^4y^2}$

   d. $\frac{9a^4b^2c^6}{21a^5b^4c^3}$

4. The following students ran for student council president. Bruce received 43 votes, Carrie received 32 votes, Nathan received 33 votes, Kaitlan received 48 votes, and Tracy received 40 votes. Write the fraction of votes each student received in its simplest form. Who won?

5. Simplify and evaluate the following expressions where $x = 4$.

   a. $\frac{5x^2}{15x}$

   b. $\frac{34x^2}{17x^4}$

   c. $\frac{-33x^6}{44x^6}$

   d. $\frac{16x^8}{64x^7}$

6. Simplify and evaluate the following expressions.

   a. $\frac{4x^2y^2}{28xy^3}$, where $x = 3$ and $y = 4$

   b. $\frac{-36a^2b}{-63a^3b^2}$, where $a = 2$ and $b = 4$

   c. $\frac{52m^4n^2}{20m^2n^4}$, where $m = 2$ and $n = 6$

   d. $\frac{25r^4s^6}{15rs^6}$, where $r = 3$ and $s = 2$

7. There are 4 errors in the evaluation below where $x = 2$, $y = 3$, and $z = 1$. Find the errors and correct them. What is the correct solution?

   $$\frac{-24x^6y^2z}{40x^3y^4z} = \frac{3x^3z}{5y^2} = \frac{216}{225}$$

Bobcat Review

1. Are the following fractions equivalent? If not, rewrite the 2nd fraction to make the expression True.

   a. $\frac{8}{56} = \frac{3}{21}$

   b. $\frac{32}{56} = \frac{9}{21}$

   c. $\frac{112}{64} = \frac{161}{92}$

   d. $\frac{64}{160} = \frac{56}{142}$

2. Write an equivalent fraction for the following...

   a. $\frac{3}{4}$

   b. $\frac{12}{20}$

   c. $\frac{120}{300}$

   d. $\frac{24}{96}$

3. Write the following fractions in their simplest forms...

   a. $\frac{26}{104}$

   b. $\frac{36}{60}$

   c. $\frac{189}{441}$

Bobcat Stretch

1. In the same election for student council president, the following students ran for student council vice-president. Liam received $\frac{1}{7}$ of the vote, Rachel received $\frac{5}{28}$ of the vote, Kristen received $\frac{1}{4}$, and Tom and Brett both received $\frac{3}{14}$ of the vote. How many votes/ballots did each student receive if a total of 196 ballots were cast and who won?

2. Simplify the following expressions.

     a. $0.3x^5y^4z^3 \div 0.15x^3y^3z^2$

     b. $1.234r^2s^5t^2 \div 7.404r^2s^2t$

     c. $\frac{-2.5m^2n^2o^4}{0.5m^4n^2o^5}$

3. Evaluate the expressions from problem 2 given the following data.

     a. $x = 2, y = 10, z = 3$

     b. $r = 6, s = 2, t = 3$

     c. $m = 3, n = 5, o = 2$

Further Review

For more videos and practice problems,

- click here to go to Khan Academy .
- search for "simplifying rational expressions with exponent properties" on Khan Academy (www.khanacademy.org).

Watch this video for a review of simplifying and evaluating expressions.

 **Multimedia**

MEDIA

Click image to the left or use the URL below.
URL: https://www.ck12.org/flx/render/embeddedobject/105610

Answers

1. a. $9x$

   b. -12

   c. -4a

   d. $\frac{2}{a}$

2. $\frac{-3ab^2}{2}$

3. a. $\frac{16}{7x^2}$

   b. $\frac{7xyz}{-4abc}$

   c. $\frac{11y}{14x^2}$

   d. $\frac{3c^3}{7ab^2}$

4. $\frac{43}{196}, \frac{8}{49}, \frac{33}{196}, \frac{12}{49}, \frac{10}{49}$, Kaitlan.

5. a. $\frac{x}{3} = \frac{4}{3}$

   b. $\frac{2}{x^2} = \frac{1}{8}$

   c. $-\frac{3}{4}$

   d. $\frac{x}{4} = 1$

6. a. $\frac{x}{7y} = \frac{3}{28}$

   b. $\frac{4}{7ab} = \frac{1}{14}$

   c. $\frac{13m^2}{5n^2} = \frac{13}{45}$

   d. $\frac{5r^3}{3} = 45$

7. $\frac{-3x^3}{5y^2} = -\frac{8}{15}$

Bobcat Review

1.a Yes, $\frac{1}{7} = \frac{1}{7}$

  b. No, $\frac{4}{7} \neq \frac{3}{7}$

  c. Yes, $\frac{7}{4} = \frac{7}{4}$

  d. No, $\frac{2}{5} \neq \frac{28}{71}$

2. Variable answers, here are some examples, a. $\frac{9}{12}$, b. $\frac{24}{40}$, c. $\frac{2}{5}$, d. $\frac{12}{48}$

3. a. $\frac{1}{4}$

  b. $\frac{3}{5}$

  c. $\frac{3}{7}$

Bobcat Stretch

1. Liam - 28, Rachel - 35, Kristen - 49, Tom - 42 and Brett - 42. Kristen won.

2. a. $2x^2yz$

  b. $\frac{1}{6s^3t}$

  c. $\frac{-5}{m^2o}$

3. a. 240

  b. 4

  c. $\frac{-5}{18}$

1.6 Least Common Multiple of Monomials

Find the least common multiple of two monomials.By the end of this lesson, you should be able to define and give an example of the following vocabulary words:

- **Common Multiple** - A number that is a multiple of two or more natural numbers. For example, 60 is a common multiple of 5 and 6.
- **Least Common Multiple (LCM)** - The least common multiple of two numbers or algebraic expressions is the smallest of their common multiples. For example, $6a^2b$ is the common multiple of $2\,ab$ and $3a^2$.

Example 1

What are the common multiples of 3 and 4?

To start to find the common multiples, we first need to write out the multiples for 3 and 4. To find the most common multiples that we can, we can list out multiples through multiplying by 12.

3, 6, 9, **12**, 15, 18, 21, **24**, 27, 30, 33, **36,...**

4, 8, **12**, 16, 20, **24**, 28, 32, **36**, 40, 44, 48,...

The common multiples of 3 and 4 are 12, 24, 36....

Example 2

If we wanted to find the LCM of two numbers without listing out all of the multiples, we could do it by using prime factorization.

What is the LCM of 9 and 12?

First, factor both numbers to their primes.

$9 = 3^2$

$12 = 2^2 \cdot 3$

Second, multiply each prime factor with the greatest power to find the LCM.

So, $3^2 \cdot 2^2 = 36$.

The LCM of 9 and 12 is 36.

Example 3

Find the LCM of $12a^2b^3$ and $9a^2b^4$.

First, factor each monomial and write it in exponent form.

$12a^2b^3 = 2^2 \cdot 3 \cdot a^2 \cdot b^3$

$9a^2b^4 = 3^2 \cdot a^2 \cdot b^4$

Second, multiply each prime factor with the greatest power to find the LCM.

So, $2^2 \cdot 3^2 \cdot a^2 \cdot b^4 = 36a^2b^4$.

The LCM of $12a^2b^3$ and $9a^2b^4$ is $36a^2b^4$.

Tips & Tricks

- Circle the greatest power of each factor as an easy way to identify what you need to multiply to find the LCM.

Practice

1. Find two common multiples of each pair of numbers.

    a. 3 and 5

    b. 4 and 8

    c. 5 and 10

2. Find the LCM of the following numbers by listing multiples.

    a. 6 and 9

    b. 4 and 14

    c. 8, 6, and 16

    d. 3, 6, and 21

3. EGJH's student council is planning an art show. Each grade has formed an art committee to create art for the show and meet in the art room. Seventh graders meet every 3 days and eighth graders meet every 2 days (Monday thru Friday - they don't meet on weekends). Chaos struck on Monday, August 22nd, when both committees were in the art room at the same time and there weren't enough art supplies to go around. The art teacher wants to be better prepared for the next time the groups overlap. How often do the groups overlap and on what date will they overlap next? Which method did you use to solve the problem (mental math, listing multiples, or prime factorization)? Why?

4. Find the LCM of the following numbers using prime factorization.

    a. 18 and 20

    b. 8 and 10

    c. 14, 26, and 28

    d. 20, 25, and 35

5. Your teacher wants to create online study groups with either 4, 5, or 6 students in each group. What is the minimum number of students needed to create the study groups with no students leftout? Which method did you use to solve the problem (mental math, listing multiples, or prime factorization)? Why?

6. Find the LCM of the following monomials.

   a. $2x^2y$ and $6xy^2$

   b. $12a^3b^2$ and $30a^4b^2$

   c. $14m^2n^3$, $24mn^4$, and $28m^4n^3$

   d. $9x^2y^2z^2$, $18x^3y^2z^4$, and $32xy^4z$

   e. $10r^4s^3$, $15r^3st^2$, $25r^3s^2t^4$

7. A bus comes to the 4th Ave pizza place at 3:00, 3:15, and 3:30. A trolley comes at 3:00, 3:12, and 3:24. What is the first time they will arrive together at the pizza place again? Which method did you use to solve the problem (mental math, listing multiples, or prime factorization)? Why?

Bobcat Review

1. An orchard is planting 50 apple trees and 30 peach trees. If they want the same number and type of trees per row. What is the maximum number of trees that can be planted per row?

2. Samantha has two pieces of cloth. One piece is 72 inches wide and the other piece is 90 inches wide. She wants to cut both pieces into strips of equal width that are as wide as possible without any scraps. How wide should she cut the strips?

3. Find the GCF of $48x^2y^4z$ and $18x^4y^3z^2$.

Bobcat Stretch

1. A teacher has a stack of colored paper collated in this order: red, yellow, pink, and orange. She has 3 test forms (A, B, and C). Form A is on the first red, Form B is on the second color (yellow), and Form C is on the third color, Form A on the fourth color, etc...

   a. What color is the 3rd Form A on?

   b. What color and form will the 13th test be on?

   c. How may As will be on red paper if 58 tests are printed?

   d. Which method did you use to solve the problem (mental math, listing multiples, or prime factorization)? Why?

2. There are four conveyer belts of cookies at the Oreo factory. The first belt has strawberry, vanilla, and chocolate cookies spread out every 2 inches. The second belt has mint, strawberry, chocolate, and vanilla spread out every 2 inches. The third belt has vanilla, strawberry, chocolate, mint, and vanilla/chocolate swirl spread out every 2 inches. The fourth belt has strawberry, mint, chocolate, vanilla, vanilla/chocolate swirl, and vanilla/mint swirl spread out every 2 inches. Today the factory is producing snack packs each containing 4 cookies - one from each conveyor belt.

   a. What flavors does the first snack pack of the day contain?

   b. When will the next snack pack be produced with exactly the same flavors as the first snack pack?

   c. Which method did you use to solve the problem (mental math, listing multiples, or prime factorization)? Why?

3. What is the LCM of $180x^3y^2z^6$, $200x^2yz^4$, and $320x^2s^3z$.

Further Review

For more videos and practice problems,

   • click here to go to Khan Academy.
   • search for "least common multiple" on Khan Academy (www.khanacademy.org).

Watch this video for a review of LCM.

MEDIA
Click image to the left or use the URL below.
URL: https://www.ck12.org/flx/render/embeddedobject/105911

Answers

1. a. 15 and 30

   b. 16 and 32

   c. 10 and 20

2. a. 18

   b. 28

   c. 48

   d. 42

3. They overlap every 6 days and they will overlap again on Tuesday, August 30th. Variable answers.

4. a. 180

   b. 40

   c. 364

   d. 700

5. 60 - variable answers.

6. a. $6x^2y^2$

   b. $60a^4b^2$

   c. $168m^4n^4$

   d. $288x^3y^4z^4$

   e. $150r^4s^3t^4$

7. 4:00pm - variable answers.

Bobcat Review

1. 10 per row

2. 18 inches

3. $6x^2y^3z$

Bobcat Stretch

1. a. Pink

   b. Form A on Red

   c. 5

   d. Variable answers

2. a. strawberry, mint, vanilla, and strawberry

   b. The 61st snack pack will be the exact same as the first.

   c. Variable answers

3. $14400x^3y^2s^3z^6$

1.7 Exponent Properties

Multiply and divide expressions with exponents.

By the end of this lesson, you should be able to define and give an example of the following vocabulary words:

- **Product Rule for Exponents:**

    $x^n \cdot x^m = x^{n+m}$

- **Quotient of Powers Property:**

    $\frac{x^n}{x^m} = x^{n-m}$

Example 1

Simplify the following expression:

So what happens when we multiply one power of x by another? You can use the full factored form for each:

$$\underbrace{(x \cdot x \cdot x \cdot x \cdot x)}_{x^5} \cdot \underbrace{(x \cdot x \cdot x)}_{x^3} = \underbrace{(x \cdot x \cdot x \cdot x \cdot x \cdot x \cdot x \cdot x)}_{x^8}$$

A much simpler way is to use the product rule for exponents:

$x^5 \times x^3 = x^{5+3} = x^8$

Example 2

Simplify the following expression:

$\frac{x^{12}}{x^5}$

Use the quotient rule:

$\frac{x^{12}}{x^5} = x^{12-5} = x^7$

Tips & Tricks

- When we have a mix of numbers and variables, we apply the rules to each number or each variable separately. For example, $\frac{6x^2y^3}{2xy^2} = \frac{6}{2} \cdot \frac{x^2}{x} \cdot \frac{y^3}{y^2}$, which simplifies to $3xy$.

Practice

1. Simplify the following expressions - keep in a^b format:

    a. $x^2 \cdot x^7$

    b. $6^3 \cdot 6^2$

    c. $2^2 \cdot 2^4 \cdot 2^6$

    d. $y^4 \cdot y^5$

    e. $(-2y^4)(-3y)$

2. If Pima County was a perfect rectangle, then what would be the square mile area of the county given the following data: One side is 2^7 miles long and another side is 2^6 miles long.

3. Simplify the following expressions - keep in a^b format::

    a. $\frac{4^5}{4^2}$

    b. $\frac{x^8}{x^4}$

    c. $\frac{-2^4}{2^2}$

    d. $\frac{-y^6}{y^3}$

    e. $\frac{-3^4}{-3^2}$

4. 5^6 trees are planted in the garden by 5^4 people on Arbor day, how many trees are planted on average by each person.

5. Simplify the following expressions - keep in a^b format:

    a. $\frac{15x^5y^6}{-5x^2y^4}$

    b. $\frac{(5m^2n^3)\cdot(4m^2n^2)}{2m^2n^2}$

    c. $2x^2y^2z^2 \cdot 3x^3y^3z \cdot 4x^2y^3z^2$

    d. $\frac{(3m^2n^2p^2)\cdot(2mn^4p^6)}{(m^2n^3p^2)\cdot(-2n^2p^2)}$

    e. $\frac{(5r^2st)\cdot(2r^4s^3t^2)\cdot(6s^3)}{(2r^2st)\cdot(2rs^4t^2)\cdot(3s^2)}$

6. A solar farm in Arizona has 15 rows of solar panels with 15 solar panels per row. Each solar panel contains 6 rows of modules with 6 modules per row.

    a. How many solar panels does the solar-powered farm contain? Write the answer as a power.

    b. How many modules are in each panel? Write the answer as a power.

    c. How many modules are in the solar farm? Write your answer as an expression then solve.

7. True or False. If False, correct the mistake to make the statement True.

    a. $3^2 \cdot 3^3 = 9^5$

    b. $3x^2 \cdot 3x^3 = 9x^5$

    c. $\frac{6x^8y^9}{-2x^4y^3} = 3x^2y^3$

    d. $\frac{-8m^3np^2}{-4m^2n} = -2mn$

8. How many Kilometers are in a Gigameter? Write your answer in exponent form. (Hint: Kilometer is 1,000 m and a Gigameter is 1,000,000,000,000 m)

Bobcat Review

1. Factor the following monomials and write in exponent form.

    a. $150a^2b^2$

    b. $490m^3n^2p^6$

    c. $675x^3y^4z^5$

2. Classify the following numbers as rational, irrational, whole, integer, and/or natural. Note - some numbers may fall in more than one category.

    a. 0

    b. $\sqrt{3}$

    c. -4

    d. $3.\overline{23}$

    e. $\frac{3}{7}$

3. Estimate the value of $\sqrt{8}$ to the nearest tenth.

Bobcat Stretch

If we have a product of more than one term inside the parentheses, then we have to distribute the exponent over all the factors, like distributing multiplication over addition. For example:

$$(x^2 y)^4 = (x^2)^4 \cdot (y)^4 = x^8 y^4.$$

Power Rule for Exponents: $(x^n)^m = x^{(n \cdot m)}$

Use the power rule of exponents to simplify the following expressions.

1. $(x^2)^2 \cdot x^3$

2. $(a^2 b^3)^2 \cdot (2ab^4)^3$

3. $\frac{(2a^3 b^3)^3}{(4a^2 b^3)^2}$

Further Review

For more videos and practice problems,

- click here to go to Khan Academy.
- search for "evaluating expressions with exponents" on Khan Academy (www.khanacademy.org).
- go to Khan Academy's Common Core page standard 8.EE.A.1 (www.khanacademy.org/commoncore/grade -8-EE).

Watch this video for a review of rules of exponents.

| MEDIA |
| Click image to the left or use the URL below. |
| URL: https://www.ck12.org/flx/render/embeddedobject/105969 |

Answers

1. a. x^9

   b. 6^5

   c. 2^{12}

   d. y^9

   e. $6y^5$

2. $2^{13} = 8192$ square miles

3. a. 4^3

   b. x^4

   c. -2^2

   d. $-y^3$

   e. 3^2

4. $5^2 = 25$ trees per person

5. a. $-3x^3y^2$

   b. $10m^2n^3$

   c. $24x^7y^8z^5$

   d. $-3mnp^4$

   e. $5r^3$

6. a. 15^2

   b. 6^2

   c. $15^2 \cdot 6^2 = 8,100$ modules in the solar farm

7. a. False, it would equal 3^5

   b. True

   c. False, it would equal $-3x^4y^6$

   d. False, it would equal $2mp^2$

8. 10^9

Bobcat Review

1.a. $2 \cdot 3 \cdot 5^2 \cdot a^2 \cdot b^2$

   b. $2 \cdot 5 \cdot 7^2 \cdot m^3 \cdot n^2 \cdot p^6$

   c. $3^3 \cdot 5^2 \cdot x^3 \cdot y^4 \cdot z^5$

2. a. rational, whole, integer

   b. irrational

   c. rational, integer

   d. rational

   e. rational

3. 2.8

Bobcat Stretch

1. $x^4 \cdot x^3 = x^7$

2. $(a^2 b^3)^2 \cdot (2ab^4)^3$

   $\{(a^2)^2 \cdot (b^3)^2\} \cdot \{(2)^3 \cdot (a)^3 \cdot (b^4)^3\}$

   $\{a^4 \cdot b^6\} \cdot \{8 \cdot a^3 \cdot b^{12}\}$

   $8a^7 b^{18}$

3. $\frac{(2a^3 b^3)^3}{(4a^2 b^3)^2}$

   $\frac{(2)^3 \cdot (a^3)^3 \cdot (b^3)^3}{(4)^2 \cdot (a^2)^2 \cdot (b^3)^2}$

   $\frac{8 \cdot a^9 \cdot b^9}{16 \cdot a^4 \cdot b^6}$

   $\frac{a^5 b^3}{2}$

1.8 Negative and Zero Exponents

Simplify expressions with zero and negative exponents.

By the end of this lesson, you should be able to define and give an example of the following vocabulary words:

- **Zero Exponent Property**:

$a^0 = 1, a \neq 0$

- **Negative Exponent Property**:

$\frac{1}{a^m} = a^{-m}$ and $\frac{1}{a^{-m}} = a^m, a \neq 0$

Example 1

Evaluate $\frac{5^6}{5^6}$ by using the Quotient of Powers property.

$\frac{5^6}{5^6} = 5^{6-6} = 5^0$

What is a number divided by itself?

$\frac{5^6}{5^6} = 1$

So, $\frac{a^m}{a^m} = a^{m-m} = a^0 = 1$

Example 2

Evaluate $\frac{3^2}{3^7}$ by using the Quotient of Powers property.

$\frac{3^2}{3^7} = 3^{2-7} = 3^{-5}$

Now evaluate $\frac{3^2}{3^7}$ by writing it in expanded form and canceling out the common 3's.

$\frac{3^2}{3^7} = \frac{\cancel{3}\cdot\cancel{3}}{\cancel{3}\cdot\cancel{3}\cdot3\cdot3\cdot3\cdot3\cdot3} = \frac{1}{3^5}$

$\frac{1}{3^5} = 3^{-5}$

So, $\frac{1}{a^m} = a^{-m}$ and $\frac{1}{a^{-m}} = a^m$

Tips & Tricks

- Anything to the zero power is one.
- Negative exponents indicate placement. If an exponent is negative, it needs to be moved from where it is to the numerator or denominator

Practice

1. Refer to the following sequence to answer the following questions:

$5^{-4}, 5^{-3}, 5^{-2}, 5^{-1}, 5^0, 5^1, 5^2, 5^3, 5^4$

    a. Rewrite the pattern using only positive exponents.

    b. Evaluate each term in the pattern.

    c. Fill in the blank. As the numbers increase, you _____ the previous term by 5.

    d. Fill in the blank. As the numbers decrease, you _____ the previous term by 5.

2. Evaluate the expression.

    a. 2^{-5}

    b. 3^0

    c. $(-3)^{-3}$

    d. $6^0 \cdot 6^{-2}$

    e. $(-4)^{-3} \cdot 4^{-1}$

3. Simplify the following expressions. Answers cannot have negative exponents.

    a. $\frac{8^2}{8^4}$

    b. $\frac{x^6}{x^{15}}$

    c. $\frac{7^{-3}}{7^{-2}}$

    d. $\frac{y^{-9}}{y^{10}}$

    e. $\frac{x^0 y^5}{xy^7}$

4. The magnitude of an earthquake represents the exponent m in the expression 10^m. Valdivia, Chile has suffered two major earthquakes. The 1575 Valdivia earthquake had a magnitude of 8.5. The world's largest earthquake was the 1960 Valdivia earthquake at a magnitude of 9.5.

What was the size of the 1575 earthquake compared to the 1960 one?

5. True or False. Identify if each expression below is equivalent to $\frac{5^{-6}}{5^{-3}} =$ _____ .

    a. 5^{-9}

    b. 5^{-3}

    c. 5^{-2}

    d. $\frac{1}{5^3}$

    e. $\frac{1}{5^9}$

    f. $\frac{1}{5^2}$

6. Simplify the following expressions. Answers cannot have negative exponents.

    a. $x^3 \cdot x^{-6}$

    b. $3^2 \cdot 3^{-3}$

    c. $n^{-7} \cdot n^{-2}$

    d. $a^5 \cdot a^{-6} \cdot a^{-2}$

    e. $(-3)^0 \cdot (-3)^{-3} \cdot 3^{-2}$

7. Simplify the following expressions. Answers cannot have negative exponents.

    a. $\frac{x^7 y z^{12}}{x^{12} y z^7}$

    b. $\frac{a^4 b^0}{a^8 b}$

    c. $\frac{x y^5}{8 y^{-3}}$

    d. $\frac{27 g^{-7} h^0}{18 g}$

8. Multiply the two fractions together and simplify. Your answer should only have <u>positive</u> exponents.

$$\frac{4x^{-2}y^5}{20x^8} \cdot \frac{-5x^6y}{15y^{-9}}$$

Bobcat Review

1. Find the value of n.

    a. $\frac{11}{5} = \frac{n}{10}$

    b. $\frac{8}{7} = \frac{32}{n}$

    c. $\frac{40}{n} = \frac{10}{2}$

2. Which fraction is larger?

    a. $\frac{5}{6}$ or $\frac{2}{3}$

    b. $\frac{11}{8}$ or $\frac{16}{11}$

    c. $\frac{6}{7}$ o $\frac{7}{9}$

3. Order the following numbers on a number line.

    -3.68, $1\frac{4}{5}$, $-\sqrt{10}$, 1.12, $\frac{15}{13}$

Bobcat Stretch

Evaluate the follwoing expressions and simplify. Your answer should only have positive exponents.

1. $\frac{g^9 h^5}{6gh^{12}} \cdot \frac{18h^3}{g^8}$

2. $\frac{4a^{10}b^7}{12a^{-6}} \cdot \frac{9a^{-5}b^4}{20a^{11}b^{-8}}$

3. $\frac{-g^8 h}{6g^{-8}} \cdot \frac{9g^{15}h^9}{-h^{11}}$

4. $\left(\frac{5}{6}\right)^{-2}$

Further Review

For more videos and practice problems,

- click here to go to Khan Academy.
- search for "negative exponents" on Khan Academy (www.khanacademy.org).
- go to Khan Academy's Common Core page standard 8.EE.A.1 (www.khanacademy.org/commoncore/grade-8-EE).

Watch this video for a review of negative exponents.

MEDIA
Click image to the left or use the URL below.
URL: https://www.ck12.org/flx/render/embeddedobject/105997

Answers

1. a. $\frac{1}{5^4}, \frac{1}{5^3}, \frac{1}{5^2}, \frac{1}{5^1}, 5^0, 5^1, 5^2, 5^3, 5^4$

   b. $\frac{1}{625}, \frac{1}{125}, \frac{1}{25}, \frac{1}{5}, 1, 5, 25, 125, 625$

   c. Multiply

   d. Divide

2. a. $\frac{1}{32}$

   b. 1

   c. $\frac{1}{-27}$

   d. $\frac{1}{36}$

   e. $-\frac{1}{256}$

3. a. $\frac{1}{64}$

   b. $\frac{1}{x^9}$

   c. $\frac{1}{7}$

   d. $\frac{1}{y^{19}}$

   e. $\frac{1}{x^1 y^2}$

4. The the size of the 1575 earthquake was $\frac{1}{10}$ the 1960 one.

5. a. False

   b. True

   c. False

   d. True

   e. False

   f. False

6. a. $\frac{1}{x^3}$

   b. $\frac{1}{3}$

   c. $\frac{1}{n^9}$

   d. $\frac{1}{a^3}$

   e. $-\frac{1}{243}$

7. a. $\frac{x^7 y z^{12}}{x^{12} y z^7} = \frac{y^{1-1} z^{12-7}}{x^{12-7}} = \frac{y^0 z^5}{x^5} = \frac{z^5}{x^5}$

   b. $\frac{a^4 b^0}{a^8 b} = a^{4-8} b^{0-1} = a^{-4} b^{-1} = \frac{1}{a^4 b}$

   c. $\frac{xy^5}{8y^{-3}} = \frac{xy^5 y^3}{8} = \frac{xy^{5+3}}{8} = \frac{xy^8}{8}$

   d. $\frac{27 g^{-7} h^0}{18 g} = \frac{3}{2 g^1 g^7} = \frac{3}{2 g^{1+7}} = \frac{3}{2 g^8}$

8. $\frac{4x^{-2} y^5}{20 x^8} \cdot \frac{-5x^6 y}{15 y^{-9}} = -\frac{20 x^{-2+6} y^{5+1}}{300 x^8 y^{-9}} = -\frac{x^{-2+6-8} y^{5+1+9}}{15} = -\frac{x^{-4} y^{15}}{15} = -\frac{y^{15}}{15 x^4}$

Bobcat Review

1. Find the value of n.

   a. 22

   b. 28

   c. 8

2. a. $\frac{5}{6}$

   b. $\frac{16}{11}$

   c. $\frac{6}{7}$

3. -3.68, $-\sqrt{10}$, 1.12, $\frac{15}{13}$, $1\frac{4}{5}$

Bobcat Stretch

1. $\frac{3}{h^4}$

2. $\frac{3b^{19}}{20}$

3. $\frac{3g^{31}}{2h}$

4. $\frac{36}{25}$

1.9 Scientific Notation

Read and write numbers using scientific notation. Perform operations with numbers expressed in scientific notation. By the end of this lesson, you should be able to define and give an example of the following vocabulary word:

- **Scientific Notation** - a number represented as a product of two factors: a number between 1 and 10 (including 1) and a power of 10.

    - A positive real number 'x' is said to be written in **scientific notation** if it is expressed as

$$x = a \times 10^n$$

    where

$$1 \leq a < 10 \text{ and } n \, \varepsilon \, I.$$

Example 1

Write 2,679,000 using scientific notation.

$$2679000 = 2.679 \times 1,000,000$$
$$2.679 \times 1,000,000 = 2.679 \times 10^6$$

Note: The exponent, $n = 6$, represents the decimal point that is 6 places to the left of the standard position of the decimal point.

Example 2

Write 0.00005728 using scientific notation.

$$0.00005728 = 5.728 \times 0.00001$$

$$5.728 \times 0.00001 = 5.728 \times \frac{1}{100,000}$$

$$5.728 \times \frac{1}{100,000} = 5.728 \times \frac{1}{10^5}$$

$$5.728 \times \frac{1}{100,000} = 5.728 \times 10^{-5}$$

The exponent, $n = -5$, represents the decimal point that is 5 places to the right of the standard position of the decimal point.

Example 3

When working with numbers written in scientific notation, you can use the following rules.

$$(A \times 10^n) + (B \times 10^n) = (A + B) \times 10^n$$

$$(A \times 10^n) - (B \times 10^n) = (A - B) \times 10^n$$

$$(A \times 10^m) \times (B \times 10^n) = (A \times B) \times (10^{m+n})$$

$$(A \times 10^m) \div (B \times 10^n) = (A \div B) \times (10^{m-n})$$

Complete the following table.

TABLE 1.2:

Expression in Scientific Notation	Expression in Standard Form	Result in Standard Form	Result in Scientific Notation
$1.3 \times 10^5 + 2.5 \times 10^5$			
$4.6 \times 10^4 - 2.2 \times 10^4$			
$(3.6 \times 10^2) \times (1.4 \times 10^3)$			
$(4.4 \times 10^4) \div (2.2 \times 10^2)$			

Solution:

TABLE 1.3:

Expression in Scientific Notation	Expression in Standard Form	Result in Standard Form	Result in Scientific Notation
$1.3 \times 10^5 + 2.5 \times 10^5$	$130,000 + 250,000$	380,000	3.8×10^5
$4.6 \times 10^4 - 2.2 \times 10^4$	$46,000 - 22,000$	24,000	2.4×10^4
$(3.6 \times 10^2) \times (1.4 \times 10^3)$	360×1400	504,000	5.04×10^5
$(4.4 \times 10^4) \div (2.2 \times 10^2)$	$44,000 \div 220$	200	2.0×10^2

One advantage of scientific notation is that calculations with large or small numbers can be done by applying the laws of exponents. For example,

- for addition and subtraction problems, the numbers in the last column have the same power of 10 as those in the first column. Note: the powers of 10 <u>must</u> be the same.
- for multiplication, the power of 10 is the result of adding the exponents of the powers in the first column.

- for division, the power of 10 is the result of subtracting the exponents of the powers in the first column.

Example 4

According to scientists, the Earth's volume is 1.083×10^{12} km^3. The volume of the Sun is 1.412×10^{18} km^3. How many times larger is the Sun than the Earth?

"How many times larger" means to set-up a division problem - how many Earths fit into the Sun? So, the Sun's volume is the numerator and the Earth's volume is the denominator.

$\frac{1.412 \times 10^{18}}{1.083 \times 10^{12}}$

Use the properties of exponents to divide the volumes. (We rounded to the nearest $\frac{1}{100}$)

1.304×10^6

In standard format, the sun is 1,304,000 times larger than the Earth. This means 1.3 million Earths fit into the Sun (and the Sun is a medium size star).

Note: you can use mental math to estimate the answer by rounding and dividing the decimal, then looking at the exponent for place value. For example,

Rounding $\frac{1.412}{1.083} = \frac{1}{1} = 1$

$\frac{10^{18}}{10^{12}} = 10^6 = 1,000,000$

Using mental math, we can easily estimate that 1 million Earths fit into the Sun, which is close to the calculated answer.

Tips & Tricks

- Scientific notation is a convenient way to represent very large and very small quantities and measures. Some examples include representing distances between stars or the distance between electrons.

- A number in scientific notation is a single nonzero digit followed by a decimal point and other digits, all multiplied by a power of 10.

- Before the addition and subtraction rule can be used, the powers of 10 must be the same. The numbers must be rewritten (by moving the decimal point) to make the powers equal.

$$(A \times 10^n) + (B \times 10^n) = (A + B) \times 10^n$$

- Move the decimal point to the left of the standard position for larger numbers (e.g. 10^6). "Left for Large numbers"

- Move the decimal point to the right of the standard position for smaller numbers (e.g. 10^{-6}).

- When performing operations with scientific notations, make sure your answers are written in the correct scientific format. If an answer is written as 12.4×10^5, then rewrite it in correct scientific notation accordingly. In this case, move the decimal to the left one space and adjust the exponent up one: 1.24×10^6.

Practice

1. Write the following measurements in scientific notation.

    a. The distance between the Sun and Neptune is 4,500,000,000 km.
    b. The diameter of an electron is approximately 0.000 000 000 000 22 inches.
    c. A nanometre is one billionth (10^{-9}) of a meter.
    d. The mass of the Sun is 1,989,100,000,000,000,000,000,000,000,000 kg.
    e. There are an average of 37,200,000,000,000 cells in the human body.

2. Express each of the following in standard form:

    a. 4.26×10^5

    b. 8×10^4

    c. 5.967×10^{10}

    d. 1.482×10^{-6}

    e. 7.64×10^{-3}

3. Complete the following table.

TABLE 1.4:

Expression in Scientific Notation	Expression in Standard Form	Result in Standard Form	Result in Scientific Notation
$(5.4 \times 10^{-4}) + (2.7 \times 10^{-4})$			
$(8.2 \times 10^8) - (6.3 \times 10^8)$			
$(2.5 \times 10^3) \times (1.1 \times 10^{-6})$			
$(6.8 \times 10^{-4}) \div (3.2 \times 10^{-2})$			

4. Calculate each of the following:

    a. $4.6 \times 10^5 + 5.3 \times 10^5$

    b. $4.7 \times 10^{-3} - 2.4 \times 10^{-3}$

    c. $(7.3 \times 10^5) \times (6.8 \times 10^4)$

    d. $(4.8 \times 10^9) \div (5.79 \times 10^7)$

5. In Russia, the population was 290.9 million in 2002. The total health care costs for the country at that time were 1.7 trillion. Calculate the average amount spent per person on health care. Write your answer in scientific notation. (Remember to write your answer in the correct scientific notation format and adjust the exponent as needed)

6. Express the following quotient in scientific notation: $\frac{6,400,000}{0.008}$.

7. The speed of light is 3×10^8 meters/second. If the sun is 1.5×10^{11} meters from earth, how many seconds does it take light to reach the earth? Express your answer in scientific notation.

8. For the given values, find an approximate value for $\frac{ab}{c}$. Express the answer in scientific notation.

   a. a = 0.000415, b = 521, and c = 71640

   b. a = 76.1, b = 818,000,000, c = 0.000016

   c. a = 9.13 X 10^9, b = 5.45 X 10^{-23}, c = 1.62

9. Last year, we noticed that the population of Tamworth was 5.6 X 10^3. The population of Liverpool was 1.3 X 10^4. Which town had a larger population? How many times larger?

10. Jane read this answer from her calculator (written in scientific notation). Write this number in standard form.

1.25e-9

11. The bedroom of our house is 1,200 cubic meters. We know that there are 3.4 X 10^9 particles of dust per cubic meter. How many particles of dust are present in the bedroom of our house? Express the answer in scientific notation.

Bobcat Review

1. Steve buys hot dogs (which come in packages of 8) and buns (which come in packages of 10) for a picnic. If he wants to have one bun for one dog, what is the least amount he can buy for it come out even?

2. If Steve is having 132 people at the picnic, and each will eat exactly one hot dog, what's the least amount he can buy so any extra hot dogs or buns are "even" as well (the same number of extra hot dogs and buns)?

3. How many people at Steve's picnic will be able to have seconds?

Bobcat Stretch

1. Calculate each of the following:
    a. $4.4 \times 10^3 + 2.2 \times 10^5$
    b. $5.5 \times 10^{-2} - 3.1 \times 10^{-4}$
    c. $(8.2 \times 10^5) \times (2.5 \times 10^{-4})$
    d. $(8.1 \times 10^{-4}) \div (4.5 \times 10^7)$

2. If we suppose that the volume of Lake Rason is approximately $2.56 \times 10^5 \ km^3$ and Lake Rason is 20 times the volume of Lake Rushy. What is the volume of Lake Rushy (approximately)?

Further Review

For more videos and practice problems,

- click here to go to Khan Academy.
- search for "scientific notation" on Khan Academy (www.khanacademy.org).
- go to Khan Academy's Common Core page standard 8.EE.A.4 for more videos and practice problems. You can also try standard 8.EE.A.3 for more challenging problems. (www.khanacademy.org/commoncore/grade -8-EE)

Watch this video for further review on scientific notation.

| MEDIA |
| Click image to the left or use the URL below. |
| URL: https://www.ck12.org/flx/render/embeddedobject/106058 |

Answers

1. a. 4.5×10^9 km

   b. 2.2×10^{-13} inches

   c. 1×10^{-9} of a meter

   d. 1.9891×10^{30} kg

   e. 3.72×10^{13}

2. a. 426,000

   b. 80,000

   c. 59,670,000,000

   d. 0.000001482

   e. 0.00764

3.

TABLE 1.5:

Expression in Scientific Notation	Expression in Standard Form	Result in Standard Form	Result in Scientific Notation
$(5.4 \times 10^{-4}) + (2.7 \times 10^{-4})$	$0.00054 + 0.00027$	0.00081	8.1×10^{-4}
$(8.2 \times 10^8) - (6.3 \times 10^8)$	$820,000,000 - 630,000,000$	$190,000,000$	1.9×10^8
$(2.5 \times 10^3) \times (1.1 \times 10^{-6})$	2500×0.0000011	0.00275	2.75×10^{-3}
$(6.8 \times 10^{-4}) \div (3.2 \times 10^{-2})$	$0.00068 \div 0.032$	0.02125	2.125×10^{-2}

4. a. 9.9×10^5

   b. 2.3×10^{-3}

   c. 4.964×10^{10}

   d. 8.29×10^1

5. 5.8×10^3 or 5,800 spent per person

6. 8×10^8

7. 5×10^2 seconds

8. a. 3.018×10^{-6}

   b. $3.8855 \times 10^{1}5$

   c. $3.071512345679012 \times 10^{-13}$

9. Liverpool is 2.32 times larger than Tamworth.

10. 0.000 000 001 25

11. 4.08×10^{12}

Bobcat Review

1. 40 (4 package of buns and 5 packages of hot dogs)

2. 160 (4 sets of 40)

3. 28

Bobcat Stretch

1. a. 2.244×10^5 - Remember you can't add numbers written in scientific notation with different exponents straight across. You either have to change the numbers to standard form and then calculate the answer or move the decimal of one of the numbers until the exponents match and then add across as usual.

   b. 5.469×10^{-2}.

   c. 2.05×10^2

   d. 1.8×10^{-11}

2. 1.28×10^4

1.10 References

1. . http://msdoddsmathematicsclasses.weebly.com/real-number-system.html .
2. . http://traylork.home.comcast.net/~traylork/mathtech/FactorTreefor136a3b6.HTM .
3. . http://hotmath.com/hotmath_help/topics/greatest-common-factor-of-monomials.html .
4. . webb.grandblanc.east.schoolfusion.us/.../get_group_file.phtml?gid - East Middle school .
5. . http://www.beaconlearningcenter.com/documents/11131_5114.pdf .
6. . http://en.wikipedia.org/wiki/List_of_earthquakes .
7. . http://www.mathworksheetsland.com/8/6scinot/ip.pdf .
8. . http://www.mathworksheetsland.com/8/6scinot/guided.pdf .
9. . http://www.mathworksheetsland.com/8/6scinot/ip.pdf .
10. . http://www.mathworksheetsland.com/8/6scinot/guided.pdf .
11. . http://www.mathworksheetsland.com/8/6scinot/ip.pdf .

CHAPTER 2

Solving Equations

2.1 Equations and Solutions

Write and solve equations using integers, fractions, and decimals. Estimate reasonable solutions.

By the end of this lesson, you should be able to define and give an example of the following vocabulary words:

- **Expression** - an expression that can consist of numbers, variables, and operations $(3x + 1)$.
- **Equation** - a mathematical sentence formed by placing an equal sign between two expressions $(3x + 1 = 7)$.
- **Solution** - a number that you can substitute for a variable to make the equation true.
- **Solving the equation** - finding all the solutions of an equation.
- **Order of Operations**- a set of rules for evaluating an expression involving more than one operation.

Example 1

Is $x = 12$ a solution for $5 - x = 17$?

Substitute 12 for x and evaluate.

$5 - 12 = 17$

$5 + (-12) = 17$

$-7 \neq 17$

So, 12 is <u>not</u> a solution for this equation.

Is $x = (-12)$ a solution for the equation?

$5 - (-12) = 17$

$5 + 12 = 17$

$17 = 17$

So, (-12) is a solution for $5 - x = 17$.

Example 2

Ben and his brother Jason are having their annual medical checkups. The nurse records their heights and weights. She tells Ben that he is 5 feet 7 inches tall and weighs 3 times as much as Jason. If Ben weighs 120 pounds, how much does Jason weigh? Write and solve an equation.

First, write the equation and define your variables.

$3j = b$, where $j =$ Jason and $b =$ Ben.

Second, let's substitute the known numbers. We know Ben weighs 120 pounds.

$3j = 120$

Third, now evaluate the equation for j.

$j = \frac{120}{3}$

$j = 40$

Jason weighs 40 pounds.

Tips & Tricks

- Remember Order of Operations:
    - First, evaluate any groupings (anything within brackets, parentheses, etc...).
    - Second, evaluate any exponents and/or roots.
    - Third, multiply/divide from left to right.
    - Fourth, add/subtract from left to right.

- Begin all word problems by defining your variable. State clearly what you want each variable to represent.

- Break complicated problems into smaller parts or try working them with simpler numbers.
- One advantage of working with equations is that you can always check your work. Think of it like a balance. When we solve an equation, we want the scale to balance. One side will be equal to the other side. When you think you know the value of a variable, plug it into the equation. If your value for the variable is the correct one, both sides will be equal. The two expressions will balance!

Practice
---

1. What is the difference between an expression and an equation? Write an example of each.

2. Do the given solutions make the following equations true? If not, explain the error and find a solution that does make the equation true.

   a. $-x + 9 = 15$, where $x = (-6)$.

   b. $7 + y = 3$, where $y = (-4)$.

   c. $3t - 8 = 19$, where $t = (-9)$.

   d. $\frac{x}{5} - 2 = 10$, where $x = 40$.

   e. $\frac{a-8}{11} = 2$, where $a = 30$.

3. The speed of sound through steel is 5,200 meters per second (m/s). This is 2,520 m/s faster than the speed of sound through silver. Write and solve an equation to find the speed of sound through silver.

4. Do the given solutions make the following equations true? If not, explain the error and find a solution that does make the equation true.

   a. $-\frac{1}{3}b + 3 = 4$, where $b = (-3)$.

   b. $0.75a - 7 = 2$, where $a = (16)$.

   c. $\frac{4}{5}t - 0.2 = 7$, where $t = (9)$.

   d. $\frac{1}{6}c - 5 = 3$, where $c = (-12)$.

   e. $\frac{2(a-1.8)}{6} = 0.9$, where $a = 4.5$.

5. The most snowfall in one day ever recorded in Arizona was 38 inches on Dec 14, 1967 at Heber Ranger Station. Sitgreaves National Forest (where the ranger station is located) is in the midst of another snowstorm. It's 8am and it has already snowed 14.75 inches since midnight. How many more inches will it have to snow before midnight in order to beat the record? Write and solve an equation.

6. The United States population in 2005 was twice the population in 1949. The population of the United States in 2005 was 296 million. Write and solve an equation to find the population in 1949 (in millions).

7. Sam saves at a rate of $15 per month. Write and solve an equation to answer the following questions.

   a. How long will it take him to save $135?

   b. Two video games cost 5 months of savings. His grandmother gave him $45 for his birthday, how many more months will it take him to save up for a video games?

8.   Jason is mixing the GORP "Good ole' Raisins and Peanuts" for his whole group. He makes GORP a bit differently. Jason adds 3.3 pounds of peanuts, 5.8 pounds of M&M's, 3.4 pounds of cashews, 1.2 pound of raisins, and a questionable amount of dried fruit. When he weighs the GORP it weighs 22 pounds. How may pounds of dried fruit were added? Write and solve an equation to answer this question.

9. Monica had some cookies. She gave seven to her sister, then she divided the remainder in half. She gave one half to her dad and kept the other half for herself. She ate all five of her cookies. Write and solve an equation that represents how many cookies Monica had to start.

10. Write a question that represents the equation: $\frac{32-x}{4} = 7$, and then find the solution.

Bobcat Review

Simplify the following expressions:

1. $\frac{54a^2b^2c}{18ac}$

2. $\frac{-21x^3y^6}{3y}$

3. $\frac{-8rs^2t^2}{-16rst^4}$

Bobcat Stretch

1. Paulo has a certain amount of money. If he spends six dollars, then he has one-quarter of the original amount left. Write and solve an equation for how much money Paulo has to start.

2. Write an equation that represents a whole number that when the square of half the number is subtracted from five times the number, we get back to the number itself. (You don't need to solve it.)

3. Write and solve an equation that represents the sum of three consecutive integers equals 372.

4. Write an equation that represents the square of the product of five and a number is equal to 3 more than that number. (You don't need to solve it.)

Further Review

For more videos and practice problems,

- click here to go to Khan Academy.
- search for "integer sums" on Khan Academy (www.khanacademy.org).
- go to Khan Academy's Common Core page standard 8.EE.C.7b (www.khanacademy.org/commoncore/grade -8-EE).

Watch this video for further review of age problems.

MEDIA
Click image to the left or use the URL below.
URL: https://www.ck12.org/flx/render/embeddedobject/106979

Answers

1. Variable answers. Example: Expression $200x + 300$ (no equal sign), Equation $200x + 300 = 700$ (equal sign).

2. a. True

   b. True

   c. False, $t = 9$

   d. False, $x = 60$

   e. True

3. $s + 2520 = 5200$, $s = 2,680$ m/s

4. a. True

   b. False, $a = 12$

   c. True

   d. False, $c = 48$

   e. True

5. $14.75 + s = 38$, s = 23.25 more inches of snow.

6. $2p = 296$, $p = 148$ million

7. a. 15m=135, m = 9 months

   b. 15m+45=15 (5), m=2 months

8. $3.3 + 5.8 + 3.4 + 1.2 + x = 22$, x = 8.3 pounds of fruit were added.

9. $\frac{1}{2}(x - 7) = 5$ or $\frac{x-7}{2} = 5$, x = 17

10. Variable answers. x = 4. A word problem example question: There are 32 students in a class with an uknown number of students absent today. They are doing a project today and divided up into 4 even group with 7 students in each group. How many students are absent today?

Bobcat Review

1. $3ab^2$

2. $-7x^3y^5$

3. $\frac{s}{2t^2}$

Bobcat Stretch

1. $x - 6 = \frac{1}{4}x$ or $x = \frac{1}{4}x + 6$, x = \$8

2. $5x - \left(\frac{x}{2}\right)^2 = x$

3. $x + (x+1) + (x+2) = 372$ or $3x + 3 = 372$, x = 123, 124, 125

4. $(5x)^2 = x + 3$

2.2 Number Properties

Use number properties to help solve equations.

By the end of this lesson, you should be able to define and give an example of the following vocabulary words:

- **Commutative Property of Addition** - In a sum, you can add terms in any order (change the order).
- **Commutative Property of Multiplication** - In a product, you can multiply factors in any order (change the order).
- **Associative Property of Addition** - In a sum, changing the groupings of terms does not change the sum (change the grouping).
- **Associative Property of Multiplication** - In a product, changing the groupings of terms does not change the product (change the grouping).
- **Inverse Operations** - operations that "undo" each other.
- **Inverse Properties** - Addition/Subtraction and Multiplication/Division.

Example 1

The Commutative Property

The Commutative Property of Addition states that the order of the addends does not change the sum. Let's test the property using simple whole numbers.

$$1+2+3 = 6 \qquad 2+1+3 = 6 \qquad 2+3+1 = 6$$
$$3+2+1 = 6 \qquad 3+1+2 = 6 \qquad 1+3+2 = 6$$

The Commutative Property of Multiplication states that the order of the factors does not change the product. Let's test the property using simple whole numbers.

$$1 \cdot 2 \cdot 3 = 6 \qquad 2 \cdot 1 \cdot 3 = 6 \qquad 2 \cdot 3 \cdot 1 = 6$$
$$3 \cdot 2 \cdot 1 = 6 \qquad 3 \cdot 1 \cdot 2 = 6 \qquad 1 \cdot 3 \cdot 2 = 6$$

As you can see, we added and multiplied by three numbers (1, 2, and 3) in many different orders, which had no effect on the answer. The Commutative Property also works for fraction, integers, and decimals too.

Example 2

The Associative Property

The Associative Property of Addition states that the way in which addends are grouped does not change the sum. Once again, let's test the property using simple whole numbers.

$$(1+3)+2 = 6 \qquad\qquad (2+3)+1 = 6 \qquad\qquad (2+1)+3 = 6$$

The Associative Property of Multiplication states that the way in which factors are grouped does not change the product. Once again, let's test the property using simple whole numbers.

$$(1\cdot 3)\cdot 2 = 6 \qquad\qquad (2\cdot 3)\cdot 1 = 6 \qquad\qquad (2\cdot 1)\cdot 3 = 6$$

Clearly, the different way the numbers are grouped has no effect on the final answer. The associative property works for fractions, integers, and decimals too.

Example 3

Another tool you can use to solve equations is inverse operations. Remember what you do to the left side of an equation, you must do to the right.

For subtraction, the inverse operation is addition (and vice versa - if this was an addition problem $x + 27 = 43$, then you would subtract 27 from both sides).

$$
\begin{aligned}
x - 27 &= 43 \\
+27 &= +27 \\
\hline
x + 0 &= 70 \\
x &= 70
\end{aligned}
$$

For multiplication, the inverse operation is division (and vice versa - if this was a division problem $\frac{x}{5} = 30$, then you would multiply 5 by both sides).

$$
\begin{aligned}
5x &= 30 \\
\frac{5x}{5} &= \frac{30}{5} \\
x &= 6
\end{aligned}
$$

This gives us a couple of properties that hold true for all equations. The *properties of equality* tell us that adding, subtracting, multiplying, or dividing the same number to each side of an equation gives us an equivalent equation. They are respectively called the addition property of equality, the subtraction property of equality, etc... This gives us a way to change an equation to our own liking. Anything is acceptable as long as you do the same thing on both sides.

Tips & Tricks

- The Commutataive Property and Associative Property are extremely useful when multiplying fractions. If you are multiplying three fractions and two of the fractions contain factors that you can divide out, you can multiply those two fractions together and have a new fraction in simplest terms, then simply multiply your new simpler fraction with the third fraction.

$$\left(\frac{6}{8} \cdot \frac{1}{2} \cdot \frac{16}{18}\right) = \left(\frac{6}{8} \cdot \frac{16}{18}\right) \cdot \frac{1}{2} = \frac{1}{1} \cdot \frac{2}{3} \cdot \frac{1}{2} = \frac{1}{3}$$

- When you are working with variable expressions, you can use the Commutative and Associative Properties of multiplication to simplify the expression. Let's see how it works.

$$\frac{2}{3} \cdot x \cdot \frac{7}{8} = \frac{2}{3} \cdot \frac{7}{8} \cdot x = \frac{1}{3} \cdot \frac{7}{4} \cdot x = \frac{7}{12} \cdot x$$

- Rewrite subtraction by adding the opposite before using the Commutative and Associative Properties of addition.
- Rewrite division by multiplying by the reciprocal before using the Commutative and Associative Properties of multiplication.

Practice

1. Name the property represented by the following equations.

    a. $(4.5 + 2.3) + 8.2 = 4.5 + (2.3 + 8.2)$

    b. $\frac{1}{3}x + \frac{3}{4} = 2$

       $\frac{1}{3}x + \frac{3}{4} + (-\frac{3}{4}) = 2 + (-\frac{3}{4})$

    c. $(-2) \cdot (-3) \cdot 5 = 5 \cdot (-2) \cdot (-3)$

    d. $3x = 6$

       $\frac{3x}{3} = \frac{6}{3}$

    e. $(-4) + 2.3 + (-3.4) = 2.3 + (-4) + (-3.4)$

    f. $(3 \cdot 4) \cdot 2 = 3 \cdot (4 \cdot 2)$

2. Evaluate the following expressions and name the property(-ies) used to solve each one.

    a. $2 \cdot 0.54 \cdot 5$

    b. $(47 + (-34)) + (-16)$

    c. $\frac{2}{3} \cdot ((-142) \cdot \frac{3}{2})$

    d. $(\frac{1}{2} - \frac{1}{3}) - \frac{2}{3}$

    e. $-6 \cdot (9 \cdot 5)$

3. By applying the Commutative and Associative Property, Alexander says that 3x + 4y is equivalent to (3)(4) + xy. Is he correct? Why or Why not?

4. Evaluate the following equations using inverse operations to isolate (put by itself on one side) the variable.

    a. $\frac{x}{7} = 4$

    b. $3.3x = -6.6$

    c. $\frac{4}{5} + x = \frac{9}{5}$

    d. $-3.5 - y = 4.2$

5. Crazy Sal's is having a Delirious Discount Sale. He is selling everything in his store for $\frac{3}{5}$ of the marked price. Rowena pays $30.99 for a pair of jeans. What was the original price of the jeans? Write and solve an equation to find the original price.

6. Evaluate the following expressions and label each step used to solve.

    a. $0.\overline{33} \cdot -3.48 \div \frac{1}{3}$

    b. $(58 - 273.48) - (-42 - 73)$

    c. $\frac{7}{8} \cdot x \cdot \frac{4}{5}$

    d. $\left(\frac{9}{18} \cdot \frac{6}{7}\right) \cdot \frac{1}{3}$

    e. $(-36.5 - 82.2) + (32.2 + 16.5)$

7. A group of 4 friends purchased 24 tokens that cost 0.25 cents a piece, a round of golf for \$48.00, and a large popcorn for \$4. How much did each friend pay? Write an equation and solve. Label each step used to solve the problem.

8. During TVHS's 1st half of the football game, the hawks passed for 13 yards, 35 yards, 11 yards, and 12 yards. They rushed for 5 yards, 9 yards, 8 yards, -3 yards, and 15 yards. How many total offensive yards did they have at the end of the 1st half? Write an equation and solve. Label each step used to solve the problem.

Bobcat Review

1. Evaluate the following expressions and write your answer in exponent format. Use only positive powers.

    a. $\frac{4^5}{4^3}$

    b. $6^4 \cdot 6^2$

    c. $\frac{5^2}{5^5}$

    d. $7^4 \cdot 7^{(-6)} \cdot 7^5$

    e. $\frac{12^4}{12^4}$

Bobcat Stretch

1. Write and simplify the equation that represents the following statements. Justify each step.

   a. Find the sum of $\frac{1}{5}x + \frac{7}{8}$ and $\frac{3}{10}x - \frac{7}{8}$.

   b. Find the product of $10.6x + 18.55$ and the multiplicative inverse of 5.3.

   c. Find the difference of $\frac{5}{6}c - \frac{5}{6}$ and $\frac{6}{5} - \frac{6}{5}c$.

   d. Find the quotient of $10.6x + 18.55$ and 5.3.

Further Review

For more videos and practice problems,

- click here to go to Mathopolis or MathisFun (scroll to bottom of page). (www.mathsisfun.com/associative-commutative-distributive).
- search for "Commutative law" or "Associative law" on Khan Academy (www.khanacademy.org). Khan Academy only has videos on this topic.

Watch this video to further review number properties.

MEDIA
Click image to the left or use the URL below.
URL: https://www.ck12.org/flx/render/embeddedobject/107009

Answers

1. a. Associative Property of Addition

   b. Inverse Operations using subtraction.

   c. Commutative Property of Multiplication

   d. Inverse Operations using division.

   e. Commutative Property of Addition

   f. Associative Property of Multiplication.

2. a. 5.4 - Commutative Property of Multiplication

   b. -3 - Associative Property of Addition

   c. -142 - Commutative and Associative Property of Multiplication

   d. $-\frac{1}{2}$ - Inverse Property, Commutative and Associative Property of Addition

   e. -270 - Commutative and Associative Property of Multiplication

3. No. You cannot use the Commutative and Associative Property to mix multiplication with addition. Numbers and variables that are factors within a given term must remain factors within that term. For example, if you substituted x = -2 and y = -3, then 3(-2)+4(-3)=(-18) and (3)(4)+(-2)(-3)=18. 18 does not equal (-18).

4. a. $x = 28$

   b. $x = (-2)$

   c. $x = 1$

   d. $y = (-7.7)$

5. $\frac{3}{5}x = 30.99$, x = \$51.65 - use inverse operations to solve.

6. a. -3.48 - change to multiplication problem by multiplying by the inverse (3). Use Commutative Property of Multiplication to change the order and multiply 0.33 by 3 = 1.

   b. -100.48 - change to addition problem by adding the opposite (+ (-273.48), (+42), and (+73). Use the Commutative Property and Associative Property of addition to change the order and grouping to add (42 + 58 = 100) and (-273.48+73=-200.48)

   c. $\frac{7}{10}x$ - change the order with associative property of multiplication ($\frac{7}{8} \cdot \frac{4}{5}$)

   d. $\frac{1}{7}$ - change the grouping with the associative property of multiplicaiton $\frac{9}{18} \cdot (\frac{6}{7} \cdot \frac{1}{3})$, then simplify.

   e. (-70) - change the order with the commutative property $(32.2 - 82.2) + (-36.5 + 16.5)$.

7. Each friend paid $14.50. Multiply the grouping first, then use inverse operations to multiply both sides by 4. Now we can use the Commutative Property of addition to change the order and add 4+6. Repeat inverse operations and divide both sides by 4 and simplify.

$$x = \frac{(24 \cdot 0.25) + 48 + 4}{4}$$
$$4x = 6 + 48 + 4$$
$$4x = 10 + 48$$
$$4x = 58$$
$$x = \frac{58}{4} = 14.5$$

8. 105 yards. Use the Commutative Property to change the order and the Associative Property to change the groupings.

$$(13 + 35 + 11 + 12) + (5 + 9 + 8 + (-3) + 15)$$
$$(13 + (-3)) + (35 + 5) + (11 + 9) + (12 + 8 + 15)$$
$$10 + 40 + 20 + 35$$

Bobcat Review

1. a. 4^2

   b. 6^6

   c. $\frac{1}{5^3}$

   d. 7^3

   e. $12^0 = 1$

Bobcat Stretch

1. a. $\frac{1}{2}x$ (use Associative Property and Commutative Property of addition by regrouping $\frac{7}{8} - \frac{7}{8}$ to cancel out those terms, then collect like terms $\frac{1}{5}x + \frac{3}{10}x$ to simplify.)

   b. $(10.6x + 18.55)\frac{1}{5.3} = 2x + 3.5$ (use Distributive Property to multiply each term by $\frac{1}{5.3}$, use Multiplicative Inverse to simplify.)

   c. $\frac{29}{15}c + \frac{-29}{15}$ (rewrite the subtractions as an addition problem, then collect like terms and simplify).

   d. $2x + 3.5$ (rewrite the division as multiplication, which turns it into the same problem as 1b.)

2.3 The Distributive Property and Collecting Like Terms

Use the distributive property and combine like terms to simplify expressions.

By the end of this lesson, you should be able to define and give an example of the following vocabulary words:

- **Terms** - the parts of an expression that is added together.
- **Like Terms** - terms that have identical variable parts raised to the same power.
- **Coefficient** - the number part of a term that includes a variable.
- **Constant Term** - a term that has a number but no variable.
- **Distributive Property** - You can multiply a number and a sum by multiplying the number by each part of the sum and then adding these products. $a(b+c) = ab + ac$ or $a(b-c) = ab - ac$

Example 1

Determine the value of 11(2 - 6).

As you know, you can use different methods to simplify expressions correctly. Here are two examples of how you can determine the value of 11(2-6).

You can apply the Order of Operations to evaluate the amount inside the parentheses first:

$$11(2-6) = 11(-4) = -44$$

Or, you can apply the Distributive Property to get the same result by distributing the "11" to each term within the parentheses, and then simplifying:

$$11(2-6) = 11(2) - 11(6) = 22 - 66 = -44$$

The Distributive Property is one of the most common mathematical properties used in everyday life. Any time we have two or more groups of objects, the Distributive Property can help us solve for an unknown.

Example 2

Simplify $2x^2 + 3x - 4 - x^2 + x + 9$.

It is often best to group like terms together first, and then simplify:

$$2x^2 + 3x - 4 - x^2 + x + 9 \ = (2x^2 - x^2) + (3x + x) + (-4 + 9) \ = \mathbf{x^2 + 4x + 5}$$

Tips & Tricks

- When applying the Distributive Property you **MUST** take note of any **negative signs!**
- When combining like terms, make sure you don't overdo it by adding terms together that can't actually be combined (for example, $4x + 3 \neq 7x$, $7x^2 + 3x \neq 10x^2$ both of these contain different terms that can't be combined).

Practice

1. Use the Distributive Property to simplify the following expressions.

   a. $4(3+2)$

   b. $4(x-2)$

   c. $-2(7+2a-3)$

   d. $x(-8-2x+4)$

   e. $-5(x-4)$

2. Combine like terms to simplify the following expression.

   a. $5a+3c+3-3a$

   b. $-4x+5x^2-3+x$

   c. $8x-3y+4y-2x+5$

   d. $7y^2+8y+4y^2+z+3$

   e. $3b^2-4b-2b+2b^2+a$

3. At the end of the school year, a teacher makes a gift bag for each of his students. Each bag contains one class photograph, two party favors and five pieces of candy. The teacher will distribute the bags among his 28 students. How many of each item does the teacher need? Write an equation and use the Distributive Property to find how many of each item the teacher needs to buy.

4. A stop-sign is in the shape of an octagon with eight sides. Each side is $2x + 1$ units. Write and simplify an algebraic expression to represent the perimeter of this stop sign in terms of x.

5. A rectangle has a width of x - 3 units and a length of 2x units. Write and simplify an algebraic expression to represent the perimeter of this rectangle in terms of x.

6. Which of the following expressions are equivalent to $3 + 2a + 5 + 3 + 5 + 2a$?

  a. $2(3) + 2(2a+5)$

  b. $2(2a + 3 + 5)$

  c. $4a + 16$

  d. $16 + 4a$

  e. $20a$

7. Simplify the following expressions.

  a. $3(x-4)+5x-2$

  b. $-3.2a - 2(1.4a - 6) + 4.5$

  c. $-8b^2 + 3b - 3(2 - b)$

  d. $5c(3c - 2) - 2(5c + c^2)$

  e. $\frac{1}{2}(4z + 6)$

8. A bookcase has five shelves, and each shelf contains seven poetry books and eleven novels. How many of each type of book does the bookcase contain?

9. Each student on a field trip into a forest is to be given an emergency survival kit. The kit is to contain a flashlight, a first aid kit, and emergency food rations. Flashlights cost $12 each, first aid kits are $7 each and emergency food rations cost $2 per day.

  a. Explain how to use mental math to figure out the total cost per item to equip 5 students for 3 days with their emergency survival kits.

  b. For a class of 17 students, how many days worth of rations can be provided with each kit if they have a budget of $500 to spend on emergency survival kits?

10. Jose wants new flooring for his living room and dining room. His living room is an 8 m by 12 m rectangle. His dining room is an 8 m by 10 m rectangle. The flooring he wants to use costs $4.15 per square meter. How much will the flooring cost.

Bobcat Review

1. Use the following expression to answer the questions below: $-4a + 3b - 5b^2 + 7a - 2b + 6$

    a. What is the constant term?

    b. What is the coefficient of the 2nd term?

    c. What are the like terms?

    d. What are the variables?

    e. What is the coefficient of the squared variable?

Bobcat Stretch

1. Simplify $\frac{2x+8}{4} + 3x + 5$.

2. Simplify $\frac{2}{7}(3y^2 - 11)$.

3. Simplify $\frac{2x}{7}\left(3y^2 - \frac{11}{xy}\right)$.

Further Review

For more videos and practice problems,

- click here to go to Khan Academy to review distributive property.
- click here for more "collect like terms" practice problems to form equivalent expressions.
- search for "Combining like terms with distribution" on Khan Academy (www.khanacademy.org).
- go to Khan Academy's Common Core page standard 7.EE.A.1 (www.khanacademy.org/commoncore/grade-7-EE).

Watch this video to further review the distributive property.

MEDIA
Click image to the left or use the URL below.
URL: https://www.ck12.org/flx/render/embeddedobject/107043

Watch this video to further review collecting like terms.

MEDIA
Click image to the left or use the URL below.
URL: https://www.ck12.org/flx/render/embeddedobject/107045

Answers
---

1. a. 20

   b. $4x - 8$

   c. $-4a - 8$

   d. $-4x - 2x^2$

   e. $-5x + 20$

2. a. $2a + 3c + 3$

   b. $-3x + 5x^2 - 3$

   c. $6x + y + 5$

   d. $11y^2 + 8y + z + 3$

   e. $5b^2 - 6b + a$

3. First, we can write an expression for the contents of each bag: Items = (photo + 2 favors + 5 candies), or simply $I = (p + 2f + 5c)$.

For all 28 students, the teacher will need 28 times that number of items, so $I = 28(p + 2f + 5c)$.

Next, **the Distributive Property** tells us that when we have a single term multiplied by a sum of several terms, we can rewrite it by multiplying the single term by each of the other terms separately. In other words, $28(p + 2f + 5c) = 28(p) + 28(2f) + 28(5c)$, which simplifies to $28p + 56f + 140c$. So the teacher needs 28 class photos, 56 party favors and 140 pieces of candy.

4. $8(2x + 1) = 16x + 8$

5. $2(x - 3) + 2(2x) = 2x - 6 + 4x = 6x - 6$

6. a, b, c, and d are all equivalent.

7. a. $3x - 12 + 5x - 2 = 8x - 14$

   b. $-3.2a - 2.8a + 12 + 4.5 = -6a + 16.5$

   c. $-8b^2 + 3b - 6 + 3b = 8b^2 + 6b - 6$

   d. $15c^2 - 10c - 10c - 2c^2 = 13c^2 - 20c$

   e. $2z + 3$

8. $5(7p + 11n) = 35p + 55n = 35$ poetry books and 55 novels

9. a. You must multiply 5 (for the 5 students) by the cost for each item for the flashlight and first aid kit (there's only 1 needed). For the rations, you must first calculate the total cost for 1 person by multiplying \$2 by 3 days for a total cost of \$6. Then, you multiply \$6 by 5 to get the total cost for the rations for 5 students. $5(12f + 7k + 6r) = 60f + 35k + 30r = \$60$ for flashlights, \$35 for first aid kits, and \$30 for emergency food rations.

9. b. 5 days worth of emergency rations can be purchased with each survival kit.

The unknown quantity in this problem is the number of days' rations. This will be x in our expression. Each kit will contain **one** $12 flashlight, **one** $7 first aid kit, and x times $2 worth of rations, for a total cost of $(12+7+2x)$ dollars. With 17 kits, therefore, the total cost will be $17(12+7+2x)$ dollars. We can use the Distributive Property on this expression:

$$17(12+7+2x) = 204+119+34x$$

Since the total cost can be at most $500, we set the expression equal to 500 and solve for x. (You'll learn in more detail how to solve equations like this in the next chapter.)

$$204+119+34x = 500$$
$$323+34x = 500$$
$$323+34x-323 = 500-323$$
$$34x = 177$$
$$\frac{34x}{34} = \frac{177}{34}$$
$$x \approx 5.206$$

Since this represents the number of days' worth of rations that can be bought, we must **round to the next lowest whole number**. We wouldn't have enough money to buy a sixth day of supplies.

10. $730.40

Bobcat Review

1. a. 6

   b. 3

   c. -4a + 7a, 3b - 2b

   d. a, b

   c. -5

Bobcat Stretch

1. 3.5x + 7 - PEMDAS directs to do division grouping first $\frac{2x+8}{4}$ can be re-written as $\frac{1}{4}(2x+8)$. Then we can distribute the $\frac{1}{4}$:

   $\frac{1}{4}(2x+8) = \frac{2x}{4} + \frac{8}{4} = \frac{x}{2} + 2 = 0.5x + 2$

   Now simplify the expression by collecting like terms.

   $0.5x + 2 + 3x + 5 = 3.5x + 7$

2. $\frac{2}{7}(3y^2 - 11) = \frac{2}{7}(3y^2) + \frac{2}{7}(-11) = \frac{6y^2}{7} - \frac{22}{7}$

3. $\frac{2x}{7}\left(3y^2 - \frac{11}{xy}\right) = \frac{2x}{7}(3y^2) + \frac{2x}{7}\left(-\frac{11}{xy}\right) = \frac{6xy^2}{7} - \frac{22x}{7xy}$, then simplify by canceling out the x's $\frac{6xy^2}{7} - \frac{22}{7y}$

2.4 Two-Step Equations

Solve two-step equations.

By the end of this lesson, you should be able to define and give an example of the following vocabulary words:

- **Equation** - a mathematical sentence formed by setting two expressions equal.
- **Solution** - a number that makes the equation true when substituted for the variable in the equation.

Example 1

Solve: $3x + 2 = 29$

Solution

Two inverse operations are required to solve this equation.

$$3x + 2 = 29$$
$$\underline{\quad -2 = -2}$$
$$3x = 27$$

Subtract 2 from both sides :

$$\frac{3x}{3} = \frac{27}{3}$$
$$x = 9$$

Divide both sides by 3

Example 2

Solve: $6(x+4) = 12$

Solution

This equation has the *x buried* in parentheses. In order to extract it we can proceed in one of two ways: we can either distribute the six on the left, or divide both sides by six to remove it from the left. Since the right hand side of the equation is a multiple of six, it makes sense to divide.

$$6(x+4) = 12$$ 　　　　　Divide both sides by 6.

$$\frac{\cancel{6}(x+4)}{\cancel{6}} = \frac{12}{6}$$

$$x \cancel{+4} = 2$$ 　　　　　Subtract 4 from both sides.

$$\underline{\quad \cancel{-4} \quad -4 \quad}$$

$$x = -2$$

Example 3

Solve: $\frac{5}{4}x + 5 = 20$

Solution:

$$\frac{5}{4}x + 5 = 20$$

$$\underline{\quad -5 = -5 \quad} \qquad \text{Add 5 to both sides.}$$

$$\frac{5}{4}x = 15$$

$$\frac{4}{1} \cdot \frac{5}{4}x = 15 \cdot 4 \qquad \text{Multiply both sides by 4.}$$

$$5x = 60$$

$$x = 12$$

Tips & Tricks

- Remember what you do to the left side of the equation, you must do to the right.
- Take care of any constants first. Generally it, is good to go from the outside in. If there are parentheses around an expression with a variable in it, divide out what is outside the parentheses first.
- Remember - terms with the same variable in them raised to the same power (or no variable in them) are like terms. Combine like terms (adding or subtracting them from each other) to simplify the expression and solve for the unknown.

Practice
---

1. Solve the following equations for the unknown variable.

    a. $-5w - 11 = -21$

    b. $11 - 3a = 44$

    c. $32 = 2 - 5p$

    d. $33.3t - 133.2 = 0$

    e. $8.2z + 5.4 = (-11)$

2. True or False. If False, identify the error, then find the solution to make the statement true.

$$8a - 4 = 12$$
$$8a = 8$$
$$a = 1$$

3. Solve the following equations for the unknown variable.

    a. $14 + \frac{4}{5}b = 18$

    b. $\frac{x}{3} - 7 = (-14)$

    c. $\frac{3a}{4} - 6 = (-3)$

    d. $5q - 7 = \frac{2}{3}$

    e. $-3y - 8 = -6$

4. Write an equation that represents the perimeter of this rectangle. Solve for x, when P (perimeter) $= 132$.

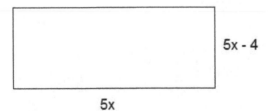

5x - 4

5x

5. Solve the following equations for the unknown variable.

    a. $5x - (3x + 2) = 1$

    b. $4(x + 3) = 1$

    c. $0.1y + 11 = 0$

    d. $7a + \frac{2}{3} + 6a + \frac{1}{4} = 2$

6. Robert's mom is planning a surprise birthday party for him. She will hire a DJ, and will provide party food for all the guests. The DJ costs $240.35 including tax for the afternoon, and the food will cost $3.95 per person. Robert's mom has a budget of $450. Write an equation to help her determine the maximum number of guests she can invite.

7. Solve the following equations by using either the distributive property or inverse operations as your first step. Explain your choice.

    a. $5(2.5a + 6) = 30$

    b. $4(1.5b - 3) = 2.4$

    c. $7c - (2.7c - 6.3) = 27.8$

8. Solve the following equations for the unknown variable.

    a. $\frac{5(q-7)}{12} = \frac{2}{3}$

    b. $\frac{5q-7}{12} = \frac{2}{3}$

    c. $s - \frac{3s}{8} = \frac{5}{6}$

9. Jenny wants to save $999 to go to Puerto Rico. She saves $47.50 each week and now has $237.50. How many more weeks (w) it will take to save $999? Write an equation and solve to find how many more weeks Jenny must save before she can book a trip to Puerto Rico.

10. At an amusement park, each student is given $18 for food. This covers the cost of 2 meals at x dollars each plus $7 worth of snacks. Solve x to find how much money the school expects each student will spend per meal.

Bobcat Review

For each step in the following equations, justify (label) each step taken to solve the equation.

1. Solve $\frac{2}{3}a - 10 = 20$.

$$\frac{2}{3}a - 10 = 20$$
$$+10 = +10$$
$$\frac{2}{3}a = 30$$
$$\frac{3}{1} \cdot \frac{2}{3}x = 30 \cdot 3$$
$$\frac{2x}{2} = \frac{90}{2}$$
$$x = 45$$

2. Solve $4.5(2b + 4) = -18$.

$$4.5(2b) + 4.5(4) = -18$$
$$9b + 18 = -18$$
$$-18 = -18$$
$$9b = -36$$
$$\frac{9b}{9} = \frac{-36}{9}$$
$$b = -4$$

3. Solve $4.5(2b + 4) = -18$.

$$\frac{4.5(2b + 4)}{4.5} = \frac{-18}{4.5}$$
$$2b + 4 = -4$$
$$-4 = -4$$
$$2b = -8$$
$$\frac{2b}{2} = \frac{-8}{2}$$
$$b = -4$$

Bobcat Stretch

Solve the following equations.

1. $-2(2y+4) = -5.\overline{33}y$

2. $-16.6y = 5 - 3(5y+3)$

3. $-15 - 6a - 8a = 8 - 5(3+3a)$

4. The ages of three brothers are consecutive integers. The sum of their ages is 39. Find their ages.

Further Review

For more videos and practice problems,

- click here to go to Khan Academy.
- search for "Two-step equations" on Khan Academy (www.khanacademy.org).

Watch this video for a review of how to solve two-step equations.

 **Multimedia**

MEDIA
Click image to the left or use the URL below.
URL: https://www.ck12.org/flx/render/embeddedobject/107103

Answers

1. a. $w = 2$

   b. $a = -11$

   c. $p = -6$

   d. $t = 4$

   e. $z = -2$

2. False. Using Inverse operations 4 should have been added to both sides (not subtracted), so $a = 2$.

3. a. $b = 5$

   b. $x = -21$

   c. $a = 4$

   d. $q = \frac{23}{15}$

   e. $y = -\frac{2}{3}$

4. $x = 7$

5. a. $x = 1.5$ or $\frac{3}{2}$

   b. $x = -2.75$ or $-\frac{11}{4}$

   c. $y = -110$

   d. $a = \frac{1}{12}$

6. $x = 53.08$, so she can invite 53 guests to the party.

7. a. $a = 0$, Inverse operations since 30 is easily divided by 5.

   b. $b = 2.4$, Distributive Property since it was easier to multiply out 4 by each term in the parentheses, then divide 2.4 by 4 if using inverse operations.

   c. $c = 5$, Distributive Property since it's easier to remove the parentheses first.

8. a. $q = \frac{43}{5}$

   b. $q = 3$

   c. $s = \frac{4}{3}$

9. a little over 16 weeks, w = 16.03 weeks

10. $x = 5.5$, so the school expects each meal to cost $5.50.

Bobcat Review

1. Inverse operations to cancel out (-10) by adding 10 to both sides. Inverse operations to cancel out 3 by multiplying each side by 3. Inverse operations to cancel out 2 by multiplying each side by 2.

2. Distributive Property to multiply out 4.5 by each term in parentheses. Inverse operations to cancel out 18 by subtracting 18 from both sides. Inverse operations to cancel out 9 by dividing both sides by 9.

3. Inverse operations to cancel out 4.5 by dividing each side by 4.5. Inverse operations to cancel out 4 by subtracting 4 from both sides. Inverse operations to cancel out 2 by dividing both sides by 2.

Bobcat Stretch

1. $y = 6$

2. $y = 2.5$

3. $a = 8$

4. 12, 13, 14

2.5 Multi-Step Equations

Solve equations by using two or more steps.

Example 1

Solve for *m*: $6(1+2m) - 3m = 24$

Apply the Distributive Property to the left side of the equation. Multiply each of the two numbers inside the parentheses by 6 and then add those products.

$$6(1+2m) - 3m = 24$$
$$(6 \times 1) + (6 \times 2m) - 3m = 24$$
$$6 + 12m - 3m = 24$$

Next, subtract the like terms—$12m$ and $3m$—on the left side of the equation.

$$6 + 12m - 3m = 24$$
$$6 + (12m - 3m) = 24$$
$$6 + 9m = 24$$

Finally, solve as you would solve any two-step equation. Subtract 6 from both sides of the equation.

$$6 + 9m = 24$$
$$6 - 6 + 9m = 24 - 6$$
$$0 + 9m = 18$$
$$9m = 18$$

Now, divide both sides of the equation by 9.

$$9m = 18$$
$$\frac{9m}{9} = \frac{18}{9}$$
$$1m = 2$$
$$m = 2$$

The value of *m* is 2.

Example 2

Solve for *a*: $\frac{-4a+6}{8} = 8$

First, clear the fractions by using inverse operations to cancel out the 8. Multiply both sides by 8.

$$\frac{-4a+6}{8} = 8$$
$$\cancel{8} \cdot \frac{-4a+6}{\cancel{8}} = 8 \cdot 8$$
$$-4a+6 = 64$$

Next, apply inverse operations again to cancel out the 6 by subtracting 6 from both sides.

$$-4a\cancel{+6} = 64$$
$$\cancel{-6} = -6$$
$$-4a = 58$$

Finally, divide both sides of the equation by -4.

$$\frac{\cancel{-4}a}{\cancel{-4}} = \frac{58}{-4}$$
$$a = -14.5$$

The value of *a* **is -14.5.**

Tips & Tricks

- When solving multi-step equations, you always want to combine everything that you can before moving on to solving the equation.

Practice
---

1. Solve for the variable, then check the solution.

    a. $2(x+3)-4=8$

    b. $6a+4+7a=30$

    c. $6(x+4)+3x-6=54$

    d. $6y+3(y-4)=33$

    e. $5(a+3)+6(a+1)+8a=40$

2. True or False. If False, identify the error and then find a solution that makes the statement true.

$$12-3(x-8)=6$$
$$12-3x-24=6$$
$$-3x-12=6$$
$$-3x=18$$
$$x=-6$$

3. A teacher gave eight students each the same amount of candy for completing a project. The next day, six different students were each given the same amount of candy as the first group for completing their project. At the end of the week, two students were each given that same amount of candy as the first and second group plus three additional pieces of candy for "going above and beyond" with their project. The total number of pieces of candy given out was thirty-eight. How much candy did each student receive in group 1, group 2, and group 3? Write and solve an equation to find the unknown amount of candy.

4. Solve for the variable, then check the solution.

    a. $\frac{x-4}{5}=-4$

    b. $\frac{-6x+9}{5}=3$

    c. $\frac{-3(7-4x)}{-5}=-3$

5. Herman is saving up for a tablet that costs $499. He has saved $129 so far. Every week he earns $32.00 bagging groceries and $12 for walking his neighbor's dog, but spends $7 on lunches. Write and solve an equation to find how many weeks it will take Herman to save enough money to purchase the tablet. Solve for x and y.

6. Solve for the variable, then check the solution.

    a. $x + 3x + 2x + 3(x+1) = 30$

    b. $2x + 4x + 6x - 2(x+3) = 34$

    c. $3(y-1) + 2(y+3) = 13$

    d. $-4 + 3(4x-2) = 12$

    e. $5(-2x+2) + 2(-5x-5) = 25$

7. The rectangle and triangle have the same perimeter and the length of the side y is 4.

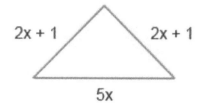 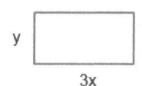

8. Solve for the variable, then check the solution.

    a. $x + 3.3x + 2.7x + 3.5(x+1) = 35$

    b. $4(a+3) - 2(a+6) = 7$

    c. $\frac{4}{5}(10x-5) - \frac{2}{5}(15x+10) = 9$

Bobcat Review

1. Convert the following decimal expansions to a rational number $\frac{a}{b}$.

   a. $0.\overline{45}$

   b. $-0.\overline{8}$

   c. $2.\overline{49}$

2. Write $\frac{7}{11}$ as a decimal.

Bobcat Stretch

1. Solve for the variable, then check the solution

   a. $\frac{2}{3}(6x - 18) - \frac{5}{6}(6x + 18) = -23$

   b. $-5(8 - x) + \frac{1}{3}(\frac{1}{2}x - 2x) = -4$

   c. $\frac{3}{5}(20x + 30) - 3x + 5(x - 4.6) = 27.2$

Further Review

For more videos and practice problems,

- click here to go to CK-12 Braingenie.
- search for "Geometeric Perimeter Problems using multi-step equations" on CK-12 Braingenie (braingenie.ck12.org/sk

Watch this video to further review multi-step equations with variables on both sides.

MEDIA
Click image to the left or use the URL below.
URL: https://www.ck12.org/flx/render/embeddedobject/107213

Answers

1. a. $x = 3$

   b. $a = 2$

   c. $x = 4$

   d. $y = 5$

   e. $a = 1$

2. $x = 10$, When the distributive property was used on the first step, -3 times -8 equals 24 (not negative 24).

3. Group 1 and 2 students each received 2 pieces of candy.

   Group 3 students received 5 pieces of candy (c + 3) for "going above and beyond"

   $c = 2$, so the unknown amount of candy was two pieces.

   $8c + 6c + 2(c + 3) = 38$

   Now solve the equation by first getting rid of the parentheses.

   $8c + 6c + 2c + 6 = 38$

   Next, combine like terms.

   $16c + 6 = 38$

   Now subtract six from both sides of the equation.

   $16c + 6 - 6 = 38 - 6$

   $16c = 32$

   $c = 2$

4. a. $x = (-16)$

   b. $x = (-1)$

   c. $x = 3$

5. 10 weeks, $499 = 129 + x(12 + 32 - 7)$

6. a. $x = 3$

   b. $x = 4$

   c. $y = 2$

   d. $x = \frac{22}{12} = \frac{11}{6}$

   e. $x = -\frac{25}{20} = -\frac{5}{4}$

7. $x = 2$ and $y = 4$

   Equation: $9x + 2 = 6x + 2y$

   Gather the x terms on the left side of the equation $9x - 6x + 2 = 2y$

   Simplify it: $3x + 2 = 2y$

   $\frac{3x+2}{2} = y$

   $\frac{3}{2}x + 1 = y$

   Solve for x. $3x = 6$, so $x = 2$.

   Substitute 2 for "x" and solve for y.

   $\frac{3}{2}(2) + 1 = y$

   $4 = y$.

8. a. $x = 3$

   b. $a = 3.5$

   c. $x = 8.5$

Bobcat Review

1. a. $\frac{5}{11}$

Where: $x = 0.\overline{45}, 100x - x = 45, 99x = 45, x = \frac{45}{99} = \frac{5}{11}$

   b. $-\frac{8}{9}$

   c. $\frac{247}{99}$

Where: $x = 2.\overline{49}, 100x = 249.\overline{49}, 100x - x = 249.\overline{49} - 2.\overline{49}, 99x = 247, x = \frac{247}{99}$

2. $0.\overline{63}$

Bobcat Stretch

1. a. $x = (-4)$

   b. $x = 8$

   c. $x = 2.3$

2.6 Equations with Square and Cube Roots

Find the square root and cube root of numbers. Solve equations containing square roots and cube roots.

By the end of this lesson, you should be able to define and give an example of the following vocabulary words:

- **Radical Sign** - the sign that indicates the square root of a number. For example, $\sqrt{2}$.
- **Square Roots** - a square root of number n is a number m which, when multiplied by itself, equals n. For example, $\sqrt{25} = \pm 5$ because $5^2 = 25$.
- **Cube Roots** - a cube root of a number n is a number m which, when multiplied by itself 3 times, equals n. For example, $\sqrt[3]{27} = 3$ because $3^3 = 27$
- **Perfect Square** - a number that is the square of an integer. For example, $\sqrt{9} = \pm 3$ because $3^2 = 9$.

Example 1

Solve $x^2 + 3 = 12$.

We want to find the value of x. First, notice that we have a two-step equation. One of the operations is multiplication with the square and the other is addition.

Let's start by subtracting three from both sides.

$$x^2 + 3 - 3 = 12 - 3$$
$$x^2 = 9$$

Now we want to get x alone. To do this, we take the square root of both sides of the equation.

$$\sqrt{x^2} = \sqrt{9}$$
$$x = \pm 3$$

Our answer is ± 3 because both multiplied by itself equal 9.

Example 2

Solve $\sqrt[3]{\dfrac{8}{27}}$.

First we distribute the cube root to both sides of the fraction.

$$\frac{\sqrt[3]{8}}{\sqrt[3]{27}}$$

Now we can evaluate the expression. We know $2^3 = 8$ and $3^3 = 27$, so our final answer is...

$\frac{2}{3}$ because $\left(\frac{2}{3}\right)^3 = \frac{8}{27}$

Tips & Tricks

- For square root equations, the answer can be both a positive or negative number.
- For positive cube roots, the answer can only be positive.
- For negative cube roots, the answer can only be negative.
- Think of a cube when dealing with cube roots:

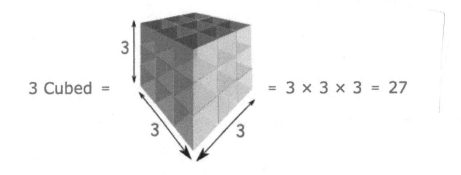

$$3 \text{ Cubed} = \qquad = 3 \times 3 \times 3 = 27$$

Practice

1. Evaluate the square root.

     a. $\sqrt{16}$

     b. $-\sqrt{36}$

     c. $\sqrt{144}$

     d. $\sqrt{\dfrac{1}{9}}$

     e. $\sqrt{\dfrac{36}{49}}$

2. The shape of a baseball infield is a square. The area of the infield is 8,100 square feet. What is the distance between each base? (Hint: the bases are the 4 corners of the square.) Write and solve an equation to find the distance between bases?

3. Evaluate the cube root.

     a. $\sqrt[3]{125}$

     b. $\sqrt[3]{\dfrac{1}{8}}$

     c. $\sqrt[3]{-64}$

     d. $\sqrt[3]{1000}$

4. A rubik's cube has a volume (length x, width x, height x) of 27 cubic inches. Write and solve an equation to find the length of a side of rubik's cube?

5. Solve the square root equations. Check your solution(s):

    a. $x^2 = 64$

    b. $q^2 = \frac{1}{100}$

    c. $m^2 - 144 = 0$

    d. $w^2 + 97 = 113$

    e. $f^2 - 64 = 161$

6. A square skating rink has an area of 3600 square feet. What is the perimeter of the rink?

7. Solve the cube root equations. Check your solutions.

    a. $x^3 = 27$

    b. $p^3 = 216$

    c. $y^3 = 125$

8. A cubic room has a volume of 1000 cubic meters. What is the length of a wall?

9. Solve for x.

$$4x(x + 3x) + x(-4x - 3x) = 36$$

Bobcat Review

1. Determine whether the square root is rational or irrational.

    a. $\sqrt{10}$

    b. $\sqrt{36}$

    c. $\sqrt{12}$

    d. $\sqrt{6.25}$

2. Order the following numbers from least to greatest: -3.56, 4.2, $\frac{13}{5}$, $\sqrt{3}$, and $-\sqrt{5}$.

Bobcat Stretch

1. The time it takes for an object dropped from a certain height to reach the ground can be modeled by the equation $t = \frac{1}{4}\sqrt{h}$, where h is the height in feet above sea level. You are standing on the top of a cliff and it takes 6 seconds for a rock you drop to reach the ground. How tall is the cliff?

2. Solve $\sqrt{x-1} = 8$

3. $6(x^3 + 2) - 2(-5 - x^3) = 49$

Further Review

For more videos and practice problems,

- click here to go to Khan Academy.
- search for "cube roots" or "square roots of perfect squares" on Khan Academy (www.khanacademy.org).
- go to Khan Academy's Common Core page standard 8.EE.A.2 (www.khanacademy.org/commoncore/grade -8-EE).

Click here to watch a video to further review cube roots.

MEDIA
Click image to the left or use the URL below.
URL: https://www.ck12.org/flx/render/embeddedobject/107227

Answers

1. a. ± 4

   b. - 6

   c. ± 12

   d. $\pm\frac{1}{3}$

   e. $\pm\frac{6}{7}$

2. 90 ft.

   $\sqrt{8100} = 90$

3. a. 5

   b. $\frac{1}{2}$

   c. -4

   d. 10

4. 3 inches, $\sqrt[3]{27}$

5. a. $x = \pm 8$

   b. $q = \pm \frac{1}{10}$

   c. $m = \pm 12$

   d. $w = \pm 4$

   e. $f = \pm 15$

6. 240 feet, $\sqrt{3600} = 60, 60 \times 4 = 240$

7. a. $x = 3$

   b. $p = 6$

   c. $y = 5$

8. 10 meters, $\sqrt[3]{1000} = 10$.

9. $x = \pm 2$

Bobcat Review

1. a. Irrational (non-terminating, non-repeating decimal)

   b. Rational (natural number, whole number, integer, terminating decimal)

   c. Irrational (non-terminating, non-repeating decimal)

   d. Rational (terminating decimal)

2. $-3.56, -\sqrt{5}, \sqrt{3}, \frac{13}{5}, 4.2$

Bobcat Stretch

1. 576 feet, $6 = \frac{1}{4}\sqrt{h}$, $24 = \sqrt{h}$, $24^2 = h$, $576 = h$

2. $x = 65$, $x - 1 = 8^2, x - 1 = 64, x = 65$

3. $x = \frac{3}{2}$

2.7 Multi-Step Equation Word Problems

Solve word problems by writing multi-step equations.

Example 1

Write a math (algebraic) model that represents the following statement and solve for the variable.

The sum of 4 times a number divided by -3 and 6 is (- 6).

First let's identify what type of problem this is, sum is our clue, so we are doing an addition problem.

Now let's translate what we know. We know the sum (-6), we know an addend is 6, and we know the other addend is equal to $\frac{4x}{-3}$ (4 times an uknown number (x) divided by -3).

$$\frac{4x}{-3} + 6 = -6$$

Finally, let's solve the equation.

$\frac{4x}{-3} = -12$ (inverse operations - subtract 6 from both sides)

$4x = 36$ (inverse operations - multiply both sides by -3)

$x = 9$ (inverse operations - divide both sides by 4)

Our answer is 9 as the solution for the unknown number in the verbal statement.

Example 2

Sarah signed 1/2 of the Christmas cards, and Richard signed 3/8 of them. If there are 32 cards in all, how many are left to be signed?

Write an equation to represent the verbal model. First, we define the variable. We're going to have "x" represent the # of cards left to be signed.

$$(\tfrac{1}{2} \cdot 32) + (\tfrac{3}{8} \cdot 32) + x = 32$$

This equation states that 1/2 of 32 cards plus 3/8 of 32 cards plus an unknown amount equals the total number of Christmas cards that need to be signed, which is 32.

Now, let's solve by evaluating inside the parentheses first (remember order of operations) and applying our other "problem-solving" properties.

$16 + 12 + x = 32$ (combine like terms)

$28 + x = 32$

$28 - 28 + x = 32 - 28$ (inverse operations)

$x = 4$

There are 4 more cards left to be signed.

Tips & Tricks

- Your first step when translating verbal models to math (algebraic) models is to clearly define the variable(s) and known terms. What do you know and what are you trying to solve?
- Then, follow the order of operations and apply "problem solving" properties to find the solution. In other words, solve for the variable.

Practice

1. Translate the following verbal models into math (algebraic) models. Don't solve!

   a. The product of 4 and a number is 28.

   b. The sum of 5 and a number is 8.

   c. The quotient of 16 divided by a number is 4.

   d. The difference between 11 and a number is 4.

   e. The difference between 6 times a number and 5 is 13.

2. Rachel and Sarah spent $8.56 for gasoline, $12.32 for a gift, and $5.25 a piece for lunch on a trip to visit their Grandma. If the girls left home with a total of $50, how much do they have for the return trip? Write and solve an equation that models this situation.

3. Translate the following verbal models into math (algebraic) models and solve.

   a. The quotient of 18 minus a number divided by 5 is 2.

   b. The product of 4 times 6 minus a number is 12.

   c. The difference of $\frac{3}{5}$ and a number is $\frac{1}{5}$.

   d. The sum of -2 times a number and $\frac{2}{9}$ is $\frac{8}{9}$.

   e. The absolute value of a number times 4 divided 3 is 8.

4. Anne earned $3.75 an hour baby-sitting, and $4.50 an hour working in the garden. Last week she baby-sat for 5 hours and completed 3.5 hours of garden work. How much more money does she need to buy a game that costs $35? Write and solve an equation that models this situation.

5. Translate the following verbal models into math (algebraic) models and solve.

   a. The difference between 2 times a number minus 4 and 5 is -17.

   b. The sum of the quotient of 14 minus a number divided by 3 and 5 is 9.

   c. The product of 2 and the quotient of 14 divided by a number is 4.

   d. The quotient of 3 times a number plus 4 divided by 4 is 4.

6. You make rubber band bracelets. You spent $13.05 including tax for rubber bands and $21.95 including tax for the loom. You are now selling the bracelets for $2 a piece. How many bracelets must you sell to make a profit of $25? Write and solve an equation that models this situation?

7. Your parents loaned you money (interest free) to buy a mountain bike that cost $176. You already paid your parents $30 and have split up the remaining amount owed into 4 equal payments. How much is each payment? Write and solve an equation that models this situation?

8. Write a word problem for the following equation and solve: $4(x + 5.50) = 30$

Bobcat Review

1. Rewrite the following numbers using scientific notation.

   a. 394,350,000.00

   b. 0.000 003 482 9

   c. 295,934,000,000

   d. 0.004 78

2. Write 4.83×10^{-5} in expanded form.

Bobcat Stretch

1. Write and simplify an algebraic expression for each verbal expression, then indicate the properties used for each step.

    a. Two times the sum of x squared and y squared, increased by three times the sum of x squared and y squared.

    b. Six times the difference of $2a$ and b, increased by $4b$.

2. A rectangular field, which is 63.6 yards long and 21.3 yards wide, is going to be fenced-in to make three separate horse corrals. A fence is needed for the perimeter of the field. Fencing is also needed to divide the field into three equal sections to make three separate horse corrals. How many feet of fencing are needed? Write and solve the equation that models this situation. (Hint: 1 yard = 3 feet)

Further Review

For more videos and practice problems,

- click here to go to Khan Academy.
- search for "multi-step word problems" on Khan Academy (www.khanacademy.org).

Watch this video to further review word problems.

MEDIA
Click image to the left or use the URL below.
URL: https://www.ck12.org/flx/render/embeddedobject/107743

Answers
---

1. a. $4 \cdot x = 28$

   b. $5 + x = 8$

   c. $\frac{16}{x} = 4$

   d. $11 - x = 4$

   e. $6x - 5 = 13$

2. You can write this model several different ways. Here's an example.

   $8.56 + 12.32 + (2 \cdot 5.25) + x = 50$

   $x = 18.62$, so they have $18.62 for their return trip home from Grandma's.

3. a. $\frac{18-x}{5} = 2, x = 8$

   b. $4(6 - x) = 12, x = 3$

   c. $\frac{3}{5} - x = \frac{1}{5}, x = \frac{2}{5}$

   d. $-2x + \frac{2}{9} = \frac{8}{9}, x = -\frac{1}{3}$

   e. $\frac{|x| \cdot 4}{3} = 8, x = \pm 6$

4. $5(3.75) + 3.5(4.50) + x = 35$

   $x = 0.50$, so she needs 50 cents more to purchase her game.

5. a. $2(x - 4) - 5 = -17, x = (-2)$

   b. $\frac{14-x}{3} + 5 = 9, x = 2$

   c. $2(\frac{14}{x}) = 4, x = 7$

   d. $\frac{3x+4}{4} = 4, x = 4$

6. $2(b) - 12.05 - 21.95 = 25$, where b equals the number of bracelets sold.

   $b = 30$, you must sell 30 bracelets to earn $25 profit.

7. $30 + 4(p) = 176$, where p equals the number of payments.

   $p = 36.50$, so you will give $36.50 to your parents to pay off the bike in 4 payments.

8. Answer will vary. Here's an example. A mom gave four sisters $30 to split to go to the movies. They spent $5.50 each for the movie ticket. How much money will each sister have left to spend on snacks?

   $x = 2$, they will have $2 each to spend on snacks.

Bobcat Review

1. a. 3.9435×10^8

   b. 3.4829×10^{-6}

   c. 2.95934×10^{11}

   d. 4.78×10^{-3}

2. 0.0000483

Bobcat Stretch

1. a. $2(x^2 + y^2) + 3(x^2 + y^2)$

   $2x^2 + 2y^2 + 3x^2 + 3y^2$, Distributive Property

   $2x^2 + 3x^2 + 2y^2 + 3y^2$, Commutative Property

   $5x^2 + 5y^2$, combine like terms

   b. $6(2a - b) + 4b$

   $6(2a) - 6(b) + 4b$, Distributive Property

   $12a - 6b + 4b$

   $12a - 2b$, combine like terms

2. $P = 3\{4(21.3) + 2(63.6)\}$, $P = 637.2$ feet of fencing

2.8 Equations with Variables on Both Sides

Solve equations with variables on both sides.

Example 1

Solve: $3(h+1) = 11h - 23$.

Solution: First you must remove the parentheses by using the Distributive Property:

$$3h + 3 = 11h - 23$$

Gather the variable terms to one side:

$$3h - 3h + 3 = 11h - 3h - 23$$

Simplify:

$$3 = 8h - 23$$

Solve by applying the appropriate number properties:

$$3 + 23 = 8h - 23 + 23$$
$$26 = 8h$$
$$\frac{26}{8} = \frac{8h}{8}$$
$$\frac{13}{4} = 3.25 = h$$

The answers is $h = 3.25$.

Example 2

Determine the lengths of the sides of the equilateral triangle below.

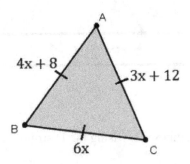

Solution: Given the fact that the triangle is equilateral, we can set any pair of sides of the triangle equal to each other. In this case, we will show that the length of side **AB** is equal to the length of side **BC** in order to solve for **x**.

$$4x + 8 = 6x$$
$$4x - 4x + 8 = 6x - 4x$$
$$\frac{8}{2} = \frac{2x}{2}$$
$$4 = x$$

You can check your solution by substituting "4" for "*x*" in the equations above to make sure they are all equal.

$4(4) + 8 = 24$

$6(4) = 24$

$3(4) + 12 = 24$

All sides equal 24, so our solution $x = 4$ is correct.

Tips & Tricks

- By now you've learned that equations come in all shapes and sizes and they all use the same "strategies" to solve.
    - Remove any parentheses by using the Distributive Property or inverse operations.
    - Simplify each side of the equation by combining like terms.
    - Isolate the ax term(s). Use inverse operations to get the variable terms on one side of the equal sign and the numerical values on the other. Combine like terms again as needed.
    - Isolate the variable. Use the inverse operations to get the variable alone on one side of the equation.
    - Check your solution.

Practice

---

1. Solve the following equations.

    a. $3t = 8t + 15$

    b. $6m - 5 = 4m + 5$

    c. $x + 6 = 2x - 3$

    d. $4s = s + 6$

    e. $-7n - 3 = -5n + 5$

2. Bill and Kate are both reading a 500-page novel. So far, Bill has read 70 pages and Kate has read 50 pages. From this point forward, Bill plans to read 25 pages per day, while Kate plans to read 29 pages per day. After how many days will they have read the same number of pages? Write an equation using the variable "d" to represent the days and solve for "d".

3. Solve the following equations.

    a. $3(x - 1) = 2(x + 3)$

    b. $7(x - 2) = 2(x - 10) + 9$

    c. $9(x - 2) = 3x + 3$

    d. $-5(5k + 7) = 25 + 5k$

    e. $21 + 3b = 6 - 6(1 - 4b)$

4. Karen and Sarah have bank accounts. Karen has a starting balance of $125.00 and is depositing $20 each week. Sarah has a starting balance of $43 and is depositing $37 each week. When will the girls have the same amount of money? Write an equation using the variable "w" to represent weeks and solve for "w".

5. An equilaterial triangle has one side that is equal to (3y - 5) and another side that is equal to (2y + 10). How long is each side of the triangle? Write an equation to solve for "y" to determine the length of each side.

6. A rectangle has a length of one side that is equal to (4x - 6) and the opposite parallel side is equal to (6x - 20). How long is the rectangle? Write an equation to solve for "x" to determine the length of the rectangle.

7. Cell phone plan A charges \$75.00 each month and \$0.05 per text. Cell phone plan B charges a flat fee of \$109 dollars, which includes unlimited texts.

     a. At how many texts will the two plans charge the same?

     b. Suppose you plan to text 700 times per month. Which plan should you choose? Why?

8. To rent a dunk tank, Modern Rental charges \$150 per day. To rent the same tank, Budgetwise charges \$7.75 per hour.

     a. After how many hours will the two companies charges be the same rate?

     b. You will need the tank for a 24-hour fund raise-a-thon. Which company should you choose?

9. Given the following possible first steps to solve this equation for "a", which step will <u>not</u> lead to a correct solution to the problem.

$$3a - \frac{11}{2} = \frac{-3a}{2} + \frac{25}{2}$$

     a. Multiply both sides of the equation by 2.

     b. Add $\frac{11}{2}$ to both sides of the equation.

     c. Subtract $\frac{3a}{2}$ from both sides of the equation.

     d. Rewrite $3a$ as $\frac{6a}{2}$.

Bobcat Review

1. 25 more than four times a number is 13. What is the number? Write an equation and solve.

2. Find the opposite of $9\frac{1}{5}$. Write your answer as an improper fraction.

3. Evaluate the expression: $(|b| - a) - (|d| - a)$. Let $a = 4$, $b = -6$, and $d = 5$.

4. Give an example of an integer that is not a counting number.

Bobcat Stretch

1. Solve the following equations.

    a. $\frac{1}{3}(8v - 21) = 2\left(\frac{3v}{2} - \frac{5}{2}\right)$

    b. $\frac{y-1}{3} = \frac{2}{5} \cdot \frac{2y+1}{3}$

    c. $4(x+3) + 1 = \frac{2(3x+1)}{5}$

    d. $0.42(3.6s + 1.6) = 2s - 1.28$

Further Review

For more videos and practice problems,

- click here to go to Khan Academy.
- search for "Equations with variables on both sides" on Khan Academy (www.khanacademy.org).
- go to Khan Academy's Common Core page standard 8.EE.C.7 (www.khanacademy.org/commoncore/grade -8-EE).

Watch this video to further review equations with variables on both sides.

 **Multimedia**

MEDIA
Click image to the left or use the URL below.
URL: https://www.ck12.org/flx/render/embeddedobject/107795

Answers

1. a. $t = (-3)$

   b. $m = 5$

   c. $x = 9$

   d. $s = 2$

   e. $n = (-4)$

2. By day 5, they will both have read the same number of pages.

   $70 + 25d = 50 + 29d$

   $d = 5$

3. a. $x = 9$

   b. $x = \frac{3}{5}$

   c. $x = 3.5$ or $\frac{21}{6}$

   d. $k = (-2)$

   e. $b = 1$

4. It will take about 4.8 weeks for Sarah and Karen to have equal amounts of money.

$$125 + 20w = 43 + 37w$$

   Solution: Using the Subtraction Property of Equality, move the variables to one side of the equation:

$$125 + 20w - 20w = 43 + 37w - 20w$$

   Simplify: $125 = 43 + 17w$

   Solve using number properties:

$$125 - 43 = 43 - 43 + 17w$$
$$82 = 17w$$
$$\frac{82}{17} = \frac{17w}{17}$$
$$4.82 \approx w$$

5. Each side is 40 units long.

   $3y - 5 = 2y + 10$.

   $y = 15$, so 3(15) - 5 = 40 and 2(15) + 10 = 40. They both equal 40, so each side of the equilateral triangle is 40 units long.

6. The rectangle is 22 units long.

$$4x - 6 = 6x - 20$$

$$x = 7$$

7. a. The plans will break even at 680 texts. $75 + 0.05(t) = 109 + 0(t)$, where $t = 680$.

   b. Plan B because texts are free and the answer to 7a tells us that if we use more than 680 texts, then Plan B becomes cheaper than Plan A. Plan A would cost \$110 and Plan B would still only cost \$109.

8. a. At 19.35 hours, the two companies cost the same amount. $150 = 7.75(h)$, where $h = 19.35$.

   b. Modern Rental as their rental will cost \$150 and Budgetwise will cost \$186 for 24 hours (7.75 x 24hours).

9. C - You must subtract $-\frac{3a}{2}$, which is equivalent to adding (not subtracting) $\frac{3a}{2}$ to both sides.

Bobcat Review

1. $25 + 4x = 13$, $x = (-3)$

2. $-\frac{46}{5}$

3. $(6 - 4) - (5 - 4) = 2 - 1 = 1$

4. Variable answers - zero and any negative integer. For example, (-3).

Bobcat Stretch

1. a. $v = (-6)$

   b. $y = 7$

   c. $x = (-4.5)$

   d. $s = 4$

2.9 Equations with Fractions and Decimals

Solve equations with fractions and decimals.

Example 1

Solve $\frac{1}{4}w - 3 = \frac{2}{3}w$.

Solution:

$$\frac{1}{4}w - 3 = \frac{2}{3}w$$

$$(12)\frac{1}{4}w - (12)(3) = (12)\frac{2}{3}w \qquad \text{(Multiply by the LCD)}$$

$$3w - 36 = 8w \qquad \text{(Simplify)}$$

$$3w - 3w - 36 = 8w - 3w \qquad \text{(Subtract 3w from both sides of the equal sign to get variables on same side)}$$

$$-36 = 5w \qquad \text{(Combine Like Terms)}$$

$$\frac{-36}{5} = \frac{5w}{5} \qquad \text{(Divide both sides by 5 to solve for the variable)}$$

$$-\frac{36}{5} = w$$

Let's check our answer $w = -\frac{36}{5}$.

$$\text{Check:}$$

$$\frac{1}{4}w - 3 = \frac{2}{3}w$$

$$\frac{1}{4}\left(\frac{-36}{5}\right) - 3 = \frac{2}{3}\left(\frac{-36}{5}\right)$$

$$\frac{-36}{20} - 3 = \frac{-72}{15}$$

$$\frac{-108}{60} - \frac{180}{60} = \frac{-288}{60}$$

$$\frac{-288}{60} = \frac{-288}{60}$$

Example 2

Solve $0.1x + 0.4 = 0.3x + 0.2$.

Solution:

At first this looks difficult because of the decimals. But multiply all of the numbers by 10 and see what happens:

$$(10)0.1x + (10)0.4 = (10)0.3x + (10)0.2$$
$$1x + 4 = 3x + 2$$
$$2 = 2x$$
$$1 = x$$

Now you can see that the answer is $x = 1$.

Tips & Tricks

- When introducing fractions into an equation, the same rules for solving any equation apply. You need to keep the equations in balance by adding, subtracting, multiplying, or dividing on both sides of the equals sign in order to isolate the variable. The goal still remains to get your variable alone on one side of the equals sign with your constant terms on the other in order to solve for this variable.

- With fractions, there is sometimes an added step of multiplying and dividing the equation by the numerator and denominator in order to solve for the variable. Or, if there are multiple fractions that do not have the same denominator, you must first find the least common denominator (LCD) before combining like terms.

- When you have decimals in an equation, you can get rid of them by multiplying by 10 (if one decimal place), 100 (if two decimal places), or 1000 (if three decimal places), and then solve the equation as usual.

- Remember that if you feel confident with adding, subtracting, multiplying, and dividing decimals, you can also solve equations with decimals by isolating the variable and solving without first removing the decimals.

Practice

1. Name the number used to multipy each side of the equation to clear the fractions or decimals, then solve for the variable.

  a. $9.6y - 15.4 = -4.3y + 26.3$

  b. $\frac{y}{4} + \frac{1}{12} = \frac{y}{3} - \frac{1}{6}$

  c. $3.4z + 6.3 = -1.7z + 47.1$

  d. $0.4x - 1.2 = 0.15x + 0.8$

  e. $\frac{3}{4}x - \frac{2}{5} = \frac{1}{2}$

2. True or False. If this statement is false, correct the error to find the solution that makes the statement true.

$$\frac{1}{8}x + \frac{1}{4} + \frac{1}{2}x = 4$$

$$(8)\frac{1}{8}x + (8)\frac{1}{4} + (8)\frac{1}{2}x = 4$$

$$x + 2 + 4x = 4$$

$$5x + 2 - 2 = 4 - 2$$

$$5x = 2$$

$$x = \frac{2}{5}$$

3. Solve the following equations.

  a. $\frac{2}{3}x + 4 = \frac{4}{3} + 4x$

  b. $\frac{3}{4}x - 5 = 19$

  c. $\frac{2}{5}x - 4 = -\frac{1}{5}x + 8$

  d. $1 = -\frac{2}{5}x + \frac{6}{4}x$

  e. $\frac{5}{8}x + \frac{2}{3} = \frac{13}{12}x - \frac{1}{4}$

4. True or False. If this statement is false, correct the error to find the solution that makes the statement true.

$$x - 0.58 = -0.26 + 0.96x$$
$$x - 58 = 26 + 96x$$
$$x = 74 + 96x$$
$$-95x = 74$$
$$x = -\frac{74}{95}$$

5. Solve the following equations.

    a. $3.5 - 2.4x = 4.7$

    b. $0.52x + 0.12 = -0.4$

    c. $0.25z - 3.3 = 0.7$

    d. $0.6x - 1.25 = 0.4x + 0.35$

    e. $x - 0.9 - 0.5x = 0.8x$

6. In this year's student election for president, there were three candidates. The second place candidate received $\frac{2}{3}$ the votes as the winner. The third place candidate received $\frac{1}{6}$ the votes as the winner. How many votes did the winner receive if a total of 583 votes were cast in the election? Write an equation and solve to find how many votes the winner received.

7. Tina went to the movies with some of her friends the tickets cost $6.50 a piece, and each person received a $1.75 student discount. The total amount paid for all the tickets was $33.25. Write and solve an equation to find the number of people who went to the movies.

Bobcat Review

1. Find the greatest common factor (GCF) of 68 and 132.

2. Factor $192a^2b^4c$. Write your answer in both expanded and exponent form.

3. Find the least common multiple (LCM) of $36x^2y^3z^2$ and $44x^2yz$.

Bobcat Stretch

1. Solve the following equations.
   a. $\frac{1}{8}(3y+2) = \frac{1}{4}(2y+\frac{1}{2}) + \frac{1}{2}$
   b. $0.2(3y-5) = 0.15(2y+3) - 0.85$
   c. $\frac{x+9}{5} = \frac{x-7}{10}$
   d. $0.5(p+3) = 3(0.1+0.16p)$

Further Review

For more practice problems,

- click here to go to CK-12 Braingenie to further review equations with decimals.
- search for "Solving Equations with Variables on Both Sides with Decimals" on CK-12 Braingenie (braingenie.ck12.org/skills/105359)
- click here to go to CK-12 Braingenie to further review equations with fractions.
- search for "Solving Equations with Variables on Both Sides with Fractions" on CK-12 Braingenie (braingenie.ck12.org/skills/105360)

Take the "quiz" below to further review equations with decimals and fractions.

 **Multimedia**

MEDIA
Click image to the left or use the URL below.
URL: https://www.ck12.org/flx/render/embeddedobject/108006

Answers

1. a. 10; $y = 3$

   b. 12; $y = 3$

   c. 10; $z = 8$

   d. 100; $x = 8$ (Note: you could also multiply by 10, which would leave you one easy decimal to deal with - 1.5)

   e. 20; $x = \frac{18}{15}$ or 1.2

2. False, you must multiply BOTH sides by the LCD 8 to cancel out the fractions correctly.

$$\frac{1}{8}x + \frac{1}{4} + \frac{1}{2}x = 4$$
$$(8)\frac{1}{8}x + (8)\frac{1}{4} + (8)\frac{1}{2}x = (8)4$$
$$x + 2 + 4x = 32$$
$$5x + 2 - 2 = 32 - 2$$
$$5x = 30$$
$$x = 6$$

3. a. $x = \frac{8}{10} = \frac{4}{5}$ (Hint: did you multiply both sides by 3 to cancel out the fractions to make the problem easier to solve?)

b. $x = 32$

$$\frac{3}{4}x - 5 = 19$$

$$\frac{3}{4}x - 5 + 5 = 19 + 5 \qquad \text{(Add 5 to both sides of the equal sign to isolate the variable)}$$

$$\frac{3}{4}x = 24 \qquad \text{(Simplify)}$$

$$(4)\frac{3}{4}x = 24(4) \qquad \text{(Multiply both sides by the denominator}(4)\text{ in the fraction)}$$

$$3x = 96 \qquad \text{(Simplify)}$$

$$\frac{3x}{3} = \frac{96}{3} \qquad \text{(Divide both sides by numerator }(3)\text{ in the fraction)}$$

$$x = 32 \qquad \text{(Simplify)}$$

Therefore $x = 32$.

Check:

$$\frac{3}{4}x - 5 = 19$$

$$\frac{3}{4}(32) - 5 = 19$$

$$\frac{96}{4} - 5 = 19$$

$$24 - 5 = 19$$

$$19 = 19$$

3   c. $x = 20$

$$\frac{2}{5}x - 4 = -\frac{1}{5}x + 8$$

$$\frac{2}{5}x + \frac{1}{5}x - 4 = -\frac{1}{5}x + \frac{1}{5}x + 8 \qquad \left(\text{Add } \frac{1}{5}x \text{ to both sides of the equal sign to combine variables}\right)$$

$$\frac{3}{5}x - 4 = 8 \qquad \text{(Simplify)}$$

$$\frac{3}{5}x - 4 + 4 = 8 + 4 \qquad \text{(Add 4 to both sides of the equation to isolate the variable)}$$

$$\frac{3}{5}x = 12 \qquad \text{(Simplify)}$$

$$(\cancel{5})\frac{3}{\cancel{5}}x = 12(5) \qquad \text{(Multiply both sides by the denominator } (5) \text{ in the fraction)}$$

$$3x = 60 \qquad \text{(Simplify)}$$

$$\frac{\cancel{3}x}{\cancel{3}} = \frac{60}{3} \qquad \text{(Divide both sides by the numerator } (3) \text{ in the fraction)}$$

$$x = 20 \qquad \text{(Simplify)}$$

Therefore $x = 20$.

Check:

$$\frac{2}{5}x - 4 = -\frac{1}{5}x + 8$$

$$\frac{2}{5}(20) - 4 = -\frac{1}{5}(20) + 8$$

$$\frac{40}{5} - 4 = -\frac{20}{5} + 8$$

$$8 - 4 = -4 + 8$$

$$4 = 4$$

3   d. $x = \frac{20}{22} = \frac{10}{11} = 0.\overline{90}$ (Hint: multiply the equation by LCD 20 to cancel out the fractions).

3   e. $x = 2$ (Hint: multiply the equation by LCD 24 to cancel out the fractions.)

4. False, x was not multiplied by 100 like the other terms. It should have been $100x$ (not x). $x = 8$ makes the statement true.

5. a. x = - 0.5 (Hint: multiply the equation by 10 to eliminate the decimals)

   b. $x = -1$

$$(100) \cdot (0.52x) + (100) \cdot (0.12) = (100) \cdot (-0.40)$$
$$52x + 12 = -40$$
$$52x = -52$$
$$x = -1$$

   c. $z = 16$

   d. $x = 8$

   e. $x = -3$

6. The winner received 318 votes.

   $x + \frac{2}{3}x + \frac{1}{6}x = 583$

   $6x + 4x + x = 3498$, when you multiply both sides of equation by 6 (LCD) to cancel out the fractions.

   $11x = 3498$ (combine like terms)

   $x = 318$

7. 7 people went to the movies.

   $6.50p - 1.75p = 33.25$

   $650p - 175p = 3325$

   $475p = 3325$

   $p = 7$

Bobcat Review

1. 4

2. Expanded Form: $2 \cdot 2 \cdot 2 \cdot 2 \cdot 2 \cdot 2 \cdot 3 \cdot a \cdot a \cdot b \cdot b \cdot b \cdot b \cdot c$

   Exponent Form: $2^6 \cdot 3 \cdot a^2 \cdot b^4 \cdot c$

3. $396x^2 y^3 z^2$

Bobcat Stretch

1. a. $y = (-3)$, use 8 as the LCD to cancel out fractions.

   b. $y = 2$, multiply both sides by 100 to cancel out decimals.

   c. $x = (-25)$, multiply both sides by 10 (LCD) to cancel out fractions.

   d. $p = (-60)$, multiply both sides by 100 to cancel out decimals.

2.10 Equivalent Equations

Write equivalent equations using inverse operations.

By the end of this lesson, you should be able to define and give an example of the following vocabulary words:

- **Formula** - an equation that states a rule for a relationship among quantities.
- **Literal Equation** - an equation with two or more variables.

Example 1

Write an equivalent equation for $4a + 4 = 4b$ in terms of "a".

"In terms of a" means to solve for the variable "a" or isolate "a" on one side of the equation.

First, locate the variable you are asked to solve for in the equation - in this case a.

Use inverse operations to undo operations and isolate the variable.

$$4a = 4b - 4$$
$$a = \frac{4b-4}{4} = \frac{4b}{4} - \frac{4}{4}$$
$$a = b - 1$$

Example 2

The formula $P = 2(l + w)$ relates the perimeter (P) of a rectangle to its length (l) and width (w). Solve this formula for w.

First, locate the variable you are asked to solve for in the equation - in this case w.

Use Distributive Property and inverse operations to isolate the variable.

$$P = 2l + 2w$$
$$P - 2l = 2w$$
$$\frac{P-2l}{2} = \frac{P}{2} - \frac{2l}{2} = w$$
$$\frac{P}{2} - l = w$$

Tips & Tricks

- Solving for the variable:
  - Step 1 - Locate the variable you are asked to solve for in the equation.
  - Step 2 - Identify the operations on this variable and the order in which they are applied.
  - Step 3 - Use inverse operations to undo operations and isolate the variable.

Practice

1. Solve each equation for the variable indicated.

   a. $4c = d$, solve for c.

   b. $n - 6m = 8$, solve for n.

   c. $2p + 5r = 1$, solve for p.

2. The formula $K = C + 273$ is used to convert temperatures from degrees Celsius to Kelvin. Solve the formula for C.

3. The formula $C = 2\pi r$ relates to the radius r of a circle to its circumference C. Solve the formula for r.

4. The formula $y = mx + b$ is called the slope-intercept form of a line. Solve this formula for m.

5. The formula for the area of a triangle is $A = \frac{1}{2}bh$, where b represents the length of the base and h represents the height.

   a. Solve the formula for b.

   b. If a triangle has an area of 32 in^2 and the height measures 8 inches, what is the measure of the base?

6. The formula $c = 5p + 215$ relates the total cost (c) in dollars of hosting a birthday party at a skating rink to the number of people (p) attending.

   a. Solve the formula the formula for p.

   b. If Allie's parents are willing to spend \$300 for a party, how many people can attend?

7. The formula $d = rt$ relates the distance (d) an object travels, to its average rate (r) of speed, and amount of time (t) that it travels.

   a. Solve the formula for t.

   b. How many hours would it take for a car to travel 150 miles at an average rate of 50 miles per hours?

8. The formula $I = Prt$ relates Interest (I) to the principal (P) amount of money invested, the interest rate (r) of the investment, and amount of time (t) the money is invested.

   a. Solve the formula for P.

   b. How much was Uncle Sam's principal investement if he earned \$2,565 in interest on money he had invested for 6 years at 9.5%?

Bobcat Review

1. Simplify the following expressions:

   a. $x^2 \cdot x^6 \cdot x^3$

   b. $\frac{x^8}{x^3}$

   c. $\frac{x^2}{x^2}$

   d. $\frac{x^2}{x^5}$

   e. $x^2 \cdot x^{-4}$

Bobcat Stretch

1. The formula for the volume of a sphere is $V = \frac{4}{3}\pi r^3$, where r represents the radius of the sphere. Solve the formula for r.

2. The formula for the conversion of matter into energy is $E = mc^2$, where E is the energy in ergs, m the mass of the matter in grams, and c is the speed of light in centimeters per second. Solve the formula for c.

3. The formula for converting Celsius (C) to Fahrenheit (F) is $C = \frac{5}{9}(F - 32)$. Solve the formula for F.

Further Review

For more practice problems,

- click here to go to CK-12 Braingenie.
- search for "Rewriting two-variable equations for specified variables" on CK-12 Braingenie (braingenie.ck12. org/skills/105384).

Answers

1. a. $c = \frac{d}{4}$

   b. $n = 6m + 8$

   c. $p = \frac{1-5r}{2}$

2. $K - 273 = C$

3. $\frac{C}{2\pi} = r$

4. $\frac{y-b}{x} = m$

5. a. $\frac{2A}{h} = b$

   b. $b = 8$ inches

6. a. $\frac{c-215}{5} = p$ or $\frac{c}{5} - 43 = p$

   b. 17 people

7. a. $\frac{d}{r} = t$

   b. 3 hours

8. a. $\frac{I}{rt} = P$

   b. $P = \$4500$ was his initial investment

Bobcat Review

1. a. x^{11}

   b. x^5

   c. 1

   d. x^{-3} or $\frac{1}{x^3}$

   e. x^{-2} or $\frac{1}{x^2}$

Bobcat Stretch

1. $\sqrt[3]{\frac{3V}{4\pi}} = r$

2. $\sqrt{\frac{E}{m}} = c$

3. $F = \frac{9}{5}C + 32$

2.11 Inequalities with Addition and Subtraction

Solve inequalities using addition or subtraction.

By the end of this lesson, you should be able to define and give an example of the following vocabulary words:

- **Inequality** - a statement formed by placing an inequality symbol between two expressions.
- **Solution of an Inequality** - the set of numbers that you can substitute for the variable to make the inequality true.
- **Equivalent Inequalities** - inequalities that have the same solutions.
- **Addition and Subtraction Properties of Inequalities** - Adding or subtracting the same number on each side of an inequality produces an equivalent inequality.
  - If $a > b$, then $a + c > b + c$.
  - If $a > b$, then $a - c > b - c$.

Example 1

Solve this inequality and graph its solution: $-2 \leq x + 4$

Use inverse operations to isolate the variable.

$$-2 \leq x + 4$$
$$-2 - 4 \leq x + 4 - 4$$
$$-2 + (-4) \leq x + 0$$
$$-6 \leq x$$

Now, we should graph the solution. However, before we can do that, we need to rewrite the inequality so the variable is listed first.

So, $-6 \leq x$ equivalent to $x \geq -6$.

The inequality $x \geq -6$ is read as "x is greater than or equal to -6." So, the solutions of this inequality include -6 and all numbers that are greater than -6.

Place a closed circle at -6 to show that -6 *is* a solution for this inequality, then draw an arrow showing all numbers greater than -6.

Example 2

Solve this inequality and graph its solution: $n - 3 < 5$.

Solve the inequality as you would solve an equation, by using inverse operations.

$$n - 3 < 5$$
$$n - 3 + 3 < 5 + 3$$
$$n + (-3 + 3) < 8$$
$$n + 0 < 8$$
$$n < 8$$

Now, graph the solution. **The inequality $n < 8$ is read as "n is less than 8."** So, the solution set for this inequality includes all numbers that are less than 8, but it does not include 8.

Place an open circle at 8 to show that 8 is *not* a solution for this inequality, then draw an arrow showing all numbers less than 8.

Tips & Tricks

- When graphing inequalities, a <u>closed circle</u> means the number is part of the solution.
- When graphing inequalities, an <u>open circle</u> means the number is not part of the solution.

Practice

1. Write the inequality represented by each graph below.

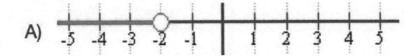

2. Write a statement that describes the following graphs.

   a.

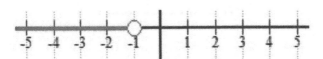

   b.

   c.

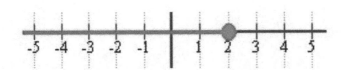

d.

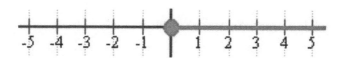

3. Solve the inequality and graph its solution.

   a. $b + 3 \geq 5$

   b. $y - 2 \leq -4$

   c. $x + 1 \geq -5$

   d. $x - 3 < 11$

   e. $x - 4 > -3$

4. At the store, Talia bought one item—a \$4.99 bottle of shampoo. Let d represent the amount in dollars that she handed the clerk. She received more than \$5 in change.

   a. Write and graph an inequality to represent d, the number of dollars Talia handed the clerk to pay for the shampoo.

   b. List three possible values of d.

5. Solve the inequality and graph its solution.

   a. $3.2x + 2.4 > 13.6$

   b. $-3.75 \geq 0.60t + 0.75$

   c. $\frac{5}{6}x + \frac{1}{2} \geq \frac{7}{9}$

   d. $\frac{11}{15} > \frac{1}{5}m + \frac{3}{5}$

6. Yellow Taxi Cab charges \$1.75 flat rate in addition to \$0.65 per mile. Katie has at most \$10 to spend on a ride.

   a. How many miles can Katie ride without going over her \$10 budget. Write and solve an inequality to find how many miles she can ride.

   b. Graph the solution.

Bobcat Review

1. Estimate the value of the following square roots to the nearest hundredth.

   a. $\sqrt{7}$

   b. $-\sqrt{2}$

   c. $\sqrt{12}$

Bobcat Stretch

1. Twice the smaller of two consecutive integers increased by the larger integer is at least 25.

   a. Model the problem with an inequality.

   b. Determine which of the given values 7, 8, and/or 9 are solutions.

   c. Find the smallest number that will make the inequality true.

2. Fred bought 3 shirts; each of them were the same price. He received less than $12 change from a $50 bill. What is the maximum cost of 1 shirt? Write and graph an inequality to find the maximum price of each shirt.

Further Review

For more videos and practice problems,

- click here to go to CK-12 Braingenie.
- search for "Solving inequalities using addition and subtraction" on CK-12 Braingenie (braingenie.ck12.org/skills/105)

Watch this video to further review inequalities with addition or subtraction.

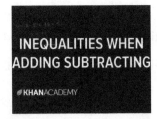

MEDIA
Click image to the left or use the URL below.
URL: https://www.ck12.org/flx/render/embeddedobject/90

Khan Academy Inequalities Using Addition and Subtraction

<hr>

Answers

<hr>

1. a. $x < -2$

   b. $x \leq -2$

   c. $x > -2$

   d. $x \geq -2$

2. a. $x < -1$, x is less than - 1.

   b. $x > 3$, x is greater than 3.

   c. $x \leq 2$, x is less than or equal to 2.

   d. $x \geq 0$, x is greater than or equal to 0.

3. a. $b \geq 2$, closed dot on 2 with arrow going to the right for greater than.

   b. $y \leq -2$, closed dot on (-2) with arrow going to the left for less than.

   c. $x \geq -6$, closed dot on -6 with arrow going to the right for greater than.

   d. $x < 14$, open dot on 14 with arrow going to the left for less than.

   e. $x > 1$, open dot on 1 with arrow going to the right for greater than.

4. a. $d - 4.99 > 5$, $d > 9.99$, open dot on 9.99 with arrow going to the right for greater than (because she received more than \$5 in change).

   b. Variable answers as long as d is \$10 or greater.

5. a. $x > 3.5$, open dot on 3.5 with arrow going to the right for greater than.

   b. $t \leq -7.5$, closed dot on (-7.5) with arrow going to the left for less than.

   c. $x \geq \frac{1}{3}$, closed dot on $\frac{1}{3}$ with an arrow going to the right for greater than.

   d. $m < \frac{2}{3}$, open dot on $\frac{2}{3}$ with arrow going to the left for less than.

6. a. 12 miles, $0.65m + 1.75 \leq 10$, $m \leq 12.69$. (Note: the answer is 12 miles because if she went 13 miles she would be over her \$10 budget)

   b. close dot on 12 with an arrow going to the left for less than.

Bobcat Review

1. a. 2.65

   b. -1.41

   c. 3.46

Bobcat Stretch

1. a. $2x + x + 1 \geq 25$

   b. $x = 7$, False, $22 \geq 25$

      $x = 8$, True, $25 \geq 25$

      $x = 9$, True, $28 \geq 25$

   c. The smallest integer is 8.

2. The maximum price of each shirt is greater than $12.67 and less than $16.67. On the graph, there should be an open dot on 12.67 and 16.67 with a line joining the 2 dots.

   $0 < 50 - 3x < 12$

   Step 1: Subtract 50 from all sides. 0-50 <50 - 50 - 3x <12 - 50

   Simplify: -50 <-3x <-38

   Step 2: Divide by -3 on all sides. -50/-3 <-3x/-3 <-38/-3

   Simplify and reverse your inequality symbol. 16.67 >x >12.67

2.12 Inequalities with Multiplication and Division

Solve inequalities using multiplication or division.

Example 1

Solve $2x \geq 12$ and graph the solution.

To find the solutions to this inequality, isolate the variable x by using inverse operations.

$$2x \geq 12$$
$$\frac{2x}{2} \geq \frac{12}{2}$$
$$x \geq 6$$

Now, graph the solution $x \geq 6$. This inequality is read as " x" is greater than or equal to 6.

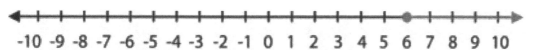

Example 2

Solve $\frac{y}{5} \leq 3$ and graph the solution.

To find the solutions, isolate the variable y by using inverse operations.

$$\frac{y}{5} \cdot \frac{5}{1} \leq 3 \cdot \frac{5}{1}$$
$$y \leq 15$$

Now, graph the solution $y \leq 15$. This inequality is read as " y" is less than or equal to 15.

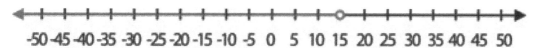

Example 3

Multiplying and Dividing an Inequality by a Negative Number

Notice that the two examples focused on positive numbers. The rules change when you are multiplying and dividing negative numbers. **This requires you to reverse (flip) the inequality sign.**

Think of it this way. When you multiply a value by -1, the number you get is the negative of the original.

$$6(-1) = -6$$

Multiplying each side of a sentence by -1 results in the opposite of both values.

$$5x(-1) = 4(-1)$$
$$-5x = -4$$

When multiplying by a negative, you are doing the "opposite" of everything in the sentence, including the verb, so you must flip the inequality sign when you divide or multiply by a negative number.

$$-2x > -4$$
$$\frac{-2x}{-2} < \frac{-4}{-2}$$
$$x < 2$$

Tips & Tricks

- **Multiplication Property of Inequality:** For all real positive numbers a, b, and c:
  If $x < a$, then $x(c) < a(c)$.
  If $x > a$, then $x(c) > a(c)$.
- **Division Property of Inequality:** For all real positive numbers a, b, and c:
  If $x < a$, then $x \div (c) < a \div (c)$.
  If $x > a$, then $x \div (c) > a \div (c)$.
- **Multiplication/Division Rule of Inequality:** For any real number a, and any **negative** number c,
  If $x < a$, then $x \cdot c > a \cdot c$
  If $x < a$, then $\frac{x}{c} > \frac{a}{c}$

Practice

1. When do you flip the inequality sign when solving for an inequality?

2. Solve the inequality and graph its solution.

    a. $3x \leq 6$
    b. $-10x > 250$
    c. $\frac{x}{-3} \leq -12$
    d. $\frac{x}{2} > 40$

3. What if the distance in miles of a bowling alley from your house is $\frac{1}{5}$ of the distance of a roller-skating rink from your house? The distance of the roller-skating rink is represented by r, and you know that the bowling alley is less than or equal to 6 miles from your house. Write and graph and inequality to find how far the roller-skating rink is from your house.

4. Solve the inequality and graph its solution.

    a. $-0.5x \leq 7.5$
    b. $\frac{x}{20} \geq -\frac{7}{40}$
    c. $\frac{x}{-3} > -\frac{10}{9}$
    d. $0.6x \geq 2.4$

5. To make one liter of an orange sports drink requires 3 spoonfuls of sports drink powder. If a container of the sports drink powder contains about 60 spoonfuls, then how many liters can you make? Write an inequality to model this situation and graph the solution.

6. Solve the inequality and graph its solution.

    a. $-3.5t + 4.2 \geq 19.95$

    b. $\frac{1}{5}m - \frac{2}{7} < \frac{6}{7}$

    c. $-\frac{1}{3}n + \frac{2}{9} > \frac{2}{3}$

    d. $-5.3p - 3.6 \leq -6.78$

    e. $3.3s + 1.2 \geq 3.84$

Bobcat Review

1. Solve for v : $v = -|2 - (-19) + 6|$.

2. A piggy bank is filled with dimes and quarters. The total amount of money is \$26.00.

    a. Write an equation that models this statement. Use "d" for the number of dimes and "q" for the number of quarters.

    b. If \$13.50 is in quarters, how many dimes must be in the piggy bank?

3. Translate the following verbal models into math (algebraic) models and solve.

    a. The difference between 3 times a number minus 2 and 6 is 3.

    b. The sum of the quotient of 21 minus a number divided by 3 and 6 is 15.

Bobcat Stretch

1. The width of a rectangle is 33cm and the perimeter is at least 776cm.

    a. Write an inequality to model this situation and graph the solution for (l) length.

    b. Using the answer from part a, write an inequality to solve for the area of the rectangle.

2. Solve and graph the solution for $-6(-2.2x - 2) - (3.2x - 2.3) \geq 39.3$

Further Review

For more videos and practice problems,

- click here to go to Khan Academy.
- search for "one step inequalities" on Khan Academy (www.khanacademy.org).

Watch this video to review inequalities with multiplication or division.

 **Multimedia**

> **MEDIA**
> Click image to the left or use the URL below.
> URL: https://www.ck12.org/flx/render/embeddedobject/108137

Answers

1. You flip the inequality sign when you are multiplying or dividing by a negative number.

2. a. $x \leq 2$, closed dot on 2 with an arrow going to the left to represent less than.

   b. $x < -25$, open dot on -25 with an arrow going to the left to represent less than. Did you remember to flip the sign?

   c. $x \geq 36$, closed dot on 36 with an arrow going to the right to represent greater than. Did you remember to flip the sign?

   d. $x > 80$, open dot on 80 with an arrow going to the right to represent greater than.

3. $\frac{1}{5}r \leq 6$, $r \leq 30$, so the roller skate rink is less than or equal to 30 miles from your house.

   The graph will have a closed dot on 30 with an arrow going to the left to represent less than.

4. a. $x \geq -15$, closed dot on (-15) with an arrow going to the right to represent greater than. Did you remember to flip the sign?

   b. $x \geq -\frac{7}{2}$, closed dot on $-\frac{7}{2}$ with an arrow going to the right to represent greater than.

   c. $x < \frac{10}{3}$, open dot on $\frac{10}{3}$ with an arrow going to the left to represent less than. Did you remember to flip the sign?

   d. $x \geq 4$, closed dot on 4 with an arrow going to the right to represent greater than.

5. It can make less than or equal to 20 liters. $3l \leq 60$, $l \leq 20$, closed dot on 20 with an arrow going to the left to represent less than.

6. a. $t \leq -4.5$, closed dot on -4.5 with an arrow going to the left to represent less than. Did you remember to flip the sign?

b. $m < \frac{40}{7}$, open dot on $\frac{40}{7}$ with an arrow going to the left to represent less than.

c. $n < -\frac{4}{3}$, open dot on $-\frac{4}{3}$ with an arrow going to the left to represent less than. Did you remember to flip the sign?

d. $p \geq 0.6$, closed dot on 0.6 with an arrow going to the right to represent greater than. Did you remember to flip the sign?

e. $s \geq 0.8$, closed dot on 0.8 with an arrow going to the right to represent greater than.

Bobcat Review

1. $v = -27$

2. a. $.10d + .25q = 26$

b. $0.10d + \$13.50 = 26$, $d = 125$, so the piggy bank has 125 dimes.

3. a. $3(x - 2) - 6 = 3$, $x = 5$

b. $\frac{21-x}{3} + 6 = 15$, $x = (-6)$

Bobcat Stretch

1. a. The length of the rectangle is greater than or equal to 355 cm. $2(33 + l) \geq 776$, $l \geq 355$, a closed dot with an arrow going to the right to represent greater than.

b. The area of the rectangle is at least $11,715\ cm^2$. $(33 \cdot 355 \geq A)$

2. $x \geq 2.5$, closed dot on (2.5) with an arrow going to the right to represent greater than.

2.13 References

1. . http://eclass1.wsd.k12.ca.us/moodle/mod/resource/view.php?id=472 .
2. . http://eclass1.wsd.k12.ca.us/moodle/mod/resource/view.php?id=472 .
3. EngageNY 8-m4-p14. .
4. EngageNY 7th grade module 3, lesson 1 p 20. .
5. . http://studentswillachievegreatness.wordpress.com/2012/09/24/homework-7-combining-like-terms-and-distributive-property-word-problems/ .
6. http://www.mathscore.com/math/practice/Perimeter%20and%20Area%20Word%20Problems/. http://www.mathscore.com/math/practice/Perimeter%20and%20Area%20Word%20Problems/ .
7. . http://www.mathplanet.com/education/pre-algebra/discover-fractions-and-factors/multiplying-polynomials-and-binomials .
8. . http://eclass1.wsd.k12.ca.us/moodle/mod/resource/view.php?id=476 .
9. . http://www.bbc.co.uk/schools/gcsebitesize/maths/algebra/formulaehirev1.shtml .
10. Pierce, Rod. "Cubes and Cube Roots" Math Is Fun. Ed. Rod Pierce. 5 Feb 2014. 15 Apr 2014
11. . http://www.mathusee.com/pdfs/Multistepword.pdf .
12. . http://www.mathusee.com/pdfs/Multistepword.pdf .
13. . http://www.mathusee.com/pdfs/Multistepword.pdf .
14. . http://tullyschools.org/hsteachers/dneuman/IntegratedAlgebra/IntegratedAlgebraNotes/01September/008ChapterWordProblems/ChapterWordProblems.pdf .
15. . http://www.mathusee.com/pdfs/Multistepword.pdf .
16. . http://www.montereyinstitute.org/courses/DevelopmentalMath/COURSE_TEXT2_RESOURCE/U10_L1_-T2_text_final.html .
17. . http://eclass1.wsd.k12.ca.us/moodle/mod/resource/view.php?id=476 .
18. . http://bobprior.com/UCR-Ext/2.3-Lnr-Eqns-Frac-Dec.pdf .
19. . Engageny 7th grade, module 3, page 188 .
20. . http://www.algebra-class.com/inequalities-word-problem.html .
21. Karin Hutchinson - See more at: http://www.algebra-class.com/inequalities-word-problem.html#sthash.XWI8zlOg.dpuf http://www.algebra-class.com/inequality-equations.html .

CHAPTER **3** **Rates, Ratios, Proportions, and Percents**

Chapter Outline

3.1 Rates and Ratios

Find ratios and unit rates.

By the end of this lesson, you should be able to define and give an example of the following vocabulary words:

- **Ratio** - uses division to compare two numbers with the same units.
- **Equivalent Ratios** - ratios that have the same values.
- **Rate** - a ratio of two quantities that have different units.
- **Unit Rate** - a rate that has a denominator of 1 unit. To write a unit rate, find an equivalent rate with a denominator of 1 unit.

Example 1

A ratio says how much of one thing there is compared to another thing.

There are 3 blue squares to 1 yellow square.

Ratios can be shown in different ways:

- 3:1   (use : to separate the values)
- 3 to 1   (use "to" to separate the values)
- $\frac{3}{1}$ (use a fraction to separate the values)

Ratios can also be scaled up as long as both values are multiplied by the same value. We can scale up the 3:1 by multiplying both sides by 2 to get 6:2.

Example 2

Ethel picked 12 peaches in 6 minutes. How many peaches can she pick in 1 hour?

$$\frac{12 \text{ peaches}}{6 \text{ minutes}} = \frac{? \text{ peaches}}{1 \text{ hour}}$$

To change 6 minutes to one hour (60 minutes), we multiply by 10 (6 X 10 = 60 minutes). We need to do the same thing to the numerator (12 X 10 = 120 peaches).

$$\frac{12 \text{ peaches}}{6 \text{ minutes}} = \frac{120 \text{ peaches}}{60 \text{ minutes}} = \frac{120 \text{ peaches}}{1 \text{ hour}}$$

We "scaled up" the ratio to find an equivalent ratio that says if Ethel can pick 12 peaches every 6 minutes, then she can pick 120 peaches in 1 hour. Since the denominator is 1, this is her "unit rate" for how many she can pick in 1 hour.

Example 3

In the example above, we found Ethel's unit rate for picking peaches per 1 hour. What is her unit rate for 1 minute?

$$\frac{12 \text{ peaches}}{6 \text{ minutes}} = \frac{? \text{ peaches}}{1 \text{ minute}}$$

To change 6 minutes to one minute, we divide 6 by 6 (6 / 6 = 1). We need to do the same thing to the numerator (12 / 6 = 2 peaches).

$$\frac{12 \text{ peaches}}{6 \text{ minutes}} = \frac{2 \text{ peaches}}{1 \text{ minute}}$$

We "scaled down" the ratio to find an equivalent ratio that says Ethel works at the rate of picking 2 peaches per minute. Since the denominator is 1, this is her "unit rate" for how many she can pick in 1 minute.

Tips & Tricks

- **Ratio** - the relationship $\frac{a}{b}$ of two quantities a and b that have **same** unit of measure.
- **Rate** - the relationship $\frac{a}{b}$ of two quantities a and b that have **different** units of measure.

Practice

1. Write the ratio in two other ways in simplest form.

    a. $\frac{5}{15}$

    b. 24:38

    c. 5 to 7.5

    d. $\frac{36}{45}$

    e. 72 to 58

2. Michael loves to bake. Here's a picture of his latest creations.

    a. Write a ratio of the number of Vanilla Cremes (marked with the red X) to the number of Chocolate Peanut Tarts (mini-chocolate pies with a small peanut in the center).

    b. For a party, the host wants more Lemon Suzettes than Shortbread Bites. Michael figures a tray with 2 Shortbread Bites for every 5 Lemon Suzettes will work. If the finished tray contains 80 Lemon Suzettes, then how many Shortbread Bites did Michael make for the tray?

3. Write an equivalent ratio by solving for a.

    a. $\frac{11}{9} = \frac{a}{81}$

    b. $\frac{a}{14} = \frac{21}{49}$

    c. $\frac{a}{2} = \frac{8}{a}$

    d. $\frac{5}{a} = \frac{a}{125}$

4. True or False, the following ratios are equivalent. If false, find the error and correct it to make a true statement.

    $\frac{5.1}{6.3} = \frac{20.6}{25.2}$

5. Write an equivalent rate to find the missing value.

    a. $\frac{60 \; miles}{1 \; hour} = \frac{? \; miles}{1 \; minute}$

    b. $\frac{75 \; beats}{1 \; minute} = \frac{? \; beats}{1 \; second}$

    c. $\frac{\$2.45}{1 \; foot} = \frac{?}{1 \; yard}$

    d. $\frac{3859 \; g}{1 \; bag} = \frac{? \; lbs}{1 \; bag}$, (hint 454 g to 1 lb)

6. Nichole descended 42 feet every hour down a mountain. At this rate, how many feet will she descend in 5 hours?

7. Use each rate to write a unit rate for each. Remember a unit rate is compared to one.

    a. Twenty students on four teams

    b. $\frac{252 \; miles}{12 \; gallons}$

    c. $\frac{-31.8 \; degrees}{6 \; hours}$

    d. $\frac{7.6 \; lbs}{2 \; dollars}$

8. A Thomson's Gazelle runs 4,400 ft per minute, a Greyhound runs 58 ft per second, and a Pronghorn Antelope runs 445 ft in 5 seconds. Which animal is the fastest?

Bobcat Review

1. Evaluate the following roots.

    a. $\sqrt{25}$

    b. $\sqrt[3]{125}$

    c. $-\sqrt{\dfrac{25}{36}}$

    d. $\sqrt[3]{\dfrac{1}{27}}$

2. Solve $x(x+3x) = 64$.

Bobcat Stretch

1. A mule deer runs 0.58 miles per minute, a coyote runs 1,261 yards per minute, an elk runs 3,960 feet per minute, and a lion runs 50 miles per hour. (Hint: 1 mile = 1760 yards and 3 feet = 1 yard)

    a. How many yards per second does each animal run?

    b. Who is the fastest?

2. A beaker contains 578 mL of water. What is the volume in quarts? (Hint: 1 qt = 0.946 L)

Further Review

For more videos and practice problems,

- click here to go to Khan Academy.
- search for "rates and ratios" on Khan Academy (www.khanacademy.org).

Watch this video to further review rates.

MEDIA
Click image to the left or use the URL below.
URL: https://www.ck12.org/flx/render/embeddedobject/108236

Answers

1. a. $\frac{1}{3}$, 1:3, and/or 1 to 3

    b. $\frac{12}{19}$, 12:19, and/or 12 to 19.

    c. $\frac{1}{2.5}$, 1:2.5, and/or 1 to 2.5.

    d. $\frac{4}{5}$, 4:5, and/or 4 to 5.

    e. $\frac{36}{29}$, 36:29, and/or 36 to 29.

2. a. 8:8

    b. 32 Shortbread bites. $\frac{2}{5} = \frac{32}{80}$

3. a. $a = 99$

    b. $a = 6$

    c. $a = 4$

    d. $a = 25$

4. False, it should be $\frac{5.1}{6.3} = \frac{20.4}{25.2}$ as the first ratio is multiplied by 4 to equal the second ratio.

5. a. 1 mile per minute

   b. 1.25 beats per second

   c. $7.35 per yard

   d. 8.5 lbs per bag

6. 42 feet per hour multiplied by 5 hours is equal to $42 \times 5 = 210$ feet in 5 hours.

7. a. 5 students per team

   b. $\frac{21 \ miles}{1 \ gallon}$

   c. $\frac{-5.3 \ degrees}{1 \ hour}$

   d. $\frac{3.8 \ lbs}{1 \ dollar}$

8. The Pronghorn Antelope is the fastest at $\frac{89 \ feet}{1 \ second}$, then the Thomson's Gazelle at $\frac{73 \ feet}{1 \ second}$, and finally the Greyhound at $\frac{58 \ feet}{1 \ second}$.

Bobcat Review

1. a. ± 5

   b. 5

   c. $-\frac{5}{6}$

   d. $\frac{1}{3}$

2. $x = 4$

Bobcat Stretch

1. a. Mule Deer can run 17.01 yards per second.

   Coyote can run 21.02 yards per second.

   Elk can run 22 yards per second.

   Lion can run 24.44 yards per second.

   b. The lion is the fastest, followed by the Elk, Coyote and Mule Deer.

2. 0.611 qts, $\frac{0.578 \ L}{1 \ beaker} = \frac{0.611 \ qt}{1 \ beaker}$, divide Liters by 0.946 to convert Liters to Quart.

3.2 Writing and Solving Proportions

Write and solve proportions.

By the end of this lesson, you should be able to define and give an example of the following vocabulary words:

- **Proportions** - an equation that states that two ratios are equivalent.
- **Cross Products** - you can use to solve a proportion.
- **Scale Model** - dimensions that are proportional to the dimensions of the actual object.
- **Scale** - the relationship between the model's dimensions and the actual object's dimensions. A scale can be written as a ratio with or without units.

Example 1

The ratio of teachers to students in a certain school is 2 : 25. If there are 400 students in the eighth-grade class, how many teachers are there?

First set up a proportion. The problem gives a ratio of teachers to students, so set up two equivalent ratios comparing teachers to students.

$$\frac{2 \ teachers}{25 \ students} = \frac{x \ 8^{th} \ grade \ teachers}{400 \ 8^{th} \ grade \ students}$$

Now use what you know about equivalent ratios to solve the proportion.

Since $25 \times 16 = 400$ for the denominator, then we multiply $2 \times 16 = 32$ for the numerator. So, $x = 32$

There are 32 teachers in the eighth-grade class.

Example 2

Solve $\frac{x}{5} = \frac{9}{10}$.

Another way of solving a proportion is called cross-multiplying.

If $\frac{a}{b} = \frac{c}{d}$, then $ad = cb$.

Using this rule we can rewrite this proportion and use algebra to solve.

$$10(x) = (9)(5)$$
$$10x = 45$$
$$x = \frac{45}{10} = \frac{9}{2} = 4.5$$

x = 4.5 is our answer.

Example 3

A builder made scale models of both the Empire State Building and the Sears Tower (now called Willis Tower). The same scale was used for both models. If the Empire State Building is 1,250 ft tall, then how tall is the Sears Tower (a.k.a. Willis Tower)?

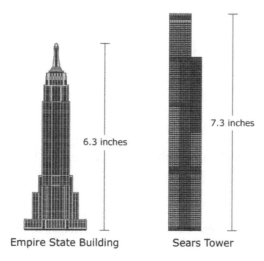

6.3 inches

7.3 inches

Empire State Building   Sears Tower

First, set-up a proportion that represents this model, since we know the ratios are equivalent (because they use the same scale).

$\frac{6.3}{1250} = \frac{7.3}{x}$

Let's cross-multiply to find our answer.

$$(6.3)(x) = (1250)(7.3)$$
$$6.3x = 9125$$
$$x = \frac{9125}{6.3} = 1448.41$$

Sears Tower (Willis Tower) is 1,448.41 ft tall.

Tips & Tricks

- When cross-multiplying, think of multiplying the values that are diagonal to each other as making an X. Remember: If $\frac{a}{b} = \frac{c}{d}$, then $ad = cb$.
- A scale model is a representation or copy of an object that is larger or smaller than the actual size of the object being represented. The scale model is usually smaller than the original and used as a guide to make the full-sized object (think blueprints for a house).

Practice

1. Solve each proportion using equivalent ratios. Check your solution.

   a. $\frac{3}{4} = \frac{x}{12}$

   b. $\frac{2}{3} = \frac{12}{y}$

   c. $\frac{a}{6} = \frac{18}{27}$

   d. $\frac{9}{10} = \frac{81}{y}$

   e. $\frac{14}{x} = \frac{35}{60}$

2. Marco makes \$25 for every 2 hours he works. If he works for 12 hours, how much will he make? Write a proportion and use equivalent ratios to find how much Marco will make in 12 hours.

3. True or False. Tell whether each statement below is true or false. If false, correct the mistake to make a true statement.

   a. $\frac{23}{8} = \frac{46}{16}$

   b. $\frac{7.1}{9.2} = \frac{21.3}{27.4}$

   c. $\frac{15}{60} = \frac{6}{22}$

4. Solve the proportion.

   a. $\frac{3}{5} = \frac{y}{2.5}$

   b. $\frac{5}{7} = \frac{3.5}{y}$

   c. $\frac{4.2}{x} = \frac{2.1}{32}$

   d. $\frac{4}{11} = \frac{14}{x}$

   e. $\frac{2}{3} = \frac{19.4}{y}$

5. Marni buys 2.5 pounds of grapefruit for \$4.48. To the nearest cent, how much would 6 pounds of grapefruit cost? Write a proportion and cross-multiply to find how much 6 pounds of grapefruit would cost.

6. Given the scale of 2 inches = 50 ft, find the actual height of the model buildings below.

    a. 4 inches

    b. 5.6 inches

    c. 8.2 inches

7. Given the scale of 3 inches = 125 ft, find the scaled model height based on the actual height of the buildings below.

    a. 450 ft

    b. 667.5 ft

    c. 937.5 ft

8. The distance between Tucson and Houston on a map is about 7 inches. The map legend says that $\frac{1}{2}$ *inch* = 75 *miles*. What is the approximate distance between Tucson and Houston based on this scale?

Bobcat Review

1. Estimate the value of the following square roots to the nearest hundredth.

    a. $\sqrt{15}$

    b. $\sqrt{30}$

    c. $\sqrt{7}$

Bobcat Stretch

1. Solve the following proportions.

    a. $\frac{x+2}{8} = \frac{20}{40}$

    b. $\frac{y-4}{11} = \frac{-12}{5}$

    c. $\frac{7.95}{17.85} = \frac{5.3}{3x+2}$

2. Beth was planning a trip to South Africa. Before going, she did some research and learned that the exchange rate is $5.70 = 7.4 Rand. How many Rand would she get if she exchanged $24.60? Round your answer to the nearest hundredth.

Further Review

For more videos and practice problems,

- click here to go to Khan Academy.
- search for "constructing proportions to solve application problems" on Khan Academy (www.khanacademy.org).

Watch this video to further review proportions.

MEDIA
Click image to the left or use the URL below.
URL: https://www.ck12.org/flx/render/embeddedobject/120827

Answers

1. a. x - 9

   b. y = 18

   c. y = 4

   d. y = 90

   e. x = 24

2. x = 150, $\frac{25}{2} = \frac{x}{12}$

3. a. True

   b. False, $\frac{7.1}{9.2} = \frac{21.3}{27.6}$

   c. False, $\frac{15}{60} = \frac{6}{24}$

4. a. y = 1.5

   b. y = 4.9

   c. x = 64

   d. x = 38.5

   e. y = 29.1

5. $10.75 for 6 lbs of grapefruit

6. a. 100 ft

   b. 140 ft

   c. 205 ft

7. a. 10.8 inches

   b. 16.02 inches

   c. 22.5 inches

8. 1,050 miles between Tucson and Houston

Bobcat Review

1.a. 3.87

   b. 5.48

   c. 2.65

Bobcat Stretch

1. a. x = 2

   b. y = (-22.4)

   c. x = 3.3

2. 31.94 Rand.

3.3 Solving Percent Problems

Solve percent problems using proportions.

By the end of this lesson, you should be able to define and give an example of the following vocabulary words:

- **Percent** - a ratio whose denominator is 100. The symbol for percent is %.
- **Base of a Percent** - The number from which a portion is to be found. In the percent equation $\frac{a}{b} = \frac{p}{100}$, the base is b. "a is p percent of b."

Example 1

Under Coach Sean Miller, the Wildcats won 96 games out of 139 games between 2009 and 2013. What is the Wildcats winning percentage during this time period?

We can use the proportion $\frac{a}{b} = \frac{p}{100}$ to solve percent problems. For almost every problem, we solve the proportion using cross products.

$$\frac{96}{139} = \frac{p}{100}$$
$$139p = (96)(100)$$
$$a = \frac{9,600}{139}$$
$$a = 69.06$$

The Wildcats won 69% (rounded) of their games between 2009 and 2013.

Example 2

34 is 3.6% of what number? Round the answer to the nearest tenth.

First, set-up a proportion to find the unknown number and solve by cross-multiplying.

$$\frac{34}{b} = \frac{3.6}{100}$$
$$3.6b = (34)(100)$$
$$b = \frac{3,400}{3.6}$$
$$b = 944.4$$

34 is 3.6% of 944.4.

Tips & Tricks

- When solving percent problems, set-up a proportion using the equation $\frac{a}{b} = \frac{p}{100}$, where " a is p percent of b".

  - a is part of the base "b" and is equivalent to the percent "p" when setting up the proportion.
  - b is the base "whole" value that is equivalent to 100 when setting up the proportion.
  - p is the percent of 100.

Practice

1. Write and solve a proportion to answer the following questions. Round answers to the nearest tenth.

    a. 13 is 12% of what number?

    b. What number is 35% of 42?

    c. 54 is 65% of what number?

    d. What number is 6.5% of 20?

    e. 23 is what percent of 267?

2. Henry, a plumber, worked 203 days last year. What percent of the year did he work? Round your answer to the nearest tenth. (Hint: a year has 365 days in a non-leap year)

3. Write and solve a proportion to answer the following quesitons. Round answers to the nearest tenth.

    a. 39 is what percent of 52?

    b. 627 is 128% of what number?

    c. What number is 4.5% of 74?

    d. 82 is what percent of 42?

    e. What number is 45% of 93?

4. Bruce scored 87% on the last math test. The test had 52 questions. How many questions did he answer correctly? Round your answer to the nearest whole number.

5. Use mental math to answer the following questions.

    a. 5x is 50% of what monomial (term)?

    b. 12x is what percent of 6x?

    c. What monomial (term) is 40% of 100x?

6. Which value is greater than the other value?

  a. 45% of 232 or 53% of 204

  b. 23% of 82 or 35% of 57

  c. 76% of 120 or 96% of 94

  d. 10% of 120 or 7.5% of 160

Bobcat Review

1. Solve the following equations.

  a. $x^2 + 5 = 21$

  b. $25 - x^3 = 17$

  c. $x(3x + 8x) = 99$

Bobcat Stretch

1. Bob took a test and missed 12 questions out of 65 questions overall. What grade (percent correct) did he get on the test? Round your answer to the nearest tenth.

2. In Rachel's eighth grade there are 328 students. She knows that 152 are boys. What percentage of the class are girls? Round your answer to the nearest tenth.

3. Herman's 7th grade has 234 students. 52.1% are girls. How many boys are in his grade? Round your answer down to the nearest whole number (as you can't have partial students).

Further Review

For more videos and practice problems,

- click here to go to Khan Academy.
- search for "finding percents" on Khan Academy (www.khanacademy.org).

Watch this video for further review of percent problems

MEDIA

Click image to the left or use the URL below.
URL: https://www.ck12.org/flx/render/embeddedobject/108462

Answers

1. a. b = 108.3

   b. a = 14.7

   c. b = 83.1

   d. a = 1.3

   e. p = 8.6%

2. p = 55.6%

3. a. p = 75%

   b. b = 489.8

   c. a = 3.3

   d. p = 195.2%

   e. a = 41.9

4. 45 correct questions

5. a. 10x

   b. 200%

   c. 40x

6. a. 53% of 204 (108.12) is greater than 45% of 232 (104.4)

   b. 35% of 57 (19.95) is greater than 23% of 82 (18.86)

   c. 76% of 120 (91.2) is greater than 96% of 94 (90.24)

   d. They are both equal (12 = 12)

Bobcat Review

1. a. $x = \pm 4$

   b. $x = 2$

   c. $x = \pm 3$

Bobcat Stretch

1. $p = 81.5\%$

2. $p = 53.7\%$

3. There are 113 boys.

3.4 Percent of Change

Solve problems with percent of increase or decrease.

By the end of this lesson, you should be able to define and give an example of the following vocabulary words:

- **Percent of Change** - shows how much a quantity has increased or decreased from the original amount.

$$\text{percent change} = \frac{\text{amount of increase or decrease (actual change)}}{\text{original amount}}$$

- **Percent of Increase** - when the new amount is greater than the original amount.
- **Percent of Decrease** - when the new amount is less than the original amount.

Example 1

A school of 500 students is expecting a 20% increase in students next year. How many students will the school have next year?

Use the percent change formula to find the number of students expected next year. Since the 20% change is an increase, we represent it in the formula as 0.20 (if it were a decrease, it would be -0.20). Remember to write the percent as a decimal.

$$0.20 = \frac{\text{actual change}}{500}$$

Multiply both sides by 500 and simplify.

$$(0.20)(500) = actual change$$

$$100 = actual change$$

So if we start out with 500 students, after an increase of 100, we know there will be a total of 600 students expected for next year.

Example 2

Another school of 850 students is expecting 680 students next year. What is the percent change from this year to next year in school enrollment?

First, plug the known numbers into the percent change formula. To calculate the actual change, subtract 850 from 680 to determine the school will have 170 less students next year.

Don't forget to include the negative sign to represent a percent decrease.

$P = \frac{-170}{850}$

$P = -\frac{1}{5}$, which is -0.20.

Move the decimal two places to the right to convert the decimal to a percentage.

$P = -20\%$

School enrollment is expected to decrease by 20% next year.

Tips & Tricks

- Here's the full percent change formula that specifically includes steps to calculate the "actual change" (by subtracting the original amount from the final amount) and to change the decimal to a percent (multiply by 100% to move the "Percent change" decimal two spaces to the right).

$$\text{Percent change} = \frac{\text{final amount - original amount}}{\text{original amount}} \times 100\%$$

- If the final answer is negative, it represents a decrease.
- If the final answer is positive, it represents an increase.

Practice

1. Find the percent change. Identify if it is a decrease or increase. Round your answer to the nearest percent.

    a. $43,500 to $46,000

    b. 305 lbs to 250 lbs

    c. $31 to $25

    d. 45 minutes to 55 minutes

2. Use mental math to solve: A decrease from 8 to 2 is what percent of decrease?

3. Find the new amount.

    a. 520 decreased by 35%

    b. 80 increased by 15%

    c. 15,300 decreased by 65%

    d. 12,800 increased by 8%

4. True or False. If false, correct the mistake to find the value that will make the statement true.

    • 4 increased by 300% is 12.

5. Find the percent increase or decrease. Round your anser to the nearest percent.

    a. x to 5x

    b. 3a to 8a

    c. 8b to 3b

    d. $\frac{1}{4}x$ to 3x

    e. b to $\frac{3}{8}b$

6. In 1995 New York had 18,136,000 residents. There were 827,025 reported crimes. By 2005 the population was 19,254,630 and there were a total of 491,829 reported crimes. (Source: New York Law Enforcement Agency Uniform Crime Reports.) Calculate the percentage change from 1995 to 2005 in the:

    a. Population of New York

    b. Total reported crimes

7. Jane has a 8" by 10" picture that she wants to reduce the dimensions by 50% for a school project.

    a. What are the dimensions of the reduced picture?

    b. Will the decrease in area be less than, equal to, or greater than 50%?

Bobcat Review

1. Compare the following numbers and list them from least to greatest.

    a. $-\frac{5}{6}, 0.35, \sqrt{3}, -0.85, 1.73$

    b. $3.4, -2.4, -\sqrt{5}, \frac{11}{4}, -\frac{9}{4}$

2. Simplify $\frac{3^5}{3^5}$.

Bobcat Stretch

1. A furniture store places a 30% markup on everything it sells. It offers its employees a 20% discount from the sales price. The employees are demanding a 25% discount, saying that the store would still make a profit. The manager says that at a 25% discount from the sales price would cause the store to lose money. Who is right?

Further Review

For more videos and practice problems,

- click here to go to Khan Academy.
- search for "Tax and tip word problems" on Khan Academy (www.khanacademy.org).
- click here to go to CK-12 Braingenie.
- search "Find the changing amount" on CK-12 Braingenie (braingenie.ck12.org).

Watch this video for further review of percent increase.

MEDIA
Click image to the left or use the URL below.
URL: https://www.ck12.org/flx/render/embeddedobject/114923

Answers

1. a. 6% increase

   b. 18% decrease

   c. 19% decrease

   d. 22% increase

2. 75% decrease

3. a. 338

   b. 92

   c. 5,355

   d. 13,824

4. False, use the percent change formula to find the error.

   $P = \frac{8}{4}$, which is 2.

   Move the decimal two spaces to the right to find 4 increased by 200% is 12.

   (You can also say 4 increased by 300% is 16. 12 is the amount changed, not the final value. You must add 12 to the original amount (12 + 4 = 16)

5. a. $p = \frac{4}{1}$, which is 4. Converted to an increase of 400%

  b. $p = \frac{5}{3}$, which is $1.\overline{66}$. Converted to an increase of 167%

  c. $p = \frac{-5}{8}$, which is -0.625. Converted to a decrease of 63%

  d. $p = \frac{2.75}{.25}$, which is 11. Converted to an increase of 1100%.

  e. $p = \frac{-0.625}{1}$, which is -0.625. Converted to a decrease of 63%

6. a. $p = \frac{1,118,630}{18,136,000}$, which is 0.06. Converted to a population increase of 6%.

  b. $p = \frac{-335196}{827025}$, which is -0.41. Convereted to a reported crime decrease of 41%.

7. a. The new picture dimensions are 4" by 5".

  b. The new area is 20 sq in, which is 75% less than the original area of 80 sq in. This is greater than a 50% reduction because changing both dimensions has a greater affect on the square area.

Bobcat Review

1. a. $-0.85, -\frac{5}{6}, 0.35, 1.73, \sqrt{3}$

  b. $-2.4, -\frac{9}{4}, -\sqrt{5}, \frac{11}{4}, 3.4$

2. $3^0 = 1$

Bobcat Stretch

1. We'll consider this problem two ways. First, let's consider an item that the store buys from its supplier for a certain price, say $1000. The markup would be 30% of 1000, or $300, so the item would sell for $1300 and the store would make a $300 profit.

And what if an employee buys the product? With a discount of 20%, the employee would pay 80% of the $1300 retail price, or $0.8 \times \$1300 = \$1040$.

But with a 25% discount, the employee would pay 75% of the retail price, or $0.75 \times \$1300 = \$975$.

So with a 20% employee discount, the store still makes a $40 profit on the item they bought for $1000—but with a 25% employee discount, the store loses $25 on the item.

Now let's use algebra to see how this works for an item of any price. If x is the price of an item, then the store's markup is 30% of x, or $0.3x$, and the retail price of the item is $x + 0.3x$, or $1.3x$. An employee buying the item at a 20% discount would pay $0.8 \times 1.3x = 1.04x$, while an employee buying it at a 25% discount would pay $0.75 \times 1.3x = 0.975x$.

So the manager is right: a 20% employee discount still allows the store to make a profit, while a 25% employee discount would cause the store to lose money.

It may not seem to make sense that the store would lose money after applying a 30% markup and only a 25% discount. The reason it does work out that way is that the discount is bigger in absolute dollars after the markup is factored in. That is, an employee getting 25% off an item is getting 25% off the original price *plus* 25% off the 30% markup, and those two numbers together add up to more than 30% of the original price.

3.5 Percent Applications and Simple Interest

Solve percent application problems and simple interest problems.By the end of this lesson, you should be able to define and give an example of the following vocabulary words:

- **Markup** - the increase in the price of an item from its wholesale price to its retail price.
- **Discount** - a decrease in the price of an item.
- **Simple Interest** - Interest (I) is the product of the Principal amount invested (P), the annual interest rate (r) written as a decimal, and the time (t) in years. $I = Prt$

Example 1

A printer that normally costs \$125 is marked down 20%. What is the sales price of the item?

Sales Price = Original Price - Discount

Let's use this formula for finding the sales price.

$$S = 125 - (0.20 \times 125)$$
$$S = 125 - 25$$
$$S = 100$$

The sales price of the printer is \$100.

Example 2

A tablet's wholesale price is \$125. Since the demand is high for the tablet, the markup for the tablet is 185%. What is the retail price of the tablet.

Retail = Wholesale + Markup

Let's use this formula for finding the retail price.

$$R = 125 + (1.85 \times 125)$$
$$R = 125 + 231.25$$
$$R = 356.25$$

The retail price of the tablet is \$356.25.

Example 3

You put \$1000 into an investment yielding 6% annual interest; you left the money in for two years. How much interest do you get at the end of those two years?

Interest is the product of the Principal amount invested (P), the annual interest rate (r) written as a decimal, and the time (t) in years. $I = Prt$

Let's use this formula for finding the retail price.

$$I = 1000(.06)(2)$$

$$I = 120$$

You earned \$120 interest on your principal investement of \$1000.

Tips & Tricks

- Sales Price = Original Price - Discount
- Retail Price = Wholesale Price + Markup
- Interest = Principal amount (P) X annual interest rate written as a decimal (r) X time in years (t)
    - $I = Prt$

Practice
---

1. Complete the following sentences.

   a. If you add a markup to a wholesale price, then you get the _____.

   b. If you subtract a discount from the original price, then you get the _____.

   c. The product of _____, _____, and _____ is the interest earned on a principal investement.

2. A $150 mp3 player is on sale for 30% off. What is the sales price of the mp3 player?

3. A shirt's wholesale price is $12. The store marked-up the shirt 80%. What is the retail price of the shirt?

4. An employee at a store is currently paid $9.50 per hour. If she works a full year, she gets a 12% pay raise. What will her new hourly rate be after the raise?

5. Find the total cost rounded to the nearest cent.

   a. $31.75 restaurant bill plus a 20% tip

   b. $14.50 retail price plus 8.1% sales tax

   c. $25.34 restaurant bill plus a 17% tip and $7.1 sales tax

6. Calculate the following amounts using the interest formula. Round to the nearest cent.

   a. What interest was earned on a principal investment of $1,400 invested at 3% for 2 years?

   b. What was the principal amount invested at 6% interest rate that yielded $235 interest over 3 years?

   c. How much interest is owed on an initial loan amount of $965 borrowed at 5.1% for 1 year?

   d. What was the interest rate for an investment of $12,000 that was invested for 5 years and yielded $2,400 in interest?

7. Calculate the following discount or markup percent. Round to the nearest percent.

   a. The retail price is \$239 for an item bought \$129 wholesale.

   b. The sales price is \$19.99 for an item that was \$29.99 originally.

   c. The sales price is \$110 for an item that was \$150 originally.

   d. The retail price is \$99 for an item bought \$45 wholesale.

8. A realtor earns 7.5% commission on the sale of a home. How much commission does the realtor make if the home sells for \$215,000?

Bobcat Review

1. List the property used at each step of solving the following equation:

$$4(x-3) = 20$$
$$4x - 12 = 20$$
$$4x = 32$$
$$x = 8$$

2. The volume of a cylinder is given by the formula $Volume = \pi(radius^2)(height)$, rewrite the formula for the radius (r). $V = \pi r^2 h$

3. Solve for w : $\frac{10}{w} = \frac{12}{3}$

Bobcat Stretch

1. You and three of your friends went out for pizza. The food bill came to $46.78 plus 15% tip and 8.1% tax. To be fair, everyone chipped in the same amount to cover the total bill. How much did you and each of your friend's pay? Round your answer to the nearest cent.

2. Store A and Store B both sell bikes, and both buy bikes from the same supplier at the same prices. Store A has a 40% mark-up for their prices, while store B has a 90% mark-up. Store B has a permanent sale and will always sell at 40% off those retail prices. Which store offers the better deal? Why?

3. Last year a company made a net profit of $20,000 on sales of $1,000,000. This year they made a net profit of $40,000 on sales of $1,000,000. When talking to the shareholders they claimed that their profit incrased by 100%, and asked for a bonus for doing so well. When they talked to their workers about a possible pay increase, they claimed their profit only increased by 2%, which hasn't event kept up with inflation. How did they determine these figures? Which one do you think is correct?

Further Review

For more videos and practice problems,

- click here to go to Khan Academy.
- search for "Percentage word problems" on Khan Academy (www.khanacademy.org).

Watch this video to further review percent application problems.

MEDIA
Click image to the left or use the URL below.
URL: https://www.ck12.org/flx/render/embeddedobject/108737

Answers

1. a. Retail Price

   b. Sales Price

   c. Principal amount (P), annual interest rate (r), time in years (t)

2. $105 is the sales price of the mp3 player.

3. $21.60 is the retail price of the shirt.

4. Her new hourly rate will be $10.64.

5. a. $38.10

   b. $15.67

   c. $31.45

6. a. $84

   b. $1,305.56

   c. $49.22

   d. 4%

7. a. Markup of 85%

   b. Discount of 33%

   c. Discount of 27%

   d. Markup of 120%

8. $16,125

Bobcat Review

1. Distributive Property (distribute the 4 to the grouping), Inverse Operations (add 12 to both sides), Inverse Operations (divide both sides by 4).

2. $\sqrt{\dfrac{V}{\pi h}} = r$

3. w = 2.5

Bobcat Stretch

1. $14.40 per person

2. Store B has the better deal. It marks up its items the most, but offers the biggest discount off the larger "marked-up" amount.

3. They calculated their profit from last year was 2% profit (20,000/1,000,000) and this year it was 4% (40,000/1,000,000). To the shareholders, they spun this as a 100% increase (after all 2+2=4), but in reality this 100% increase only represented an "actual" 2% increase. The statement to the workers was correct.

3.6 References

1. Pierce, Rod. "Ratios" Math Is Fun. Ed. Rod Pierce. 10 Feb 2014. 23 Apr 2014
2. . http://housing.ucsc.edu/ucen/photo-gallery/06.html .
3. . http://www.education.com/study-help/article/ratio-rate-word-problems_answer/ .
4. . http://ritter.tea.state.tx.us/student.assessment/resources/online/2009/taksm_g09_math/9mathm.htm .
5. Stapel, Elizabeth. "'Investment' Word Problems." Purplemath. Available from http://www.purplemath.com/modules/i Accessed 23 April 2014. .

CHAPTER 4

Functions

4.1 Relations & Functions

Identify functions using ordered pairs, table of values, and graphs. Write a function rule.

By the end of this lesson, you should be able to define and give an example of the following vocabulary words:

- **Relation** - A set of ordered pairs that relates and input (x) to an output (y).
- **Independent Variable** - the input (x) of a function.
- **Dependent Variable** - the output (y) of a function.
- **Function** - A relation in which each input (x) has exactly one output (y).
- **Domain** - A set of all possible input (x) values for a function.
- **Range** - The set of all possible output (y) values for a function.

Example 1

Determine if the relation is a function.

(1, 3), (-1, -2), (3, 5), (2, 5), (3, 4)

The easiest way to figure out if a relation is a function is to look at all the $x-$values in the list. If a value of x appears more than once, and it's paired up with different $y-$ values, then the relation is not a function.

You can see that in this relation there are two different $y-$ values paired with the same $x-$ value of 3.

This means that this relation is not a function because there is more than one output (y) per each input (x).

Example 2

Determine if the relation is a function.

(-3, -3), (-2, -1), (-1, 1), (0, 3), (1, 5)

You can write the ordered pairs in a table and graph them.

TABLE 4.1:

Input (x) (Domain)	Output (y) (Range)
-3	-3
-2	-1
-1	1
0	3
1	5

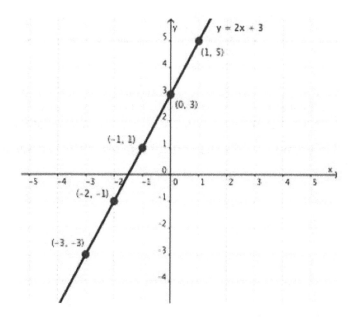

Let's see if each input (x) has only one output (y). All of the other inputs and outputs are unique.

This means that this relation is a function because each value of x has exactly one y-value.

Note: Upon closer inspection, you can see the relation between the input and output values is $y = 2x + 3$. This is the function rule for this data set. All data in this set must follow this rule for it to be a true function.

Example 3

Determine if the relation is a function.

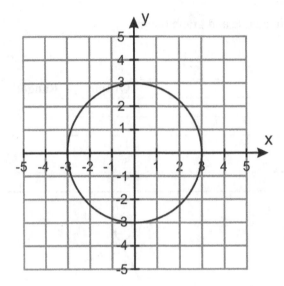

When a relation is represented graphically, we can determine if it is a function by using the **vertical line test** . If you can draw a vertical line that crosses the graph in more than one place, then the relation is not a function.

This relation is not a function because it fails the vertical line test. The red vertical line crosses the graph twice.

Example 4

Maya has an internet service that currently has a monthly access fee of \$11.95 and a connection fee of \$0.50 per hour. Represent her monthly cost as a function of connection time.

The problem is asking you to write a "function rule" that models this situation, so you can plug in any number of hours Maya is on the Internet each month to determine the total cost of her monthly bill.

When writing a function rule, try to find an equation of the form $y = (a)x + b$, where $a = \frac{change\ in\ ouput\ (y)}{change\ in\ input\ (x)}$.

The Independent Variable, $x =$ the number of hours Maya spends on the internet in one month.

The Dependent Variable, $y =$ Maya's monthly cost.

$a = \$0.50$, as the problem states Maya is charged \$0.50 per hour.

$b = \$11.95$, as the probelm states Maya is charged a flat monthly fee of \$11.95.

So, the total cost $(y) =$ hourly fee $(a) \times$ number of hours (x) + flat fee (b).

The function is $y = 0.50x + 11.95$.

Note: You can substitute a set of inputs (domain) into this function to create a set of outputs (range). For example,

TABLE 4.2:

Input (x) (Domain) in hours	Output (y) (Range) in \$
3.5	13.7
4	13.95
20	21.95

Tips & Tricks

- Remember a function is a relation in which each input (x) has exactly one ouput (y).
- The easiest way to figure out if a set of ordered pairs or a table of values is is a function is to look at all the $x-$values in the list or the table. If a value of x appears more than once, and it's paired up with different $y-$ values, then the relation is **not** a function.
- Use the vertical line test to figure out if a graph is a function. If you can draw a vertical line that crosses the graph more than one place, then the relation is **not** a function.
- When writing a function rule, try to find an equation of the form $y = ax + b$, where $a = \frac{change\ in\ ouput\ (y)}{change\ in\ input\ (x)}$. To find b, substitute an (x, y) value and solve for b.
- Domain = Set of "x" values (inputs).
- Range = Set of "y" values (outputs).
- The Independent Variable (x) often represents time.

Practice

1. Fill in the blanks:

   A _____ is a relation in which each _____ has exactly _____ ouput.

2. Determine if the following relations are a functions. Why or Why not?

   a. (1, 7), (2, 7), (3, 8), (1, 8), (5, 9)

   b. (-2, -8), (-1, -1), (0, 0), (1, 1), (2, 8), (-1, -1)

   c.

x	-4	-3	-2	-1	0
y	16	9	4	1	0

   d. (1, 1), (4, 2), (4, -2), (9, 3), (9, -3)

3. Make a table of values for the following function rules. Use the domain (-1.5), (-1), 0, 2, and 3 to find the corresponding range.

   a. $y = 3x + 4$

   b. $y = |x|$

   c. $y = 0.2x - 2$

4. Write a function rule for the table.

Number of CDs	2	4	6	8	10
Cost ($)	24	48	72	96	120

5. Determine if the following relations are functions.

a.

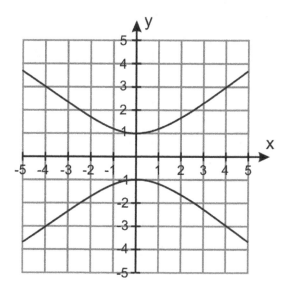

b.

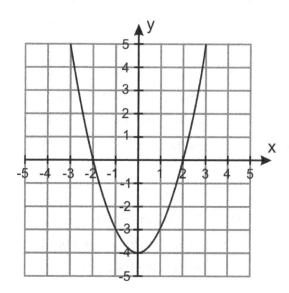

c.

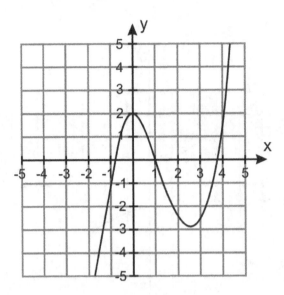

6. Sheri is saving for her first car. She currently has $515 and is saving $62 each week.

    a. Write a function rule that represents the total amount saved as a function of the number of weeks saving.

    b. Make an input/output table to find how many weeks it will take Sheri to save $1817.

7. Solomon charges a $40 flat rate and $25 per hour to repair a leaky pipe.

    a. Write a function rule that represents the total fee charged as a function of hours worked.

    b. How much does Solomon earn for a three-hour job?

8. Dave's bank charges a monthly fee of $15 for his checking account and also charges $0.10 for each check written.

    a. Write a function rule that represents the total fee charged as a function of checks written.

    b. In August, Dave wrote 12 checks, how much will his bank charge him for his checking account that month?

9. Write a function rule for each of the the following tables. (Hint: After finding "a", substitute x and y-values into the equation to solve for "b" to find the function rule y = a (x) + b).

a.

x	0	1	2	3
y	-5	-3	-1	1

b.

hours	0	1	2	3
cost	15	20	25	30

10. When the input to a function is 5, the output is 3. Which statement(s) about this function <u>must</u> be true? Choose all that apply.

a. An input of 5 has infinitely many possible outputs.

b. An input of 5 has exactly one possible output.

c. An output of 3 has infinitely many inputs.

d. An output of 3 has exactly one input.

Bobcat Review

1. Simplify: $84 \div [(18 - 16) \times 3]$.

2. Evaluate the expression $\frac{2}{3}(y + 6)$ when $y = 3$.

3. You purchased six video games for $29.99 each and three DVD movies for $22.99. What is the total amount of money you spent?

Bobcat Stretch

1. Write a function rule for each of the the following tables.

a.

qty of books	1	2	3	4	5	6
cost	4.75	5.25	5.75	6.25	6.75	7.25

b.

minutes	10	18	20	26
miles	0.6	1	1.1	1.4

2. When scuba divers come back to the surface of the water, they need to be careful not to ascend too quickly. Divers should not come to the surface more quickly than a rate of 0.75 ft per second.

a. Write a function rule that represents the relationship between the time of ascent in seconds (t) and the distance from the surface (d) if the divers start at a depth of 100 feet below the surface.

b. Will they be at the surface in 5 minutes? How long will it take the divers to surface from their dive? (Remember (t) is in terms of seconds.)

c. Make a table of values showing several times and the corresponding distance of the divers from the surface. Explain what your table shows. How do the values in the table relate to your equation?

3. When diving in the ocean, you must consider how much pressure you will experience from diving a certain depth. From the atmosphere, we experience 14.7 pounds per square inch (psi) and for every foot we dive down into the ocean, we experience another 0.44 psi in pressure.

a. Write a function rule expressing how pressure changes depending on depth underwater.

b. How far can you dive without experiencing more than 58.7 psi of pressure on your body?

Further Review

For more videos and practice problems,

- click here to go to Khan Academy.
- search for "Recognizing functions" on Khan Academy (www.khanacademy.org).
- go to Khan Academy's Common Core page standard 8.F.A.1 (www.khanacademy.org/commoncore/grade-8-F).

Watch this video to further review relations and functions.

MEDIA
Click image to the left or use the URL below. URL: https://www.ck12.org/flx/render/embeddedobject/113454

Answers

1. A **function** is a relation in which each **input** has exactly **one** output.

2. a. This is **not** a function. There are more than one output per input, for example "1" has more than one output "7" and "8".

   b. This is a function. Every input has only one output (Bonus: and is related per the function rule $y = 7x - 6$).

   c. This is a function. Every input has only one output (Bonus: and is related per the function rule $y = x^2$)

   d. This is **not** a function. Every input has more than one output, for example the input "4" as outputs "2" and "-2".

3. a. (-0.5), 1, 4, 10, 13

TABLE 4.3:

Input (x)	Output (y)
(-1.5)	(-0.5)
(-1)	1
0	4
2	10
3	13

b. 1.5, 1, 0, 2, 3

TABLE 4.4:

Input (x)	Output (y)
(-1.5)	1.5
(-1)	1
0	0
2	2
3	3

c. (-2.3), (-2.2), (-2), (-1.6), (-1.4)

TABLE 4.5:

Input (x)	Output (y)
(-1.5)	(-2.3)
(-1)	(-2.2)
0	(-2)
2	(-1.6)
3	(-1.4)

4. $y = 12x$

You pay $24 for 2 CDs, $48 for 4 CDs, and $120 for 10 CDs. That means that each CD costs $12.

x = # of CDs (Independent variable) and y = Cost (Dependent Variable)

So the function rule is Cost $= \$12 \times$ number of CDs or $y = 12x$.

5. a. No, it fails the vertical line test as a vertical line crosses the graph more than once.

b. Yes, it passes the vertical line test as a vertical line crosses the graph only once.

c. Yes, it passes the vertical line test as a vertical line crosses the graph only once.

6. a. $y = 62x + 515$

   b. 21 weeks

TABLE 4.6:

TABLE 4.6:

Input (x)	Output (y)
5	825
10	1135
15	1445
20	1755
21	1817

7. a. $y = 25x + 40$

   b. $y = 25(3) + 40$, so Solomon earned $115 for the 3-hour job.

8. a. $y = 0.10x + 15$

   b. $y = 0.10(12) + 15$, so Dave is charged $16.20 in bank charges for the month of August.

9. a. $y = 2x + 5$

   b. $y = 5x + 15$

10. b - a function has only one output per input. Did you select "d" too? Remember the vertical line test for graphs of nonlinear functions, in those cases an output may have more than one input. However, the reverse is not true - each input can only produce ONE output.

Bobcat Review

1. 14

$$84 \div [(18 - 16) \times 3]$$
$$84 \div [2 \times 3]$$
$$84 \div 6$$
$$14$$

2. 6

$$\frac{2}{3}(3 + 6)$$
$$\frac{2}{3}(9)$$
$$\frac{18}{3}$$
$$6$$

3. Total cost was $248.91

$$(6 \times 29.99) + (3 \times 22.99)$$
$$179.94 + 68.97$$
$$248.91$$

Bobcat Stretch

1. a. $y = \frac{1}{2}x + 4.25$

   b. $y = 0.05x + 0.1$

2. a. If the divers start at a depth of 100 ft below the surface, the equation $d = 0.75t - 100$ shows the relationship between the time of the ascent in seconds (t) and the distance from the surface in feet (d).

   b. First, convert 5 minutes to second as the rate of change is feet per second (not minutes). 5 minutes = 300 seconds. Substitute 300 for t and solve for distance (d). $d = 0.75 (300$ seconds$) - 100$, $d = 125$ ft, which is greater than $0 =$ surface, so yes they will be able to surface by 5 minutes .

The second question is asking to solve for (t), when (d) = 0, meaning the diver is at the surface. $0 = 0.75 (t) - 100$, $100 = 0.75 (t)$, $t = 133.33$ seconds or 2.22 minutes.

   c. Answers will vary, here are the inputs (range) 60, 120, 133, and 0 seconds. So in 60 seconds the divers are 55 feet below the surface. At 120 seconds, the divers are 10 feet below the surface, and at 133 seconds, they are only .25 feet from the surface. At 0 seconds, they start 100 ft below the surface.

t (sec)	d (ft)
60	-55
120	-10
133	-0.25
0	-100

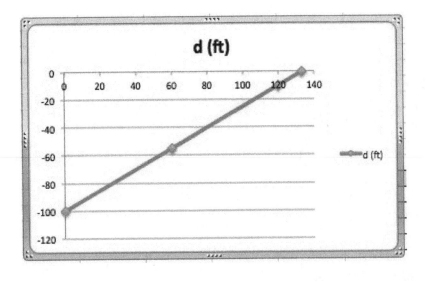

3. a. We are always experiencing 14.7 psi from the atmosphere, and that pressure increases by 0.44 psi for every foot we descend into the ocean. Let d be our depth in feet underwater. Our dependent variable is the pressure P, which is a function of d :

$P = 0.44d + 14.7$

b.) We want to know what our depth would be for a pressure of 58.7 psi.

$58.7 = 0.44d + 14.7$

Simplifying our equation by subtracting 14.7 from each side:

$44 = 0.44d$

What should d be in order to satisfy this equation? It looks like d should be 100. Let's check:

$44 = 0.44(100) = 44$

So we do not want to dive more than 100 feet, because then we would experience more than 58.7 psi of pressure.

4.2 Interpreting Graphs and Finding Rate of Change

Interpret a graph to compare properties of functions. Find and compare rates of change.

By the end of this lesson, you should be able to define and give an example of the following vocabulary word:

- **Rate of Change** - A ratio that compares the amount of change in output to the change in the input.

$$rate\ of\ change = \frac{change\ in\ output}{change\ in\ input}$$

Example 1

Two MP3 download sites, Company 1 and 2, offer the following monthly subscriptions.

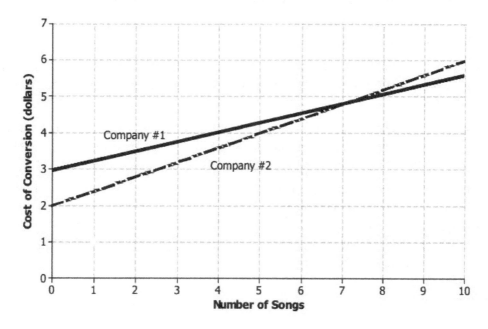

Interpret the graph to identify properties of each monthly subscription (function).

    a. Find the rate of change for each company.

    b. Identify which company's model has the more expensive cost per song.

    c. Identify the initial fee of each monthly subscription.

    d. Write a function to model the monthly subscription plans for Company #1 and Company #2.

    e. Determine which site you would choose if you only wanted to download 5 songs per month? How about 10? Explain your reasonsing.

First identify ordered pairs on each line and enter them in a table to determine the rate of change, where the x-values equal number of songs (Independent Variable) and the y-values equal the cost (Dependent Variable).

Company #1			Company #2	
# of songs (x)	Cost (y)		# of songs (x)	Cost (y)
0	3		0	2
4	4		5	4

Calculate the rate of change using the ordered pair data. Remember: *rate of change* $= \frac{change\ in\ output}{change\ in\ input}$.

    Company #1: *rate of change* $= \frac{change\ in\ cost}{change\ in\ number\ of\ songs} = \frac{4-3}{4-0} = \frac{1\ dollar}{4\ songs} = 0.25\ per\ song$

    Company #2: *rate of change* $= \frac{change\ in\ cost}{change\ in\ number\ of\ songs} = \frac{4-2}{5-0} = \frac{2\ dollars}{5\ songs} = 0.40\ per\ song$

a. So the rate of change for Company #1 is $0.25 per song and $0.40 per song for Company #2.

b. Based on the rate of change, the graph for Company #2 (0.40) is steeper than Company #1 (0.25), so Company #2 has the more expensive cost per song. $0.40 cents per song versus $0.25 cents per song.

c. Company #1 has an initial fee of $3 (0, 3) for its monthly subscription. Company #2 has an initial fee of $2 (0, 2) for its monthly subscription (where the line crosses the y-axis, when x = 0).

d. Remember the equation $y = (a) x + b$. The rule for Company #1 monthly subscription (function) is $y = 0.25x + 3$, where a = rate of change and b = initial fee for Company #1. The rule for Company #2 monthly subscription (function) is $y = 0.40x + 2$.

e. For 5 songs, Company #2 is cheaper than Company #1 as the cost point for when $x = 5$ is lower for Company #2 ($4) than Company #1 ($4.25) on the graph. You can also solve it using the function. Company #1 = $y = 0.25 (5) + 3$, so $y = \$4.25$. Company #2 = $y = 0.40 (5) + 2$, so $y = \$4$.

For 10 songs, Company #1 is cheaper than Company #2 as the cost point for when $x = 10$ is lower for Company #1 ($5.50) than Company #2 ($6) on the graph. You can also solve it using the function. Company #1 = $y = 0.25 (10) + 3$, so $y = \$5.50$. Company #2 = $y = 0.40 (10) + 2$, so $y = \$6$.

Example 2

The graph shows a roundtrip route made by a large delivery truck on a particular day. During the day, the truck made two deliveries.

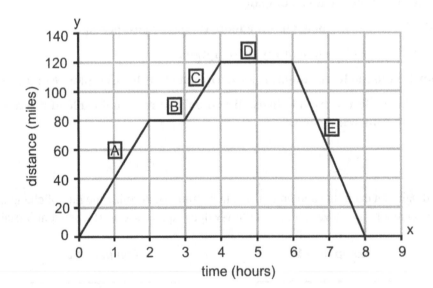

Interpret the graph to identify and compare the rates of change of each stage of the trip (stages A - E).

First, identify the independent and dependent variables.

    The Independent Variable (x) is Time (hours).

    The Dependent Variable (y) is Distance (miles) from the starting point (the garage where the delivery trucks starts out every morning).

Enter the ordered pairs for each stage of the trip in a table to help you more easily calculate the rate of change.

TABLE 4.7:

Hours	0	2	3	4	6	8
Miles	0	80	80	120	120	0

Stage A:

Rate of change $= \frac{\Delta y}{\Delta x} = \frac{80-0}{2-0} = \frac{80 \text{ miles}}{2 \text{ hours}} = 40$ miles per hour

Notice that the rate of change is a speed, so during the first part of the trip, the truck travels at a constant speed of 40 mph for 2 hours, covering a distance of 80 miles.

Stage B:

Rate of change $= \frac{\Delta y}{\Delta x} = \frac{80-80}{3-2} = \frac{0 \text{ miles}}{1 \text{ hours}} = 0$ miles per hour

The rate of change is 0 mph (noted by the horizontal line on the graph). The truck is stationary for one hour. This is the first delivery stop.

Stage C:

Rate of change $= \frac{\Delta y}{\Delta x} = \frac{120-80}{4-3} = \frac{40 \text{ miles}}{1 \text{ hours}} = 40$ miles per hour

The truck is traveling at 40mph as it drives to the next delivery stop.

Stage D:

Rate of change $= \frac{\Delta y}{\Delta x} = \frac{120-120}{6-4} = \frac{0 \text{ miles}}{2 \text{ hours}} = 0$ miles per hour

Once again the rate of change is 0 mph (noted by the horzontal line on the graph). The truck is stationary for two hours at the second delivery stop. At this point, the truck is 120 miles from the garage where it started this morning.

Stage E:

Rate of change $= \frac{\Delta y}{\Delta x} = \frac{0-120}{8-6} = \frac{-120 \text{ miles}}{2 \text{ hours}} = -60$ miles per hour

The truck is traveling at negative 60 mph as it returns back to where it started from. Wait! Does that make sense? Does that mean that the truck is reversing?

Well, probably not. The negative sign highlights that the distance from the starting position is decreasing with time because the truck is completing its round trip (returning back to its original starting position). Since it no longer has 2 heavy loads, it travels faster (60 mph instead of 40 mph), covering the 120 mile return trip in 2 hours. Its speed is 60 mph, and its velocity is -60 mph, because it is traveling in the opposite direction from where it started out.

Note: The difference between speed and velocity is that velocity has a direction, and speed does not. In other words, velocity can be either positive or negative, with negative velocity representing travel in the opposite direction.

Tips & Tricks

- The steeper the line of a graph, the greater the rate of change.
- If there is no rate of change (0), the line of the graph is horizontal.
- The initial value of a function (b) is where the line crosses the y-axis, when x = 0.

Practice

1. Calculate the rates of change for line a, b, and c in the graph below and then identify the line with the greatest rate of change. Explain your reasoning.

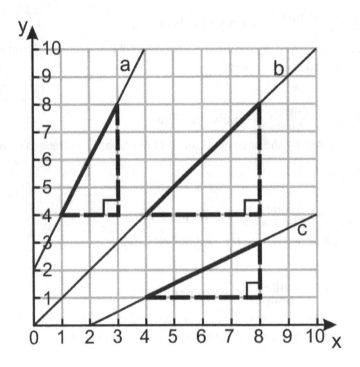

2. The population of fish in a local lake increased from 370 to 420 over 2 months. At what rate is the population increasing?

3. The graph below is a distance vs. time graph for Mark's 3.5 miles cycle ride to school. Put the following statements in the order they happened as shown in the graph. Explain your reasoning.

    1. He stopped for two-minutes at a traffic light.

    2. He rode on a hilly cycle path for a little over 6 minutes.

    3. He took a shortcut up a hill to arrive at school on time.

    4. He rode down a hill.

    5. He stopped to fix his bike chain for 5 minutes.

    6. He started out going up a hilly dirt path.

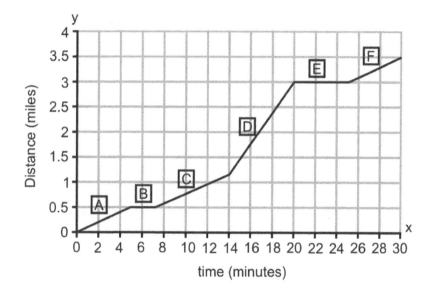

4. Two people, Adam and Bianca, are competing to see who can save the most money in one month.

   a. Use the table and the graph below to determine who will save more money by the end of the month.

   b. How much money did each person already have saved at the start of the competition.

Adam's Savings:

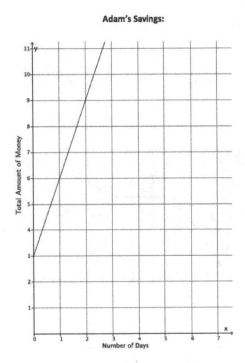

Number of Days

Bianca's Savings:

Input (Number of Days)	Output (Total amount of money)
5	$17
8	$26
12	$38
20	$62

5. The relationship between Jameson's account balance and time is modeled by the graph below.

   a. Write a story that models the situtation represented by the graph.

   b. When is the function represented by the graph increasing? How does this relate to your story?

   c. When is the function represented by the graph decreasing? How does this relate to your story?

   d. What was his initial account balance?

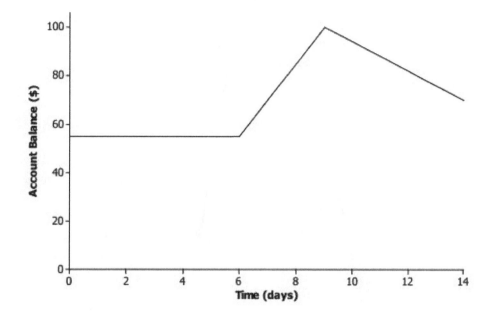

6. The graph below shows the speed of a vehicle plotted against time.

   a. Calculate and explain the rates of change between each point (A to B), (B to C), (C to D), (D to E), and (E to F).

   b. What point represents the speed at 10 seconds? What is the speed at 10 seconds? (If the input is 10, what is the output?)

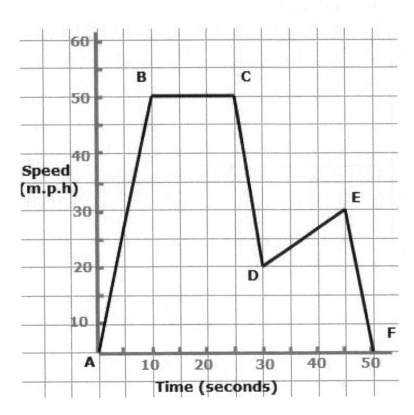

7. Which function represents a greater rate of change? a or b?

    a. $y = 3x + 7$

    b.

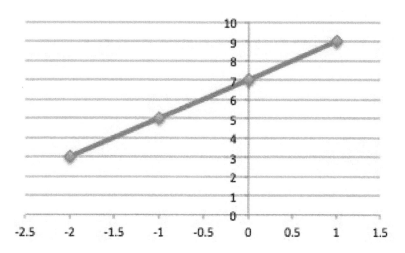

Bobcat Review

1. Identify if the following numbers are Rational, Integer, Whole, Natural, and/or Irrational. Explain your reasoning. Note: numbers may fall into more than one category.

    a. -45.89

    b. -3

    c. $3.5982957....$

    d. $\sqrt{6}$

    e. $-4.\overline{44}$

    f. 1952

2. Convert $8.\overline{88}$ to a fraction.

Bobcat Stretch

1. Siblings, Rose and Pete, walk 2 miles to school from home at constant rates. Rose can walk to school in 24 minutes. Pete has slept in again and needs to run to school. Pete's speed is shown in the graph.

    a. Which sibling is moving at a greater rate? Explain your reasoning.

    b. If Pete leaves 5 minutes after Rose, will he catch Rose before they get to school? Explain your reasoning.

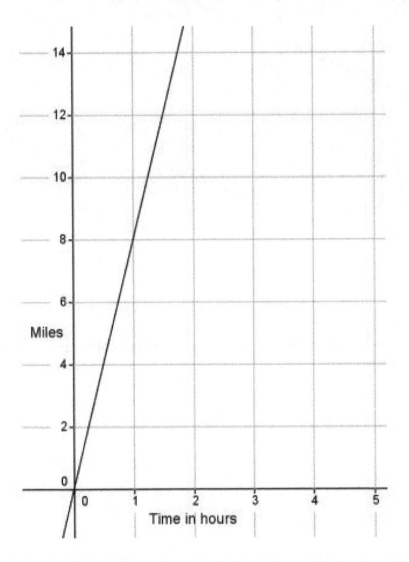

2. The rule $y = 123x$ is used to describe the function for the number of x minutes needed to produce y toys at Toys Plus. Another company, #1 Toys, has a similar function that assigned the values shown in the table below. Which company produces toys at a slower rate? Explain.

Time in minutes (x)	Toys Produced (y)
5	600
11	1,320
13	1,560

Further Review

For more videos and practice problems,

- click here to go to Khan Academy.
- search for "Interpreting graphs of linear and nonlinear functions" on Khan Academy (www.khanacademy.org).
- go to Khan Academy's Common Core page standard 8.F.A.2 and 8.F.B.4 (www.khanacademy.org/commoncore/grade-8-F).

Watch this video to further review interpreting graphs.

MEDIA

Click image to the left or use the URL below.

URL: https://www.ck12.org/flx/render/embeddedobject/113769

Answers

1. a. Rate of change $= \frac{\Delta y}{\Delta x} = \frac{8-4}{3-1} = \frac{4}{2} = 2$

   b. Rate of change $= \frac{\Delta y}{\Delta x} = \frac{8-4}{8-4} = \frac{4}{4} = 1$

   c. Rate of change $= \frac{\Delta y}{\Delta x} = \frac{3-1}{8-4} = \frac{2}{4} = \frac{1}{2}$

   Line "a" has the greatest rate of change because 2 >1 >0.5 as represented by being the steepest line on the graph.

2. The change in $y-$values, or Δy, is the change in the number of fish, which is $420 - 370 = 50$. The change in $x-$values, Δx, is the amount of time over which this change took place: two months. So $\frac{\Delta y}{\Delta x} = \frac{50 \text{ fish}}{2 \text{ months}}$, or **25 fish per month.**

3. 6. He started out going up a hilly dirt path. (a slower rate of change as he went slower up a hill)

   1. He stopped for two-minutes at a traffic light. (0 - rate of change as noted by the horizontal line)

   2. He rode on a hilly cycle path for a little over 6 minutes. (a slower rate of change as he went slower up a hill)

   4. He rode down a hill. (a steeper rate of change = a steep line since he was going faster down hill)

   5. He stopped to mend a punctured a tire. (0 - rate of change as noted by the horizontal line)

   3. He took a shortcut up a hill to arrive at school. (a slower rate of change as he went slower up a hill)

4. a. Adam's rate of change: Rate of change $= \frac{\Delta y}{\Delta x} = \frac{9-6}{2-1} = \frac{3}{1} = 3 \text{ dollars per day.}$

   Bianca's rate of change: Rate of change $= \frac{\Delta y}{\Delta x} = \frac{26-17}{8-5} = \frac{9}{3} = 3 \text{ dollars per day.}$

   Since they are both saving at the same rate ($3 per day), then they will have both saved the same amount of money by the end of the month.

   b. Adam began the competition with $3 as noted by the point (0, 3). This means on day 0 he already had $3 saved.

   Bianca began the competition with $2. This means on day 0 she already had $2 saved. (Use the function equation y = (a) x + b to solve for b (as shown in relations and functions lesson). Plug the ordered pair ($x = 5, y = 17$) and the rate of change ($a = 3$) into the equation to solve for b, so $17 = 3 (5) + b, 17 = 15 + b, 2 = b.$)

   If their previous savings were included in the contest, then Adam won because even though they saved the same amount per day - he had $1 more in savings at the beginning of the competition.

5.a. Answers will vary. For example, Jameson was sick and did not work for almost a whole week. Then he mowed several lawns over the next few days and deposited the money into his account after each job. It rained several days, so instead of working Jameson withdrew money from his account each day to go to the movies and out to lunch with friends.

b. Between 6 and 9 days. Jameson earned money mowing lawns and made a deposit to his account he day. The money earned for each day was constant for these days. This is represented by a straight line.

c. Between 9 and 14 days. Since days 9 - 14 are represented by a straight line, this means that Jameson spent the oney constantly over these days. James cannot work because it is raining.

d. His initial account balance was $55 as noted by the point $(0,55)$, when $x = 0$, then $y = 55$.

6. a. Points A and B: The rate of change is increasing quickly (at a rate of 5 miles per second) since the line is steep and going up. The car starts from a stationary position and increases speed up to 50 mph after 10 seconds per the graph.

$$\text{Rate of change} = \frac{\Delta y}{\Delta x} = \frac{50-0}{10-0} = \frac{50}{10} = 5 \text{ miles per second}$$

Points B and C: The rate of change is 0 since the line is horizontal, so the car is traveling at a constant speed which is 50 mph as shown by the graph. In this case, the 0 rate of change means the car is not increasing or decreasing in speed, but remaining at a constant speed for 15 seconds.

$$\text{Rate of change} = \frac{\Delta y}{\Delta x} = \frac{50-50}{25-10} = \frac{0}{15} = 0 \text{ miles per second}$$

Points C and D: The car is slowing down (probably breaking) to 20 mph over 5 seconds. The rate of change for the deceleration is 6 miles per second. Remember the negative sign just means that the car is decreasing in speed (not actually going - 6 miles per second).

$$\text{Rate of change} = \frac{\Delta y}{\Delta x} = \frac{20-50}{30-25} = \frac{-30}{5} = -6 \text{ miles per second}$$

Points D and E: The rate of change is speeding up from 20 to 30 mph over 15 seconds at a rate of $\frac{2}{3}$ miles per second.

$$\text{Rate of change} = \frac{\Delta y}{\Delta x} = \frac{30-20}{45-30} = \frac{10}{15} = \frac{2}{3} \text{ miles per second}$$

Points E and F: The car is slowing down and stopping over 5 seconds. The rate of change for the deceleration is 6 miles per second. Remember the negative sign just means that the car is decreasing in speed (not actually going - 6 miles per second).

$$\text{Rate of change} = \frac{\Delta y}{\Delta x} = \frac{0-30}{50-45} = \frac{-30}{5} = -6 \text{ miles per second}$$

b. Point B, where the input is 10 seconds, the output is 50 mph.

7. The "a" function has a greater rate of change, which equals 3 (a = 3 in the function rule y = (a) x + b). The "b" function's rate of change is 2 ($y = 2x + 7$).

(For function b, the rate of change is calculated by choosing two points from the graph - in this case points $(1, 9)$ and $(0, 7)$ Rate of change $= \frac{\Delta y}{\Delta x} = \frac{9-7}{1-0} = \frac{2}{1} = 2$, so "a" = 2. The b-value is 7 because the line crosses the y-axis at 7, when x = 0.)

Bobcat Review

1. a. Rational (terminating decimal)

   b. Rational, Integer (negative number)

   c. Irrational (Non-terminating, non-repeating decimal)

   d. Irrational (Non-terminating, non-repeating decimal)

   e. Rational (Repeating decimal)

   f. Rational, Whole, Natural (Whole, positive, counting number)

2. $100x = 888.\overline{88}$

  -    $x = 8.\overline{88}$

      —————————

    $99x = 880$

     $x = \frac{880}{99} = \frac{80}{9}$

Bobcat Stretch

1.a. Pete is faster as he can run 1 mile every 7.5 minutes while Rose can walk 1 mile in 12 minutes.

   Rose's rate of change: Rate of change $= \frac{\Delta y}{\Delta x} = \frac{2}{24} = \frac{1\ mile}{12\ minutes}$

   Pete's rate of change: Rate of change $= \frac{\Delta y}{\Delta x} = \frac{8-0}{60-0} = \frac{8}{60} = \frac{2\ miles}{15\ minutes} = \frac{1\ mile}{7.5\ minutes}$. Remember you have to convert hours (from the graph) to minutes, so you can accurately compare the rates of change between Rose and Pete.

   You could have graphed Rose's rate of change too on Pete's graph and compared the two lines. Pete's line would be steeper since he has the greater rate of change.

   b. Yes Pete will catch Rose before school if he wakes up 5 minutes late and runs.

   It takes Rose 24 minutes to walk 2 miles to school. Rose's function rule is y = 12 x

   It will take Pete 20 minutes to get to school as he can run the two miles to school in 15 minutes (see rate of change above) plus add 5 more minutes for him sleeping in late. So he will arrive at school in 20 minutes and will catch his sister on the way (as it takes her 24 minutes to walk to school). Pete's function rule is y = 7.5 x + 5

2. #1 Toys produces toys at a slower rate because is has a slower rate of change (120 <123).

   Toys Plus' rate of change = 123 toys per minute because in the equation $y = 123x$, 123 is the rate of change (a).

   #1 Toys' rate of change: Rate of change $= \frac{\Delta y}{\Delta x} = \frac{1320-600}{11-5} = \frac{720}{6} = 120\ toys\ per\ minute$

4.3 Constructing and Analyzing Rates of Change

Construct, graph, and analyze rates of change.

By the end of this lesson, you should be able to define and give an example of the following vocabulary word:

- **Rate of Change** - A ratio that compares the amount of change in output (y) to the change in the input (x).

$$rate\ of\ change = \frac{change\ in\ output}{change\ in\ input}$$

Example 1

Draw a graph that represents the following situation.

Mr. Peabody left home and drove his car at an average speed of 40 mph for the first 30 minutes until he reached the highway. He drove on the highway for 2 hours averaging 80 mph until he reached his exit. At his exit, he stopped to get lunch and gas for 30 minutes. He drove another 30 minutes going 50 mph until he reached his destination.

First, identify the dependent and independent variables.

The Independent Variable (x) is Time (hours).

The Dependent Variable (y) is Distance from home (miles).

Construct a table of values to graph from the verbal description above.

Time (h)	Distance (m)
0	0
0.5	20
1.5	100
2.5	180
3	180
3.5	205

(0,0) - At this point, the car is at home stationary.

(0.5, 20) - At this point, the car has driven 30 minutes (0.5 hours) at 40 mph. Since it is only an hour, divide 40 in half because only half the 40 miles per **hour** were driven.

(1.5, 100) - At this point, the car has driven 1 hour more (0.5 + 1 = 1.5 hours traveled) at 80 mph, so add 80 to the distance already covered. The total distance covered at this point is 20 + 80 = 100 miles traveled.

(2.5, 180) - At this point, the car has driven 1 more hour (1.5 + 1 = 2.5 hours traveled) at 80 mph, so add another 80 miles to the miles already covered. 100 + 80 = 180.

(3, 180) - At this point, the car stopped for 30 minutes (2.5 + 0.5 = 3 hours traveled). The distance traveled stays at 180 since the rate of change was 0.

(3.5, 205) - At this point, the car traveled 30 more minutes (3 + 0.5 = 3.5 hours traveled) at 50 mph. The distance traveled is only half of 50 (since the car only traveled for half-an-hour), so 180 + 25 = 205 total miles traveled.

Sketch a graph that models this situation by plotting the ordered pairs from the table on a graph.

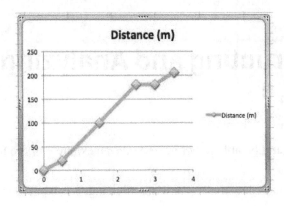

Note: the initial value of this graph is 0 (represented by point (0, 0)) since he started at home. However, if the situation changed and instead he was on a trip and started off on the day's journey 100 miles from home, then the initial value would be 100 (point 0, 100) and the entire graph would shift up from the starting point of (0, 100).

Tips & Tricks

- The steeper the line (slope), the greater the change.
- A horizontal line indicates no change or zero rate of change.
- A continuous straight line indicates a constant rate of change.
- The initial value (b) is where the line crosses the y-axis, when x = 0.

Practice

1. Tom had $500 in his savings account. Each month he added $50 to his account and withdrew nothing. Draw a graph of this function.

2. Bridget is painting a room with 400 sq. ft. to paint. She paints the room for three hours before taking a 30 minute break. During the first hour she averaged 60 sq. ft. per hour, then she ups her pace to 80 sq. ft. for the second and third hour. After her break, she paints another 2 hours averaging 90 sq. ft. per hour. Is she done painting the room or does she have to continue painting tomorrow? Draw a graph of this function with x = Time (hours) and y = Surface Area **not** yet painted to answer the question.

3. True or False. Does this graph represent the following situation? If not, correct the error to make the graph a true model of the function.

A rental car company charges $35 a day for the car as well as a one-time $20 fee for the car's GPS.

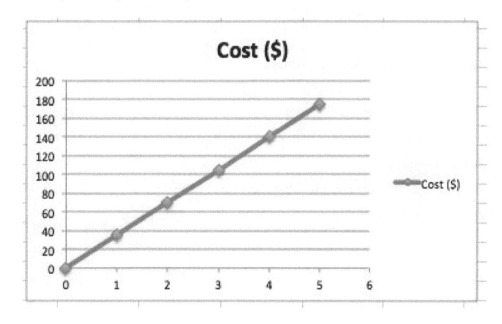

4. During a soccer game, Tracy's heart rate increased 4 beats per minute over 15 minutes from a resting heart rate of 65. For most of the game (20 minutes), her heart rate remained steady. Since her team was ahead, she was benched for the remaining 10 minutes of the game, where her heart rate decelerated at a rate of 3.5 beats per minute. What was her heart rate at the end of the game? Draw a graph to model this function and answer this question.

5. Michael started to shuck corn at the rate of 2 ears of corn per 5 minutes. After 10 minutes, Michele joined him and was able to shuck 3 ears of corn per 10 minutes. 20 minutes after Michael started, how many ears of corn were shucked? Sketch a graph to model this function and answer the question.

Bobcat Review

1. Estimate $\sqrt{12}$ to the nearest hundredth.

2. Compare the following numbers and list them from least to greatest.

   $1.56, \frac{4}{7}, \frac{3}{2}, -0.34, \sqrt{2}$

3. Plot the numbers from question #2 on a number line.

Bobcat Stretch

1. Jet 1 is parked at the terminal and takes off. It traveled 310 mph for the first 2 hours and then was slowed down for the last 3 hours going against the wind to 250 mph. Jet 2 takes off 5 minutes after Jet 1 and travels 280 mph for the first 3 hours and then catches a tail wind (with the wind) and travels 310 mph for the last 2 hours. Which Jet traveled farther? Graph the distance traveled for both jets to answer the question.

2. A candle has a starting length of 10 inches. 30 minutes after lighting it, the length is 7 inches.

   a. Graph the function.

   b. Determine the rate of change in length of the candle as it burns.

   c. Determine how long the candle takes to completely burn to nothing.

Further Review

For more videos and practice problems,

- click here to go to Khan Academy.
- search for "Interpreting features of linear functions" on Khan Academy (www.khanacademy.org).
- go to Khan Academy's Common Core page standard 8.F.B.5 (www.khanacademy.org/commoncore/grade-8-F).

- click here to go to Braingenie for simpler practice problems that you can graph to answer.
- search for "Rate challenge" on CK-12 Braingenie (braingenie.ck12.org/skills/101810)

Watch this video to further review constructing and analyzing rates of change.

MEDIA
Click image to the left or use the URL below.
URL: https://www.ck12.org/flx/render/embeddedobject/113772

Answers

1.

Time (months)	Account Balance ($)
0	500
1	550
2	600
3	650
4	700
5	750

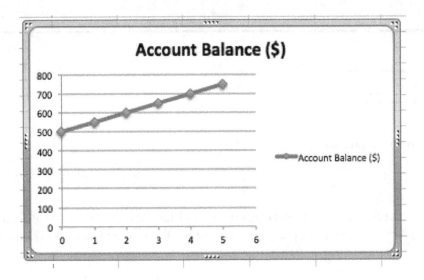

2. Yes, she is done painting the room because the final point is (5.5, 0), meaning she's painted for 5.5 hours and there is no more square feet to paint.

Time (hours)	Area to be Painted (sq ft)
0	400
1	340
2	260
3	180
3.5	180
5.5	0

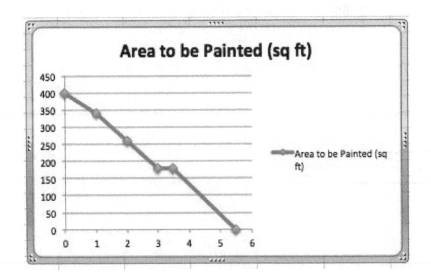

3. False. The graph starts at (0,0), which is incorrect. There is a one-time $20 fee for the GPS, so the starting point should be (0, 20). The correct graph is below.

Time (days)	Cost ($)
0	20
1	55
2	90
3	125
4	160
5	195

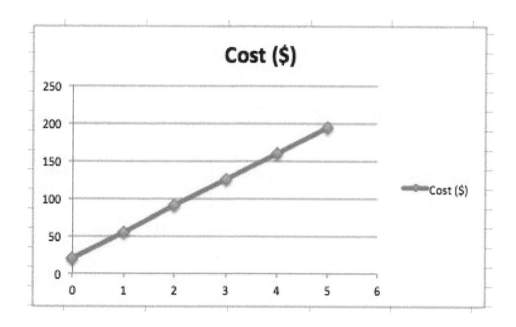

4. Her heart rate at the end of the game was 90 beats per minute.

Time (min)	Heart Rate
0	65
15	125
35	125
45	90

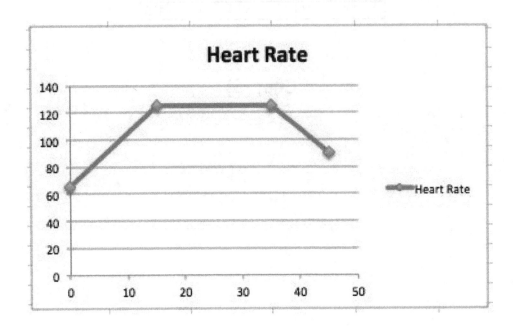

5. 11 ears of corn were shucked after 20 minutes.

Time (min)	Ears of Corn
0	0
5	2
10	4
20	11

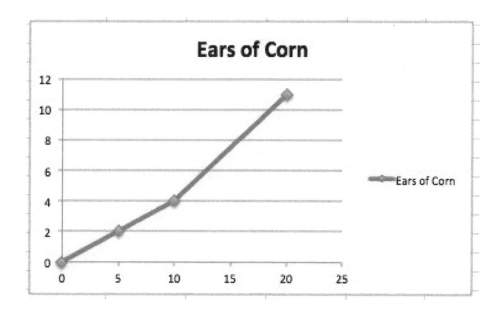

Bobcat Review

1. 3.46 ($\sqrt{9} < \sqrt{12} < \sqrt{16}$, so $3 < \sqrt{12} < 4$. $3.4 < \sqrt{12} < 3.5$, $3.45 < \sqrt{12} < 3.47$, so $\sqrt{12} \approx 3.46$)

2. -0.34, $\frac{4}{7}$, $\sqrt{2}, \frac{3}{2}$, 1.56

3. Plot the points from #2 on a number line.

Bobcat Stretch

1. Jet 2 traveled farther. It traveled 1460 miles in 5 hours while Jet 1 travels 1370 miles in 5 hours.

Time (h)	Distance (m)
0	0
2	620
5	1370

Time (h)	Distance (m)
0	0
3	840
5	1460

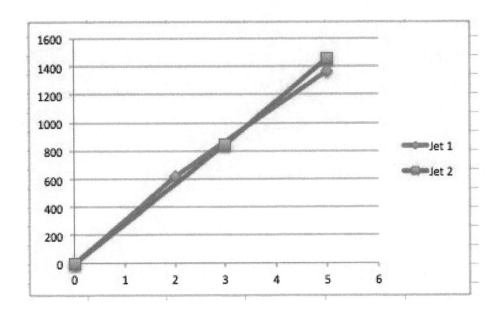

2. a. First we will graph the function to visualize what is happening. We have 2 points to start with. We know that at the moment the candle is lit (*time* = 0) the length of the candle is 10 inches, and after 30 minutes (*time* = 30) the length is 7 inches. Since the candle length depends on the time, plot time on the horizontal axis and candle length on the vertical axis.

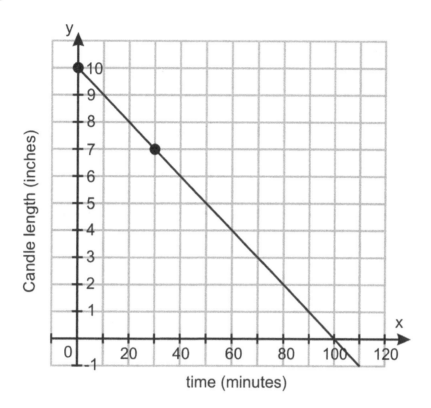

b. The rate of change of the candle's length is -0.1 inches per minute.

$$\text{Rate of change} = \frac{y_2 - y_1}{x_2 - x_1} = \frac{(7 \text{ inches}) - (10 \text{ inches})}{(30 \text{ minutes}) - (0 \text{ minutes})} = \frac{-3 \text{ inches}}{30 \text{ minutes}} = -0.1 \text{ inches per minute}$$

Note that the rate is negative. A negative rate of change means that the quantity is decreasing with time just as we would expect the length of a burning candle to do.

c. To find the point when the candle reaches zero length, we can simply read the $x-$intercept off the graph (100 minutes) for when $y = 0$. We can use the rate equation to verify this algebraically:

$$\text{Length burned} = \text{rate} \times \text{time}$$
$$10 = 0.1 \times 100$$

Since the candle length was originally 10 inches, our equation confirms that it takes 100 minutes for the candle to burn to nothing.

4.4 References

1. . http://www.wyzant.com/resources/lessons/math/algebra/graphing_linear_equations .
2. . Algebraic Functions Ck-12 .
3. . Algebraic Functions CK-12 .
4. . Engage NY Module 6 Lesson 2 p 20 .
5. . slope and rate of change - CK-12 .
6. . Slope and Rate of Change Ck-12 .
7. . Slope and rate of change Ck-12 .
8. . Engage NY Lesson 7 Module 5 p87 .
9. . Engage NY Module 6, Lesson 4, p 43 .
10. . http://www.helpingwithmath.com/by_subject/statistics_probability/sta_rate_of_change8sp3.htm .
11. . ACCRS Example problem .
12. . Engage NY Module 5 Lesson 7 p93 .
13. . Ck-12 Slope and Rate of Change .

CHAPTER **5**   Introduction to Linearity

5.1 The Coordinate Plane

Identify and plot points in a coordinate plane.

By the end of this lesson, you should be able to define and give an example of the following vocabulary words:

- **Coordinate Plane** - A coordinate system formed by the intersection of a horizontal number line, called the x-axis, and a vertical number line, called the y-axis.
- **x-axis** - The horizontal number line in a coordinate plane.
- **y-axis** - The vertical number line in a coordinate plane.
- **origin** - The point (0, 0) where the x-axis and the y-axis meet in a coordinate plane.
- **Quadrant** - One of the four regions that a coordinate plane is divded into by the x-axis and the y-axis.
- **Ordered Pair** - A pair of numbers (x, y) that can be used to represent a point in a coordinate plane. The first number is the x-coordinate, and the second number is the y-coordinate.
- **x-coordinate** - The first number in an ordered pair representing a point in a coordinate plane.
- **y-coordinate** - The second number in an ordered pair representing a point in a coordinate plane.

Example 1

Plot (-3, -2), (-2, 0), (0, 4), and (2, 8) on a coordinate plane and draw a line through the coordinates.

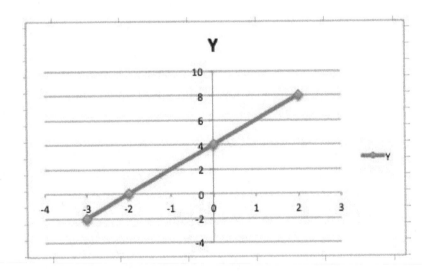

Note: the function (a.k.a. linear equation) for this line is $y = 2x + 4$, where 2 equals the rate of change and 4 equals the y-intercept (when $x = 0$). It's a linear equation because the graph forms a straight line.

Tips & Tricks

- The quadrants are named using Roman Numerals. The image below illustrates the quadrant names.

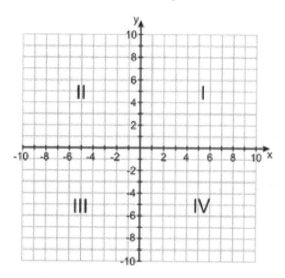

- Not all axes will be labeled for you. There will be many times you are required to label your own axes. Some problems may require you to graph using only the first quadrant. Others need two or all four quadrants.
- The tic marks on graphs vary - they are not always one. They can be marked in increments of 2, 5, or even 0.5.
- The axes do not even need to have the same increments! The increments by which you count your axes should MAXIMIZE the clarity of the graph.
- A linear equation forms a straight line when plotted on a graph.
- Note that quadrant I contains coordinates that are both positive (+, +). Quadrant II coordinates are (-, +), quadrant III coordinates are (-, -) and quadrant IV coordinates are (+, -).

Practice

1. Plot the following ordered pairs on the same graph and draw and label a line through each set (a, b, and c line).

    a. (-5, 0.5), (-2, 2), (3, 4.5), (2, 4)

    b. (-3, 4), (-2, 2), (1, -4), (2.5, -7)

    c. (2, 1), (-1, -2), (-3, -4), (3, 2)

2. Plot the following ordered pairs on the same graph and draw and label a line through each set (a, b, and c line).

    a. (-3, 11), (-1, 5), (0, 2), (1, -1)

    b. (4, 6.5), (-2, 2), (1, 4.25), (-3, 1.25)

    c. (2, -4.5), (-3, -3.25), (3, -4.75), (-10, -1.5)

3. True or False. The graph represents a line that is plotted through points (-3, -6), (0, -3), (2, -1), (4, 1). If False, correct the error(s) and graph correctly.

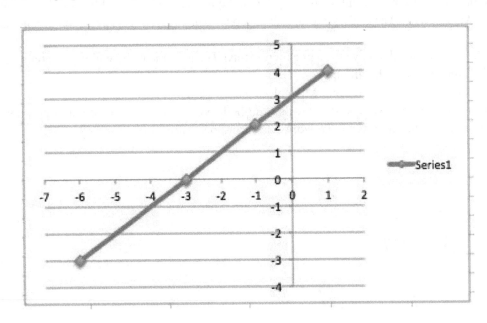

4. Plot the following ordered pairs on the same graph and draw and label a line through each set (a, b, and c line).

    a. (-3, -8), (-1, -4), (0, -2), (2, 2)

    b. (2, 5.5), (1, 4), (-1, 1), (-3, -2)

    c. (2, -3), (-3, 2), (3, -4), (1, -2)

Bobcat Review

1. Write the function rule (a.k.a. linear equation) for each line (a, b, and c) from problem 1 of the practice set.

   Hint: Remember the format is $y = (a) x + b$, where a = rate of change and $b = y$ - intercept (when $x = 0$). You can also find the value of "b" by plugging in an (x, y) value into the equation and solve for b.

Bobcat Stretch

1. Plot the points that have a domain of 2, 3, 4, and 5. Find the corresponding range using the linear equation $y = 2.5x - 10$.

Further Review

For more videos and practice problems,

- click here to go to Khan Academy.
- search for "graphing points and naming quadrants" on Khan Academy (www.khanacademy.org).

Watch this video to further review graphing linear equations.

MEDIA
Click image to the left or use the URL below.
URL: https://www.ck12.org/flx/render/embeddedobject/113793

Answers

1. Your graph may look different depending on what increments you chose to use for your x and y-axis.

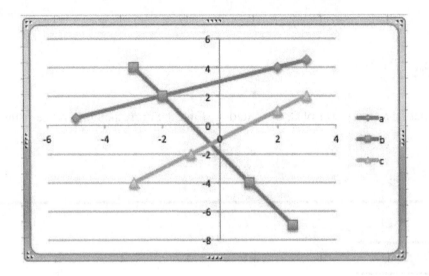

2. Your graph may look different depending on what increments you chose to use for your x and y-axis.

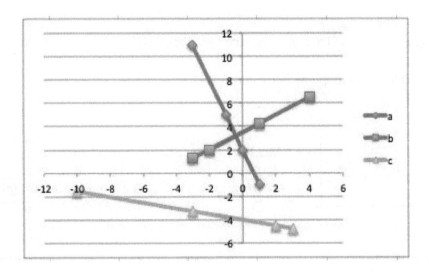

3. False, the *x*-values and *y*-values are reversed in the graph. Here's the correct graph.

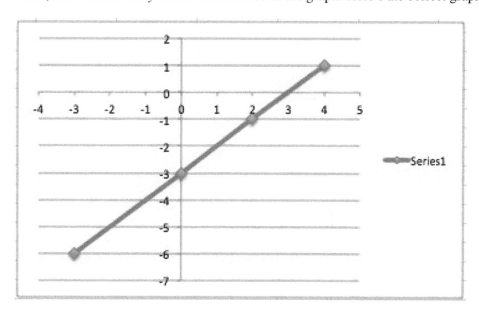

4. Your graph may look different depending on what increments you chose to use for your x and y-axis.

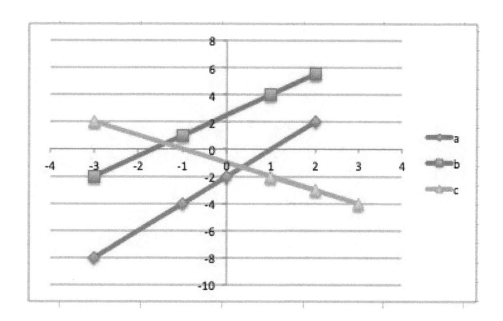

Bobcat Review

1. a. $y = 0.5x + 3$

   (Hint: Remember $y = (a) x + b$. First calculate the rate of change to solve for "a", then substitute one of the ordered pairs and solve for "b". "b" is the y-intercept when $x = 0$.)

   b. $y = -2x - 2$

   c. $y = x - 1$

Bobcat Stretch

1. The range is -5, -2.5, 0, and 2.5.

x	y
2	-5
3	-2.5
4	0
5	2.5

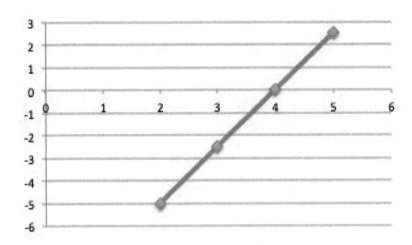

5.2 Equations in Two Variables

Find solutions of equations in two variables.

By the end of this lesson, you should be able to define and give an example of the following vocabulary words:

- **Solution of an equation in two variables** - An ordered pair whose values make the equation true.
- **Equations in Function Form** - An equation is in function form when it is solved for *y*.
    - **Function form:** $y = -x + 5$
    - **Not function (Standard) form**: $x + y = 5$

Example 1

Tell whether (-2, 4) is a solution of $x + 3y = 10$.

Write original equation.

$$x + 3y = 10.$$

Substitute -2 for *x* and 4 for *y*.

$$-2 + 3(4) = 10$$

Simplify.

$$-2 + 12 = 10$$

Solution check: $10 = 10$

The ordered pair (-2, 4) is a solution of $x + 3y = 10$.

Note: this equation was written in standard (not function form). If it were in function form, then the equivalent equation would be $y = -\frac{1}{3}x + \frac{10}{3}$.

$$4 = -\frac{1}{3}(-2) + \frac{10}{3}$$
$$4 = \frac{2}{3} + \frac{10}{3}$$
$$4 = \frac{12}{3}$$
$$4 = 4$$

So either way (function or standard form), (-2, 4) is a solution of this equation.

Tips & Tricks

- Function Form: $y = -2x - 7$
- Non-Function (Standard) Form: $2x + y = 7$

Practice

1. Fill in the blank.

   $y = 15x - 21$ is an example of a equation written in _____.

2. Given the equation, $y = -3x + 3$, complete the missing values in the table below.

X	Y
-3	
-1	
5	
	-3

3. Tell whether the ordered pair (5, -2) is a solution of the following equations. If not, write down an ordered pair that would be a solution.

   a. $y = 2x - 12$

   b. $y = -2x + 6$

   c. $-3x - y = -17$

   d. $x - y = 7$

   e. $1.5x + 0.5y = 6.5$

4. Find 4 solutions for $y = 3.5x - 4.5$. Write solutions as ordered pairs.

5. Jenna works at a retail shop. She makes $10 per hour, plus $3 for each item she sells.

   a. Write an equation in function form to model this situation for how much Jenna earns per hour.

   b. If she sold 3 items during her 1st hour, how much would she be paid for that hour?

   c. If she earned $22 for her 2nd hour of work, how many items did she sell during her second hour of work?

6. True or False. (-3, -2) is a solution of $4x - 2y = -2$. If false, make corrections to one or both coordinates to make a true statement.

7. Write the equation in function form and then find 3 solutions of the equation. Write solutions as ordered pairs.

    a. $3x + y = 24$

    b. $y - \frac{1}{2}x = 40$

    c. $2y + 12x = 36$

    d. $3x - \frac{1}{3}y = 6$

8. Tickets to a concert are $15 and the fee to rent the concert hall is $500.

    a. Write an equation in function form to model this situation.

    b. If the total profit was $5950, then how many tickets were sold?

    c. Next year, the date is moved and only half the amount of tickets are sold. Will the total profit be half the profit from last year? Explain.

9. Write an equation in function form that represents the following table.

x	y
0	2.5
1	3.25
2	4
3	4.75

Bobcat Review

1. Simplify the expression: $\frac{-8xy^2z^5}{4yz^2}$

2. Evaluate the expression $\frac{-15x^5}{-5x^3}$, when x = 5.

3. Simplify $y^9 \times y^3$.

Bobcat Stretch

1. The price of one share of stock is $10 per share, while the other stock is $5 per share. The investor spends a total of $5000.

   a. Write an equation in function form to model this situation.

   b. Find 4 possible investment options for the investor (a.k.a. find 4 solutions to the equation).

   c. If the investor wants to purchase a total of 700 shares and wants to buy at least 50 shares of each stock, how much of each stock should she buy.

2. Seats for a concert cost $10.50 for prime seats and $2.50 for "cheap" seats. The concert generated $570 in total revenue.

   a. Write an equation in function form to model this situation.

   b. Find 4 possible ticket sale distribution solutions (between $10.50 seats and $2.50 seats) that will generate $570 in revenue and at least 10 of each type of ticket must be sold. Remember, no partial tickets can be sold, so only whole numbers work as solutions.

   c. The concert hall has a capacity of 100 seats, so how many of each type of seat were sold to generate $570 in revenue?

Further Review

For more videos and practice problems,

- click here to go to Khan Academy.
- search for "ordered pair solutions to linear equations" on Khan Academy (www.khanacademy.org).

Watch this video to further review ordered pair solutions of equations.

MEDIA
Click image to the left or use the URL below.
URL: https://www.ck12.org/flx/render/embeddedobject/114096

Answers

1. function form

2.

x	y
-3	12
-1	6
5	-12
2	-3

3. a. Yes

   b. No, a correct solution of the equation would be (5, -4).

   c. No, a correct solution of the equation would be (5, 2).

   d. Yes

   e. Yes

4. Various answers: (0, -4.5), (1, -1), (2, 2.5), (3, 6)

5. a. $e = 3s + 10$, where e = Jenna's total earnings per hour and s = # of items sold per hour. **Note:** you may choose any variables for x-values and y-values as long as you clearly explain what they mean.

   b. $e = 3 (3) + 10$, $e = 19$. She earned \$19 for her 1st hour of work.

   c. $22 = 3 (s) + 10$, $12 = 3s$, $s = 4$. She sold 4 items during her 2nd hour of work to earn \$22 dollars.

6. False. (-3, -2) is not a solution of $4x - 2y = -2$. Various answers - one example of a true statement: The ordered pair (-2, -3) is a solution of $4x - 2y = -2$. Remember an ordered pair is (x, y), so the x-values and y-values need to be substituted correctly in the equation with the corresponding variable.

7. a. $y = -3x + 24$, where (0, 24), (1, 21), and (2, 18) are all solutions. Various answers for solutions are acceptable.

   b. $y = \frac{1}{2}x + 40$, where (0, 40), (1, 40.5), and (2, 41) are all solutions. Various answers for solutions are acceptable.

   c. $y = -6x + 18$, where (0 , 18), (1, 12), and (2, 6) are all solutions. Various answers for solutions are acceptable.

   d. $y = 9x - 18$, where (0, -18), (1, -9), and (2, 0) are all solutions. Various answers for solutions are acceptable.

8. a. $p = 15t - 500$, where p = Total profit from the concert and t = # of tickets sold. Note: you may choose any variables for x-values and y-values as long as you clearly explain what they mean.

   b. 430 tickets sold ($5950 = 15t - 500$, $6450 = 15t$, $6450 / 15 = t$, $t = 430$)

   c. No, because of the concert hall rent fee is a fixed fee whether 215 tickets are sold or 430 tickets. So, the profit for next year is $p = 15 (215) - 500$, where $p = \$2725$, which is less than half of the profit generated last year.

9. $y = 0.75x + 2.5$ or $y = \frac{3}{4}x + 2\frac{1}{2}$

Bobcat Review

1. $-2xyz^3$

2. $3x^2 = 3(5^2) = 3(25) = 75$

3. $y^{9+3} = y^{12}$

Bobcat Stretch

1. a. $10x + 5y = 5000$, so $y = -2x + 1000$ (function form), where $x = \$10$ share and $y = \$5$ share.

   b. Various answers: $(100, 800)$, $(200, 600)$, $(300, 400)$, $(400, 200)$, where $x = \$10$ per share stock and $y = \$5$ per share stock.

   c. $(300, 400)$. Since the x-value and y-value must equal 700 shares, then the investment mix of 300 shares of $10 per share stock and 400 shares of $5 per share stock will meet the investor's wishes.

2. a. $10.50x + 2.50y = 570$, $2.50y = -10.50x + 570$, so $y = -4.2x + 228$ (function form), where $x = \$10.50$ per ticket price and $y = \$2.50$ per ticket price.

   b. Various answers. Example solutions include: $(10, 186)$, $(20, 144)$, $(30, 102)$, $(40, 60)$.

   c. $(40, 60)$ as $40 + 60 = 100$. This means 40 seats @ $10.50 each and 60 seats @ $2.50 each were sold to generate $570 in revenue. $10.50 (40) + 2.50 (60) = 570$

5.3 Graph Linear Equations

Sketch the graph of a linear equation.

By the end of this lesson, you should be able to define and give an example of the following vocabulary word:

- **Linear Equation in two variables** - An equation in which the variables appear in separate terms and each variable occurs only to the first power. The graph of a linear equation is a straight line.

Example 1

Graph the linear equation $y = \frac{1}{3}x - 3$.

Make a table of values by substituting any number for x and solving for y.

x	y
0	-3
3	-2
6	-1
9	0

List solutions as ordered pairs: (0, -3), (3, -2), (6, -1), and (9, 0).

Plot the ordered pairs and draw a line through them.

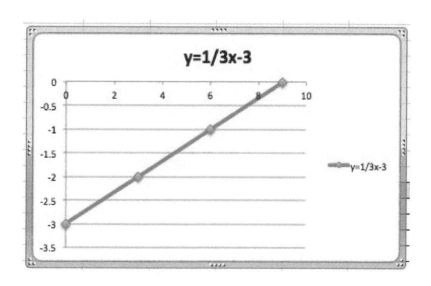

The line is the graph of $y = \frac{1}{3}x - 3$ **and is linear because it forms a straight line.**

Tips & Tricks

- An equation in "function form", for example $y = 3x + 6$, is also a linear equation in two variables.
  - linear equation: $y = mx + b$, where m is the slope of the line (a.k.a. rate of change) and b is the y-intercept (a.k.a. initial value).
- If the graph of an equation in two variables is a straight line, the equation is a linear equation.
- Every solution to the equation is located on the straight line of the graphed equation.

Practice

1. Graph $y = 3x + 2$.

2. True or False. The graph below represents the linear equation $y = -2x + 2$. If False, correct the error to make a **true** statement.

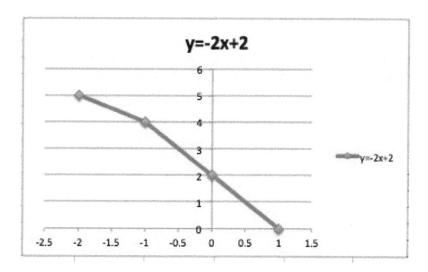

3. Graph $y = \frac{3}{4}x - 1$.

4. A recycling collection company pays 0.025 per crushed soda can and charges a flat $0.50 processing fee for each customer. Write and graph the linear equation that models this situation.

5. Graph $y = -\frac{8}{5}x + 3$.

Bobcat Review

1. Simplify $\frac{x^9}{x^4}$

2. Simplify $\frac{4^6}{4^6}$

3. Simplify $\frac{4^6}{4^8}$. Write your answer with only positive exponents.

Bobcat Stretch

1. Recycling R Us pays $0.80 per pound of aluminum cans.

    a. Write the linear equation that models this situation and graph the line.

    b. If it takes 32 aluminum cans to make a pound, then how much does Recycling R Us pay per can? Write and graph a linear equation that models price per can instead of price per pound.

    c. The next month, the demand for aluminum is higher, so Recycling R Us raises its rate to $0.88 per pound. Write and graph the linear equation that models this new situation.

    d. Compare graphs "a", "b", and "c". Which forms a steeper line? Explain?

2. Graph $2y + x = 9$.

Further Review

For more videos and practice problems,

- click here to go to Khan Academy .
- search for "graphing linear equations" on Khan Academy (www.khanacademy.org).

Watch this video to further review graphing linear equations.

 **Multimedia**

MEDIA
Click image to the left or use the URL below.
URL: https://www.ck12.org/flx/render/embeddedobject/114140

Answers

1.

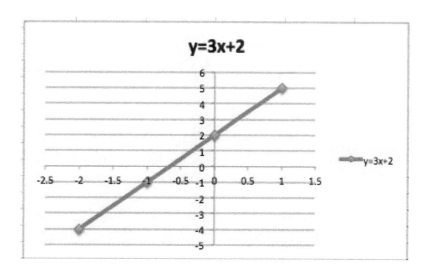

Points plotted on line:

x	y
0	2
1	5
-1	-1
-2	-4

2. False, the graph does not represent a linear equation because it is <u>not</u> a straight line. Looking closer, the point (-2, 5) is incorrect, the point should be (-2, 6) to make the statement true. The correct graph is...

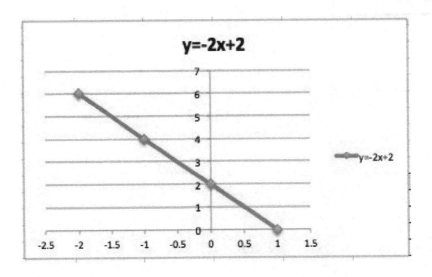

3.

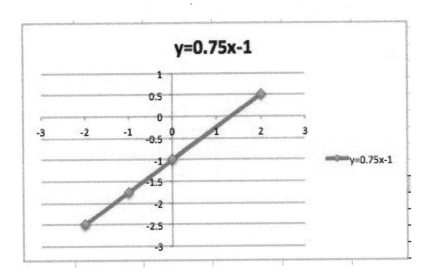

4. $y = .025x - .50$

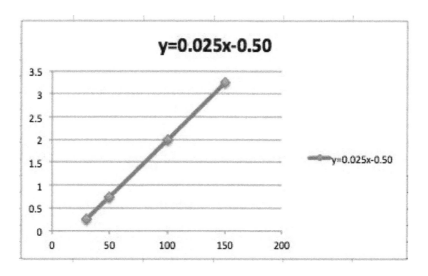

Points plotted on line:

x	y
30	0.25
50	0.75
100	2
150	3.25

5.

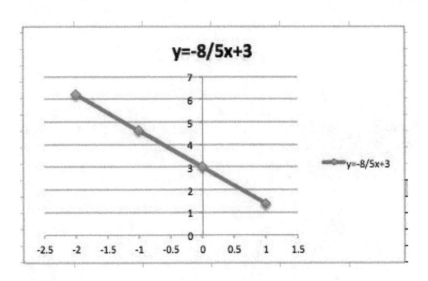

Points Plotted on line:

x	y
0	3
-1	4.6
1	1.4
-2	6.2

Bobcat Review

1. x^5

2. $4^0 = 1$

3. $4^{-2} = \frac{1}{4^2} = \frac{1}{16}$

Bobcat Stretch

1. a. $y = 0.80x$, where x = # of pounds of cans.

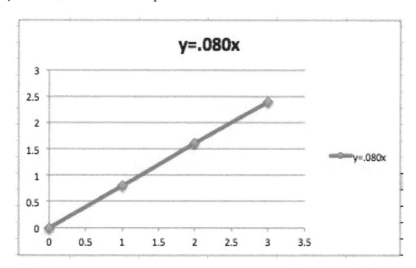

b. Recycling R Us pays $0.025 per can ($0.80 / 32 = 0.025), so the equation is $y = 0.025x$, where x = # of aluminum cans.

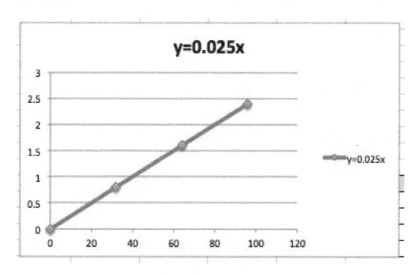

c. $y = 0.88x$, where x = # of pounds of cans.

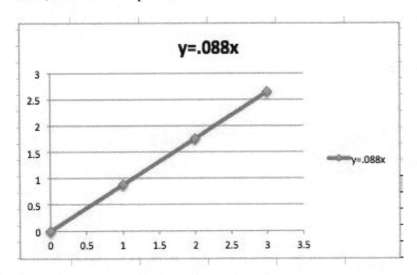

d. Graph "c" is steeper because it has a greater rate of change 0.88 >0.80/lb = 0.80/32 cans, so customers will earn more per pound/can at the higher pay rate.

2. Convert the equation to function form to make it easier to find solutions. $y = -0.50x + 4.5$. Plot points (0, 4.5), (-1, 5), (-2, 5.5), and (2, 3.5).

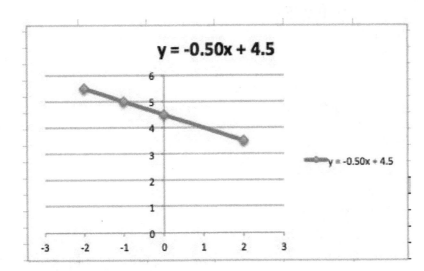

5.4 Graph Linear and Non-Linear Equations

Sketch the graph of a vertical and horizontal linear equation. Recognize the difference between linear vs. non-linear equations. Sketch the graph of a non-linear function.

By the end of this lesson, you should be able to define and give an example of the following vocabulary words:

- **Non-Linear Equation** - An equation in which the variables appear in separate terms and one or more variables occur to degrees either greater than or less than 1. The graph does <u>not</u> form a straight line (non-linear).
    - $5x^2 + 3y = 12$ is a non-linear equation because one of the variables is squared (greater than 1).
    - $3x + 2y^{\frac{1}{3}} = 10$ is a non-linear equation because one of the variables is to the $\frac{1}{3}$ degree (less than 1).
- **Vertical Line Test** - Remember you can use the vertical line test to tell whether a graph represents a function. If any vertical line intersects the graph at more than one point, then the graph does not represent a **function**.

Example 1

Graph $x = 1$　and　$y = 1$.

$x = 1$ forms a vertical line because all the ordered pairs have an x-coordinate of 1. For example, $(1, 0)$, $(1, 3)$, $(1, 4)$, and $(1, 5)$ are all on the line of $x = 1$. Note: this graph does not represent a function because it would fail the vertical line test.

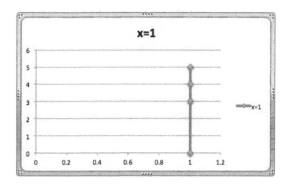

$y = 1$ forms a horizontal line because all the ordered pairs have a y-coordinate of 1. For example, (-1, 1), (0, 1), (1, 1), and (2, 1) are all on the line of $y = 1$.

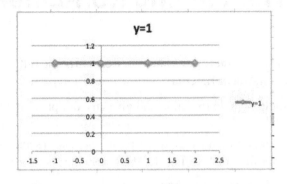

Example 2

Tell whether the equation is linear or non-linear and graph the line of the equation.

$y = x^2 - 4$

It's non-linear because one of the variables occurs to a degree greater than 1 (x^2), so the graph of this line will not be a straight line. Note: this means the line does not have a constant rate of change, so it's not a straight line.

To graph, make a table of values to graph (similar to linear equations). For this equation it would be easier to first find several values for x, then substitute the x-value into the equation and solve for y.

x	$y = x^2 - 4$	(x, y)
-3	y = (-3)^2 - 4 = 5	(-3, 5)
-2	y = (-2)^2 - 4 = 0	(-2, 0)
-1	y = (-1)^2 - 4 = -3	(-1, -3)
0	y = (0)^2 - 4 = -4	(0, -4)
1	y = (1)^2 - 4 = -3	(1, -3)
2	y = (2)^2 - 4 = 0	(2, 0)
3	y = (3)^2 - 4 = 5	(3, 5)

Plot the points from the table of values.

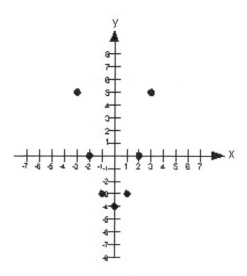

Draw a curved line through the plotted points.

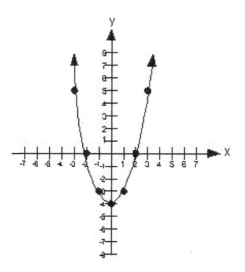

Tips & Tricks

- The graph of $x = a$ is the vertical line passing through $(a, 0)$.
- The graph of $y = b$ is the horizontal line passing through $(0, b)$.
- Remember a function has exactly one output value for each input value.
- A non-linear equation or function has a variable that occurs to a degree either less than or greater than 1.
- Use the vertical line test to determine if a linear or non-linear equation is a function. If a vertical line drawn through the graph crosses the graph more than once, then it is not a function. However, both linear and non-linear equations can be functions.

Practice

1. Match the equation with the description of the graph: a vertical line, a horizontal line, a diagonal line, or a curved line. Explain.

    a. $x = -8$

    b. $y = x - 8$

    c. $y = x^2 - 8$

    d. $y = -8$

2. Find three ordered pairs (x, y) that are solutions of the given equation.

    a. $x = 8$

    b. $y = -3$

3. Tell whether the following equations are linear or non-linear. Explain.

    a. $-3x + 2y^2 = 15$

    b. $6x + 3.3y = 10$

    c. $y = 3x^2 - 5.2$

    d. $A = \pi r^2$

    e. $y = -0.45x + 2(x + 4)$

4. Write the equation of the line.

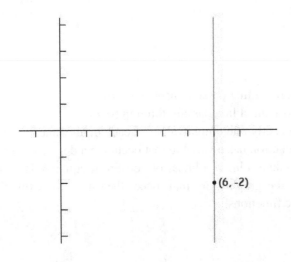

(6, -2)

5. Write the equation of the line.

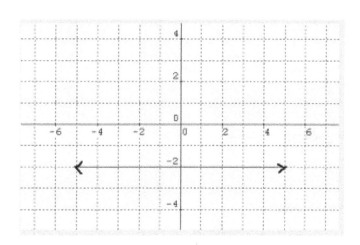

6. Graph the linear equation. Complete the table of values first for the given domain: {-10, -5, 0, 5, and 10} (see example 2 above for guidance).

$y = \frac{2}{5}x + 3$

7. Tell whether the following equations are linear or non-linear. Explain.

a. $y = -8 \times 3x$

b. $y = (3x + 5)^2$

c. $y = \frac{x}{8}$

d. $y = 5x^3 - 3$

e. $y = 3x * 3$

8. A pool is being drained at 650 gallons per hour. The pool has 16,000 gallons of water. You can determine how long it will take to drain the pool from the equation $g = -650h + 16,000$, where g is the total number of gallons **left** to be drained and h is the number of hours the pool has been draining.

a. Graph the equation using the given domain:{ 0, 6, 10, 15, and 20}. (Hint: Create a table of values first before graphing the equation.)

b. Estimate how many hours it will take to drain the pool.

9. Graph the equation using a table of values, where x = -2, -1, 0, 1, and 2.

$y = -3x^2$

10. Graph the equation using a table of values for the domain: {-3, -2, 0, 2, and 3}.

$$y = x^2 - 3$$

Bobcat Review

1. Write 367,000,000,000 using scientific notation.

2. Write 0.000 0456 using scientific notation.

3. In 1986, Japan caught 2.82×10^3 whales. In 2010, Japan caught 4.54×10^2 whales. Based on this information, the number of whales caught in 1986 is **about** how many times the number of whales caught in 2010?

Bobcat Stretch

1. Tell whether this is a linear or non-linear equation: $y = 3x(x+3) - 4^2$. Explain.

2. Two lines are graphed on the same coordinate plane. The lines intersect at the point (-2, 4).

   a. If one line is a horizontal straight line and the other line is a vertical straight line, then what is the linear equation for each line?

   b. Graph these equations on the same coordinate plane.

   c. Determine which line is a function and which one is not.

3. Graph $y = \left(\frac{1}{2}x + \frac{2}{5}\right)^2 + 4.84$.

Further Review

For more videos and practice problems,

- click here to go to Khan Academy.
- search for "linear and nonlinear functions" on Khan Academy (www.khanacademy.org).

Watch this video to further review the difference between linear and nonlinear equations.

MEDIA
Click image to the left or use the URL below.
URL: https://www.ck12.org/flx/render/embeddedobject/114285

Answers

1. a. A vertical line because $x = a$ is always a vertical line.

   b. A diagonal line because it is a linear equation.

   c. A curved line because it is a non-linear equation.

   d. A horizontal line because y = b is always a horizontal line.

2. a. Various answers as long as the x-value is always 8: (8, 0), (8, 1), (8, 2).

   b. Various answers as long as the y-value is always - 3: (0, -3), (1, -3), (2, -3).

3. a. It's a non-linear equation because the y occurs to the 2nd degree, so the graph will be a curved line.

   b. It's a linear equation because all the variables are only to the 1st degree, so the graph will be a straight line.

   c. It's a non-linear equation because the x occurs to the 2nd degree, so the graph will be a curved line.

   d. It's a non-linear equation because the r occurs to the 2nd degree, so the graph will be a curved line.

   e. It's a linear equation because all the variables are only to the 1st degree, so the graph will be a straight line.

4. $x = 6$

5. $y = -2$

6. The ordered pairs are (-10, -1), (-5, 1), (0, 3), (5, 5), (10, 7).

x	y=0.4x+3	(x, y)
-10	y = 0.4 (-10) + 3	(-10, -1)
-5	y = 0.4 (-5) + 3	(-5, 1)
0	y = 0.4 (0) + 3	(0, 3)
5	y = 0.4 (5) + 3	(5, 5)
10	y = 0.4 (10) + 3	(10, 7)

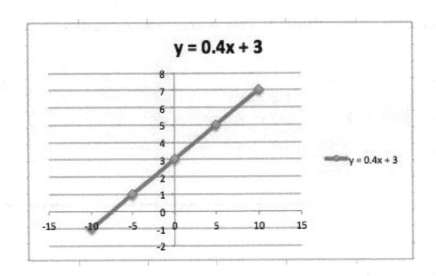

7. a. linear - all the variables are only to the 1st degree, so the graph will be a straight line.

   b. non-linear - once the grouping is squared, there will an x^2 variable, so the graph will be a curved line.

   c. linear - all the variables are only to the 1st degree, so the graph will be a straight line.

   d. non-linear - the x is cubed, so the graph will be a curved line.

   e. linear - all the variables are only to the 1st degree, so the graph will be a straight line.

8. a.

h	g
0	16000
6	12100
10	9500
15	6250
20	3000

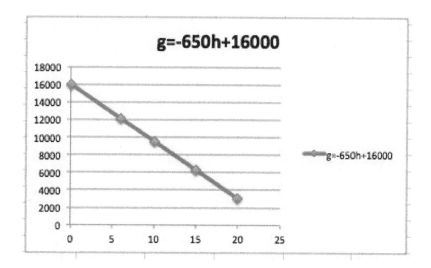

b. Look at the graph, if you were to extend the line to the x-intercept, where $y = 0$ (means the pool was drained), it would cross the x-axis around 25 hours. You can check your estimation by solving $0 = -650h + 16000$, where $h = 24.6$ hours.

9.

x	y
-2	-12
-1	-3
0	0
1	-3
2	-12

Note, both graphs are correct, they are just drawn on different scales. The red line graph is a better example of how the line should be drawn for a non-linear graph - it should be a smooth curved line.

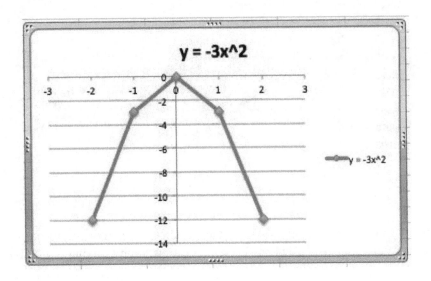

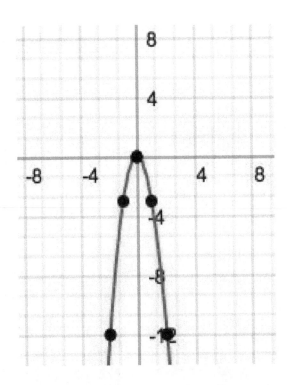

10.

x	y
-3	6
-2	1
0	-3
2	1
3	6

Note, both graphs are correct, they are just drawn on different scales. The red line graph is a better example of how the line should be drawn for a nonlinear graph - it should be a smooth curved line.

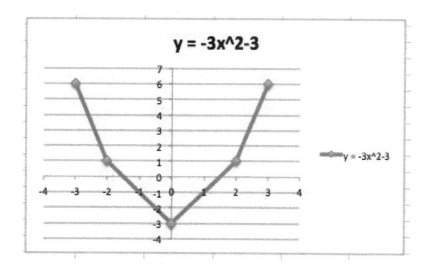

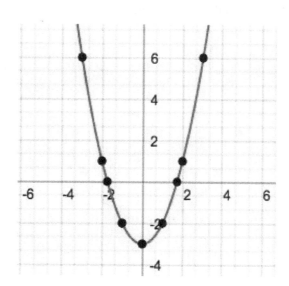

Bobcat Review

1. 3.67×10^{11}

2. 4.56×10^{-5}

3. In 1986, Japan caught about 6 times the number of whales as caught in 2010. 2820/454 = 6.21. You can also use the exponent properties to find the answer 2.82/4.5 = 0.621 and $\frac{10^3}{10^2} = 10^1$, so move the decimal one space to the right for 6.21.

Bobcat Stretch

1. It is a non-linear equation because it simplifies to $y = 3x^2 + 9x - 16$, where x occurs to the 2nd degree.

2. a. The two linear equations are x = -2 (vertical line) and y = 4 (horizontal line) .

    b.

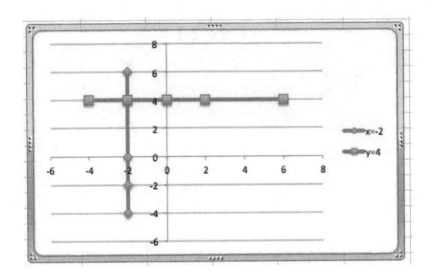

    c. The equation x = -2 is not a function and y = 4 is a function.

3.

$$(-5, 11.25), (-4, 9), (-3, 7.25), (-2, 6), (-1, 5.25), (1, 5.25), (2, 6), (3, 7.25), (4, 9), (5, 11.25)$$

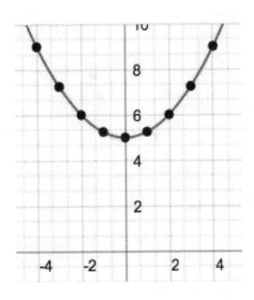

5.5 Using Intercepts

Find x- and y-intercepts of lines and interpret what they mean given the context of the data.

By the end of this lesson, you should be able to define and give an example of the following vocabulary words:

- **x-intercept** - The x-coordinate of the point where the graph crosses the x-axis. The graph of $y = -\frac{3}{2}x + 3$ crosses the x-axis at (2,0), so its x-intercept is 2.
- **y-intercept** - The y-coordinate of the point where the graph intersects the y-axis. The graph of $y = -\frac{3}{2}x + 3$ crosses the y-axis at (0, 3), so its y-intercept is 3.

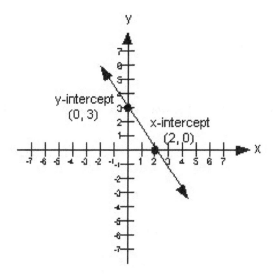

- **Standard Form of a Line -** This is another way of writing an equation of a line: $Ax + By = C$. It gives all the same information as the function form ($y = ax + b$), but is just written differently.

Example 1

Robbie has \$12 to spend on snacks at the movie theater for him and his friends. The candy costs \$3 per item and the popcorn costs \$2 per box. The linear equation representing this situation is $3x + 2y = 12$, where $x =$ the number of candy items and $y =$ the number of boxes of popcorn.

Find and graph the intercepts of $3x + 2y = 12$ and explain what they mean given the context of the situation.

To find the x-intercept of a graph, substitute 0 for y into the equation of the line and solve for x.

$$3x + 2(0) = 12$$
$$3x + 0 = 12$$
$$x = \frac{12}{3}$$
$$x = 4$$

The x-intercept is 4, which means that if Robbie doesn't buy any popcorn, then he can buy 4 candy items to share.

To find the y-intercept of a graph, substitute 0 for x into the equation of the line and solve for y.

$$3(0) + 2y = 12$$
$$0 + 2y = 12$$
$$y = \frac{12}{2}$$
$$y = 6$$

The y-intercept is 6, which means that if Robbie doesn't buy any candy, then he can buy 6 boxes of popcorn to share.

Graph the x-intercept (4, 0) and the y-intercept (0, 6) and draw a line through the two points to graph the line $3x + 2y = 12$.

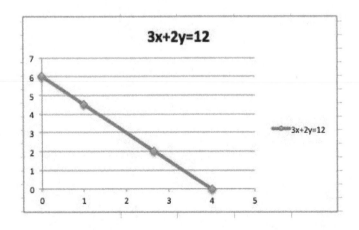

Tips & Tricks

- To find the *x*-intercept of a graph, substitute 0 for *y* into the equation of the line and solve for *x*.
- To find the *y*-intercept of a graph, substitute 0 for *x* into the equation of the line and solve for *y*.
- Remember: The Standard Form equation of a line ($Ax + By = C$) is usually the easiest form to work with when finding the intercepts of a line. (You have to do more work to find the *x*-intercept if the equation is in Function Form: $y = ax + b$, but the *y*-intercept is still easy (*b*) to identify in this format.)

Practice

1. Identify the *x*- and *y*-intercept in the graph.

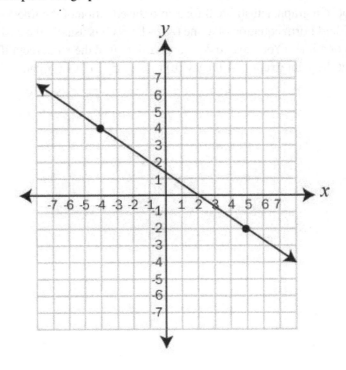

2. Find the *x*- and *y*-intercepts of the following linear equations.

    a. $2x + 6y = 18$

    b. $y = -3x + 5$

    c. $3.5x - 2.8y = 9.8$

    d. $y = \frac{2}{5}x - 5.7$

    e. $y = -2$

3. Emily is going to the rodeo and has $30 to spend on the rides and games. The games cost $2 each and the rides cost $5 each. The equation that represents *x* games and *y* rides is $2x + 5y = 30$. Identify the *x*- and *y*-intercepts and explain what each means.

4. Graph the line that has a *x*-intercept of -2 and a *y*-intercept of 3.

5. Identify the *y*-intercepts for the following equations and order them from least to greatest.

   a. $-4x - 3y = 24$

   b. $y = \frac{5}{6}x - \frac{5}{8}$

   c. $3.4x + 4.2y = -35.7$

6. The average lifespan of American women has been tracked, and the model for the data is $y = 0.2t + 73$, where $t = 0$ corresponds to 1960. Identify and explain the meaning of the *y*-intercept.

7. For 8 weeks, Molly has been saving $25 per week from babysitting. At the end of the 8 weeks, her bank account balance was $245. The linear equation to model this situation is $y = 25x + b$, where *x* is the number of weeks she saved (8 weeks) and *y* is the current balance of her savings account ($245).

   a. Solve for *b* and explain what the variable "*b*" means in the context of this situation.

   b. What if her current balance was $195 instead of $245? Solve for *b*, given $y = \$195$ at the same savings rate of $25 per week for 8 weeks, and explain what the variable '*b*" means in the context of this different situation.

Bobcat Review

1. Solve for c: $3.1(2c + 4) + 1.2c = 38.3$

2. Solve for d: $\frac{d-5}{3} = 7$

Bobcat Stretch

1. Fisherman in the Finger Lakes Region have been recording the dead fish they encounter while fishing in the region. The Department of Environmental Conservation monitors the pollution index for the Finger Lakes Region. The model for the number of fish deaths "y" for a given polution index "x" is $y = 9.607x + 111.958$. What is the meaning of the y-intercept?

2. The equation for the speed (not the height) of a ball that is thrown straight up in the air is given by $v = 128 - 32t$, where "v" is the velocity (in feet per second) and "t" is the number of seconds after the ball is thrown. With what initial velocity was the ball thrown?

3. Find the x- and y-intercepts of $25x^2 + 4y^2 = 9$.

Further Review

For more videos and practice problems,

- click here to go to Khan Academy.
- search for "linear function intercepts" on Khan Academy (www.khanacademy.org).

Watch this video to further review finding x- and y-intercepts.

 Multimedia

MEDIA
Click image to the left or use the URL below.
URL: https://www.ck12.org/flx/render/embeddedobject/114347

Answers

1. The *x*-intercept is 2, where the line passes through the *x*-axis at (2, 0).

   The *y*-intercept is 1.5, where the line passes through the *y*-axis at (0, 1.5).

2. a. The *x*-intercept is 9 and the *y*-intercept is 3.

   b. The *x*-intercept is $\frac{5}{3}$ and the *y*-intercept is 5.

   c. The *x*-intercept is 2.8 and the *y*-intercept is -3.5.

   d. The *x*-intercept is 14.25 and the *y*-intercept is -5.7.

   e. There is no *x*-intercept (because the line never crosses the *x*-axis) and the *y*-intercept is -2.

3. The *x*-intercept is 15 and means that if she doesn't ride any rides, then she can play 15 games (0, 15). The *y*-intercept is 6 and means that if she doesn't play any games, then she can ride 6 rides (6, 0).

4. The points are (-2, 0) and (0, 3).

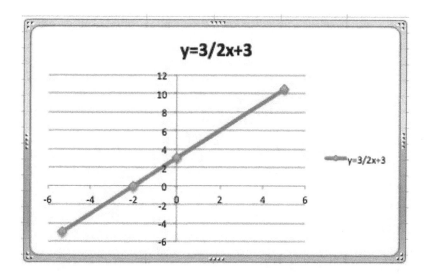

5. c. *y*-intercept = -8.5

   a. *y*-intercept = - 8

   b. *y*-intercept = $-\frac{5}{8}$

6. The *y*-intercept is 73, which means that in 1960, when they started to track the data, the average lifespan of an American woman was 73 years.

7. Hint: this question is asking you to find the *y*-intercept, which in this case is "b".

   a. *b* = 45, which means Molly's initial savings account balance was $45.

   b. *b* = -5 This means Molly's initial savings account balance was -$5.00 dollars, but that doesn't really make sense. If *b* is a negative number, then it probably means the bank charged her an initial fee to open her savings account of $5, which is why her account balance is only $195.

Bobcat Review

1. $c = 3.5$

2. $d = 26$

Bobcat Stretch

1. The y-intercept is 111.958. This means that even if the index were zero (that is, even if the water was pure), there would still be about 112 fish deaths a year anyway.

2. This is really asking to interpret the y-intercept of the graph, which is 128. This means that the ball was released ($t = 0$ seconds) at a velocity "v" of 128 feet per second.

3. The x-intercepts are $\pm \frac{3}{5}$. The y-intercepts are $\pm \frac{3}{2}$.

5.6 Slope & Midpoint Formulas

Find and interpret the slope of a line. Relate steepness of a line and constant rate of change to slope. Find the midpoint of a line.

By the end of this lesson, you should be able to define and give an example of the following vocabulary words:

- **Slope** - The ratio of the rise (change in y) to the run (change in x). Slope $= \frac{rise}{run} = \frac{y_2 - y_1}{x_2 - x_1}$
  - **Rise** - means up and down (vertical change) - it's how much y has changed
  - **Run** - means how far left and right (horizontal change) - it's how much x has changed.
- **Midpoint** - The midpoint of a line segment between two points marks the half-way point or middle of the segment.
  - $Midpoint = \left(\frac{x_1 + x_2}{2}, \frac{y_1 + y_2}{2} \right)$

Example 1

Find the slope of a line given the points (-2, 1) and (1, 3).

Plot the points and draw a line through them. Since the line forms a straight line, then this represents a linear equation that has a constant rate of change.

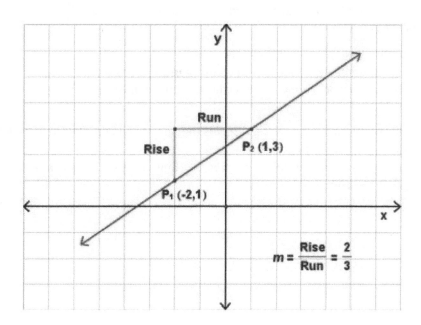

Find the slope by counting the $\frac{rise}{run}$ between the two points. To get from the first point to the second, count up (rise) +2 and over to the right (run) +3.

The slope (m) of the line is $\frac{2}{3}$. This means for every 1 unit "x" increases, then "y" increases $\frac{2}{3}$ of a unit.

Note: the linear equation ($y = mx + b$) of this line is $y = \frac{2}{3}x + \frac{7}{3}$, where (slope) $m = \frac{2}{3}$ and (y-intercept) $b = \frac{7}{3}$.

Example 2

Find the midpoint of the line segment between (-2, 1) and (1, 3).

$$Midpoint = \left(\frac{x_1 + x_2}{2}, \frac{y_1 + y_2}{2}\right)$$

$$\left(\frac{-2+1}{2}, \frac{1+3}{2}\right)$$

$$\left(\frac{-1}{2}, \frac{4}{2}\right)$$

$$\left(\frac{-1}{2}, 2\right)$$

The midpoint of the line segment between (-2, 1) and (1, 3) is point $\left(-\frac{1}{2}, 2\right)$.

Tips & Tricks

- Note: the rate of change equation: $a = \frac{y_2 - y_1}{x_2 - x_1}$ is equal to the slope equation $m = \frac{rise}{run}$.
- Rise MUST be on top! Think of alphabetical order: rise comes before run. $\frac{rise}{run}$
- Slope tells you how steep a line is.
  - The larger the absolute value, the steeper the slope.
  - The smaller the absolute value, the less steep the slope.
  - The sign of the slope (+ or -) does not define how steep the line is, it determines whether the line is going uphill or downhill.
- In function form, the equation $y = ax + b$, " a " equals the rate of change. The slope of the line ($a = m$) occurs when "a" is representing a constant rate of change.
- Positive Slope - think of a walking **uphill** to the right. "Think positive, things are looking up." Note: Graphs should be read from left to right!

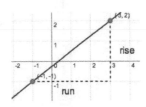

- Negative Slope - think of this as walking **downhill** to the right. "No, no, I'm falling down!"

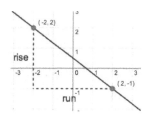

- Zero slope - this is a **horizontal** line - think of this as walking on level ground.

- Undefinded slope - this is a **vertical** line - think of this as jumping off a cliff - it would be an experience that is indescribable, unimaginable, undefined!.

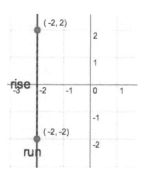

- The slope of the line can be found no matter which **two** points you choose to use in the formula.
- There is only one line passing through a given point with a given slope.

Practice

1. Describe the slope of each line: red diagonal line (, blue horizontal line (–), green diagonal line (/) , and purple vertical line (I) as positive, negative, zero, or undefined.

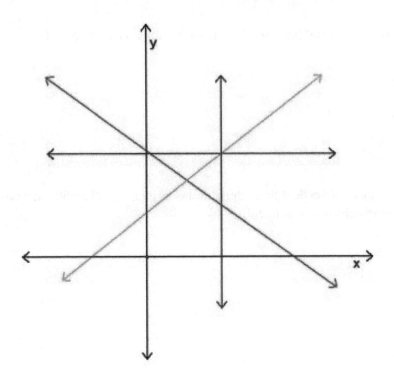

2. The slope of a non-vertical line is the ratio _____.

3. Write the coordinates of the two points and find the slope of the line shown in the graph.

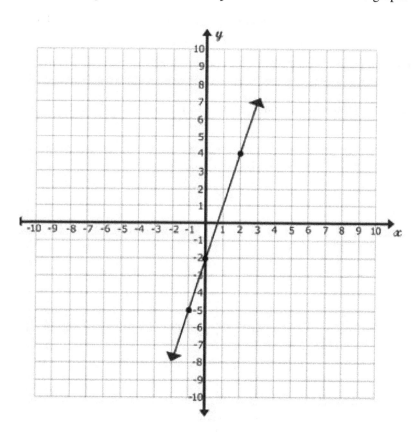

4. Given the graph below,

    a. Write the coordinates of two points on the line and find the slope of the line. Pay attention to the scale of the graph!

    b. Write down two different points on the line and find the slope of the line *again* to check your "slope" answer from part a.

    c. Explain why the slope is the same no matter what two points are used from the line.

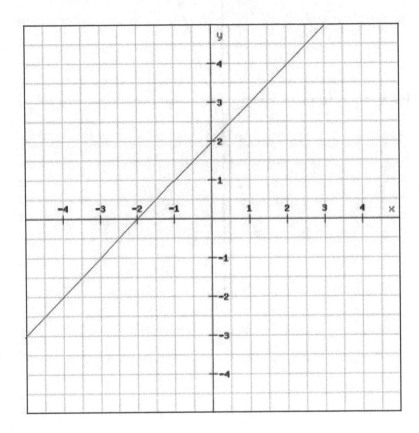

5. Find the slope of the line passing through the points and tell whether it is a positive, negative, zero, or an undefined slope.

    a. (-5, 9) and (5, 7)

    b. (9, -8) and (10, -15)

    c. (0, -2) and (7, 1)

    d. (2, 1) and (2, 5)

    e. (6, 3) and (-8, 3)

6. $\triangle ABC$ has the vertices at points A (-2, -1), B (4, -1), and C (-2, -4).

    a. Plot and connect the points on a coordinate plane.

    b. Find the slope of $\overline{AB}$.

    c. Find the slope of $\overline{BC}$.

    d. Find the slope of $\overline{CA}$.

7. Find the midpoint of the line segment connecting the points.

    a. (1, -5) and (-5, 3)

    b. (3, -4) and (2, -1)

8. Line t and $\triangle DBA$ and $\triangle ECB$ are shown on the coordinate plane. Given the graph, label each statement below as True or False.

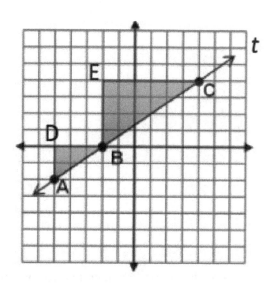

    a. The slope $\overline{AB}$ is equal to the slope of $\overline{BC}$.

    b. The slope $\overline{AC}$ is equal to the slope of line t.

    c. The slope of line t is equal to $\frac{EB}{DB}$.

    d. The slope of line t is equal to $\frac{AD}{DB}$.

    c. The slope of line t is equal to $\frac{BE}{EC}$.

9. Identify the graph that has a greater rate of change (slope), then find and compare the actual slope of **each** line to verify your original answer.

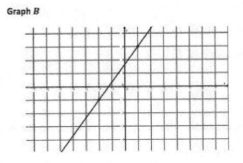

Bobcat Review

1. Evaluate $-\sqrt{15}$ to the nearest tenth and plot it on a number line.

2. Evaluate $\sqrt[3]{64}$.

3. Evaluate $\sqrt[3]{\dfrac{1}{27}}$

Bobcat Stretch

1. Identify the graph that has a greater rate of change (slope), then find & compare the actual slope of each line to check your original answer.

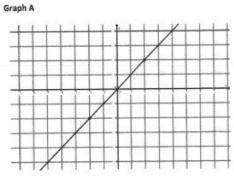
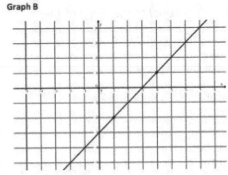

2. A line has a slope of $-\frac{1}{2}$. Name two points that might be on the line.

3. Show on a coordinate plane, using <u>similar</u> triangles, why the graph of an equation of the form $y = mx$ is a line with slope m that passes through the origin.

Further Review

For more videos and practice problems,

- Click here to go to Khan Academy for more slope practice problems (plus earn more Kahn Academy points and badges).
- Click here to go to Khan Academy for more slope and triangle similarity questions (similar to those on the PARCC).
- Click here to go to Khan Academy for challenging "midpoint of a segment" practice problems.

- search for "Slope and triangle similarity" on Khan Academy (www.khanacademy.org).

- go to Khan Academy's Common Core page standard 8.EE.B.6 (www.khanacademy.org/commoncore/grade -8-EE).

Watch this video to further review how to find the slope of a line.

 **Multimedia**

MEDIA
Click image to the left or use the URL below.
URL: https://www.ck12.org/flx/render/embeddedobject/114367

Answers

1. The red line has a negative slope (downhill).

   The blue line has a zero slope (horizontal).

   The green line has a positive slope (uphill).

   The purple line has an undefined slope (vertical).

2. $m = \frac{rise}{run}$

3. (-1, -5) and (2, 4), so the slope (rise/run) is 9/3 or $m = 3$.

4. a. Various answers (-2, 0) and (0, 2), so $m = 1$ (rise over run equals 2/2 = 1).

   b. Various answers (-1, 1) and (1, 3), so m = 1 (rise over run equals 2/2 = 1).

   c. The slope is the same because the line is straight and represents a constant rate of change. So no matter what points are chosen from the line, the line is still increasing 1 y unit for every 1 x unit.

5. a. $-\frac{1}{5}$, so the slope is negative.

   b. -7, so the slope is negative.

   c. $\frac{3}{7}$, so the slope is positive.

   d. $\frac{4}{0}$, since you can't divide by 0, then the slope is undefined. This means the points fall on a vertical line.

   e. $\frac{0}{-14}$, so the slope is zero, which represents a horizontal line.

6. a.

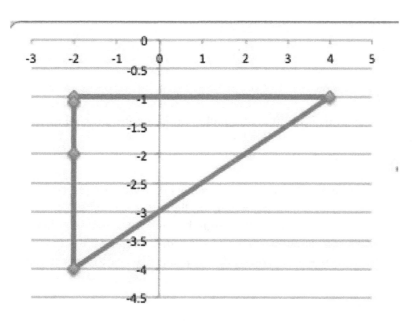

b. The slope is 0, which is a horizontal line.

c. The slope is $\frac{1}{2}$, which means y increase one-half unit for every 1 x unit.

d. The slope is undefined, which is a vertical line.

7. a. (-2, -1)

b. (2.5, -2.5)

8. a. True

b. True

c. False

d. True

e. True

9. Graph B has a greater rate of change because the line is steeper than Graph A.

The slope of Graph A is $\frac{2}{3}$, which is less than the slope of Graph B that is $\frac{4}{3}$. This confirms the initial observation that Graph B has a greater rate of change.

Bobcat Review

1. -3.9, plotted between points -3.8 and -4.0 on a number line.

2. 4

3. $\frac{1}{3}$

Bobcat Stretch

1. They have equal rates of change. The slope of Graph A is $\frac{4}{4}$ and the slope of Graph B is $\frac{3}{3}$. Since these point equal 1, then they both have the same rate of change of 1.

2. Answers will vary. (0, 0) and (2, -1).

3. Answers will vary. The line shown has a slope of 2. When we compare the corresponding side lengths of the similar triangles, we have the ratios $\frac{2}{1} = \frac{4}{2} = 2$. In general, the ratios would be $\frac{x}{1} = \frac{y}{m}$, equivalently $y = mx$, which is a line with slope m. The line passes through the origin because $b = 0$, so the y-intercept crosses the y-axis at 0 (0, 0 is the origin), which is why "b" is left out of this equation. If the line didn't pass through the origin, then the equation of the line would be $y = mx + b$, where b = the y-intercept. $y = mx$ is an example of a **direct variation**.

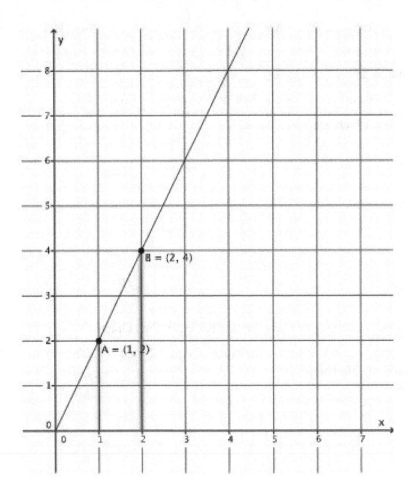

5.7 Direct Variation

Identify, write, graph, and compare direct variations.

By the end of this lesson, you should be able to define and give an example of the following vocabulary word:

- **Direct Variation** - A special type of linear relationship that can be written in the form $y = kx$, where k is a nonzero constant called the *constant of variation*.
  - $y = kx$
  - $\frac{y}{x} = k$

Example 1

Suppose a moving object travels 1 foot in 64 seconds, 2 feet in 128 seconds, 3 feet in 192 seconds, 4 feet in 256 seconds, and 5 feet in 320 seconds. Does this represent a direction variation relationship between x and y?

Make a table of values to find the ratios of y to x to determine if the data represents direct variation.

x	y	y/x
1	64	64
2	128	64
3	192	64
4	256	64
5	320	64

Since the ratio $\frac{y}{x} = 64$ for all the data points, then this situations represents direct variation. This means y is always 64 times x or $y = 64x$.

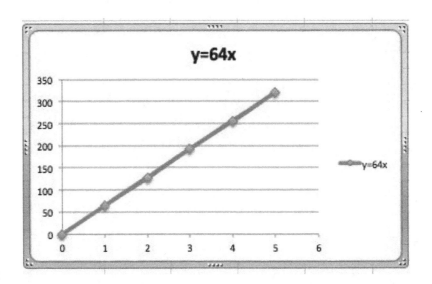

Note: the graph of $y = 64x$ passes through the origin $(0, 0)$, which is another confirmation that it is a direct variation. Direct variations must pass through the origin. In other words, the y-intercept is 0.

Example 2

True or False: $-5x + y = 4$ is a direct variation.

Write the equation in function form.

$y = 5x + 4$

The equation is <u>not</u> a direct variation because it cannot be written in the form $y = kx$. It has a y-intercept of 4 that does not equal 0, so the line does not pass through the origin $(0, 0)$.

So the answer is False, $-5x + y = 4$ is not a direct variation.

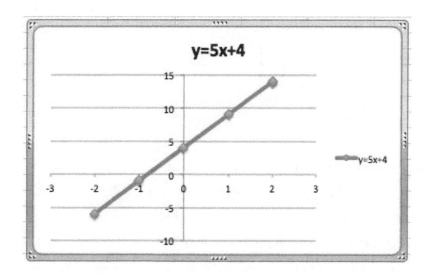

Example 3

Two different proportional relationships (direct variations) are represented by the equation and the table.

Compare the rates of change of the proportional relationships to find how much more or less one rate of change is over the other.

Proportion A		Proportion B
x	**y**	**y = 7x**
0	0	
3	28.5	
4	38	
5.5	52.25	
6	9.7	
6.5	61.75	

First find the rate of change (constant of variation) for each proportion (direct variation).

For Proportion A, use any ordered pair to find the rate of change $k = \frac{y}{x} = \frac{28.5}{3} = 9.5$.

For Proportion B, identify k in the equation $y = kx$, where $k = 7$.

Now compare the rates of change to write a comparison statement.

The rate of change in Proportion A (9.5) is 2.5 more than the rate of change in Proportion B (7).

Tips & Tricks

- Direct Variation means two variables are related in such a way that the ratio of their values always remains the same.

- $\frac{y}{x} = 5$ means that y is always 5 times more than x ($y = 5x$), so 5 is the constant of variation (k).

- In the equation, $y = kx$, "k" is the same as slope (m) of the line.

- $y = kx$ is a special case of a linear equation where the y-intercept equals 0, so the straight line of the graph always goes through the origin (0,0).
  - If a line doesn't go through the origin (0, 0), then it is **not** a direct variation.

- Note: Inverse variation is represented by the equation $y = \frac{k}{x}$. This equation **will not** create a straight line. Therefore, it is not linear.

Practice

1. Given $y = kx$, k is called the _____.

2. Identify whether the equation represents a direct variation or not. If so, find the constant of variation (k). Explain your reasoning.

    a. $-6x + y = 0$

    b. $\frac{1}{2}x - 2 = y$

    c. $\frac{x}{y} = -3$

    d. $\frac{y}{x} = \frac{2}{5}$

    e. $\frac{1}{4}x + y = 4$

3. True or False. The data represents a direct variation. Graph the data to support your answer.

x	y
1	9
2	18
3	27
4	36
5	45

4. Write the direct variation equation that represents the following data.

Time taken to complete problems (x)	5	10	15	20	25
Number of problems completed (y)	1.47	2.94	4.41	5.88	7.35

5. On Monday, Kelly performed a tune up on four cars in three hours. On Tuesday, she tuned two cars in one and one-half hours. On Wednesday, she tuned eight cars in six hours. Is the number of cars Kelly tuned **directly** proportional to the hours she works? Graph the data to support your answer.

6. Two different proportional relationships (direct variations) are represented by the equation and the table. Compare the rates of change of the proportional relationships to find how much more or less one rate of change is over the other and write a comparison statement.

Proportion A		Proportion B	
y = 4.5 x		x	y
		0	0
		1.5	4.5
		2	6
		2.5	7.5
		3	9
		3.5	10.5

7. Two different proportional relationships (direct variations) are represented by the equation and the table. Compare the rates of change of the proportional relationships to find how much more or less one rate of change is over the other and write a comparison statement.

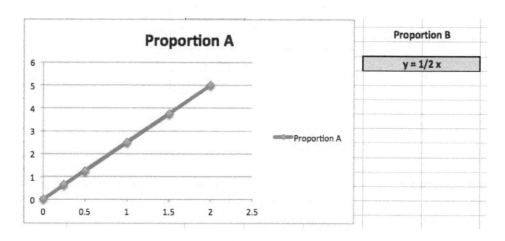

8. A solution is 10% vinegar. Write an equation and create a graph that represents all possible combinations of the number of liters of vinegar, contained in the number of liters of solution.

Bobcat Review

1. Solve $x^2 + 3 = 12$.

2. Evaluate $\sqrt[3]{\dfrac{27}{64}}$.

3. Solve $5 - a^3 = -3$

Bobcat Stretch

1. Write and graph the equation that either proves or disproves that the amount of water that flows from a faucet is a direct variation of time.

Minutes	gallons
2	7
5	17.5
7	24.5
8	28

2. Now assume you are filling a 50 gallon bath tub with the same faucet from problem 1. The tub already has 8 gallons of water in it. Write and graph the equation that represents how many minutes it will take to fill the tub. Does this situation represent a direct variation? Why or why not?

Further Review

For more videos and practice problems,

- click here to go to Khan Academy. (Note, there are inverse variation problems mixed in as well.)
- search for "direct variation" on Khan Academy (www.khanacademy.org).
- go to Khan Academy's Common Core page standard 8.EE.B.5 for more videos and practice problems. (www.khanacademy.org/commoncore/grade-8-EE)

Watch this video to further review direct variation.

MEDIA
Click image to the left or use the URL below.
URL: https://www.ck12.org/flx/render/embeddedobject/114429

Answers

1. Constant of Variation

2. a. Yes because it can be written in the form $y = 6x$, which passes through the origin $(0, 0)$. $k = 6$

 b. No because it cannont be written as a direction variation $(y = kx)$. This equation doesn't pass through the origin $(0, 0)$, instead it passed through $(0, -2)$.

 c. Yes because it can be written in the form $y = -\frac{1}{3}x$, which passes through the origin $(0, 0)$. $k = -\frac{1}{3}$

 d. Yes because it can be written in the form $y = \frac{2}{5}x$, which passes through the origin $(0, 0)$. $k = \frac{2}{5}$

 e. No because it cannont be written as a direction variation $(y = kx)$. This equation doesn't pass through the origin $(0, 0)$, instead it passed through $(0, 4)$.

3. True because $k = \frac{y}{x} = 9$ for each data point. $y = 9x$. The graph passes through the origin $(0, 0)$.

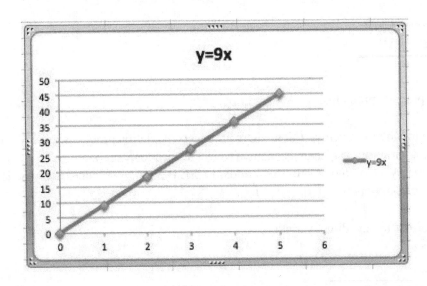

4. $y = .294x$ or $k = \frac{y}{x} = .294$

5. Yes, she tunes cars at the rate of $y = \frac{4}{3}x$. The graph passes through the origin $(0, 0)$, so this represents a direct variation relationship.

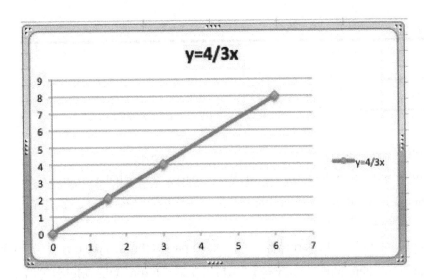

6. Proportion A rate of change is 4.5 and Proportion B is 3, so Proportion A's rate of change is 1.5 more than Proportion B's rate of change. Proportion B's rate of change is 1.5 less than Proportion A's rate of change is also an acceptable answer.

7. Proportion A has a rate of change = 2.5 and Proportion B has a rate of change = $\frac{1}{2}$, so Proportion A's rate of change is 2 more than Proportion B's rate of change. Proportion B's rate of change is 2 less than Proportion A's rate of change is also an acceptable answer.

8. $y = \frac{1}{10}x$ The x-axis is # of liters of solution and the y-axis is # of liters of vinegar.

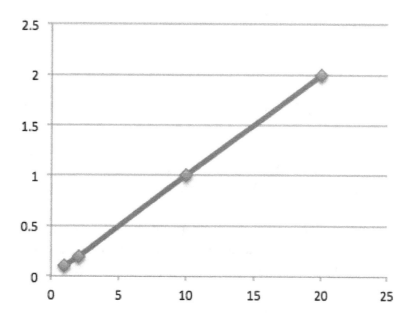

Bobcat Review

1. x = ±3

2. $\frac{3}{4}$

3. a = 2

Bobcat Stretch

1. Yes, this represents a direct variation because the graph passes through the origin $(0, 0)$ and the equation is written in $y = kx$ format so, $y = 3.5x$. This means 3.5 gallons of water flows through the faucet at a constat rate (k) every minute.

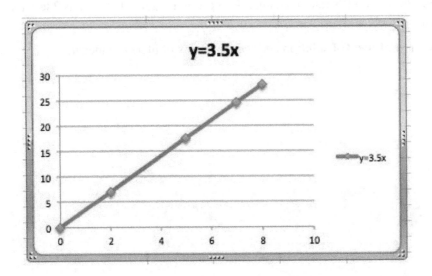

2. $y = 3.5x + 8$, where $y = 50$ gallons. If $50 = 3.5x + 8$, $x = 12$. It will take 12 minutes to fill the tub. No, this is not a direct variation, as the line does not pass through the origin $(0, 0)$. Instead it passes through $(0, 8)$ because the bath tub is already filled with 8 gallons of water to start.

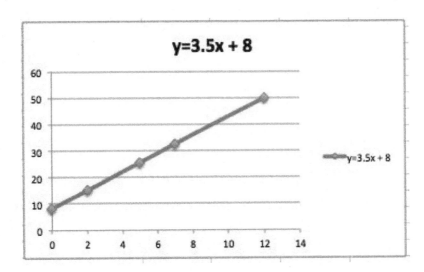

5.8 Slope-Intercept Form

Write and graph equations in slope-intercept form.

By the end of this lesson, you should be able to define and give an example of the following vocabulary word:

- **Slope-Intercept Form** - The linear equation $y = mx + b$ is written in slope-intercept form, where m is the slope and b is the y-intercept.

Example 1

Graph $-\frac{1}{4}x + y = -2$.

First rewrite the equation in slope-intercept form.

$$y = \frac{1}{4}x - 2$$

Graph the equation by starting with the easy-to-identify y-intercept (0, -2). Then use the slope $m = \frac{rise}{run} = \frac{1}{4}$ to find the next point. You count up 1 and over to the right 4 to the next point at (4, -1). Draw a straight line through the two points.

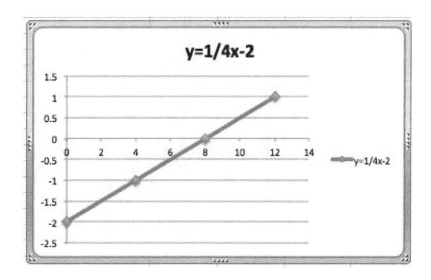

This is the graph of the equation $-\frac{1}{4}x + y = -2$.

Tips & Tricks

*

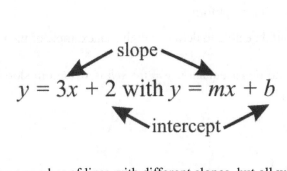

* The following graph shows a number of lines with different slopes, but all with the same $y-$intercept: $(0, 3)$.

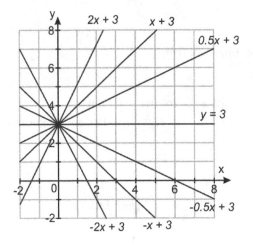

* This graph shows a number of lines with the same slope ($m = 2$), but different $y-$intercepts.

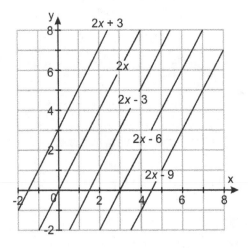

* "A rose by any other name would smell as sweet" - William Shakespeare
  - There are many terms in math that all mean the same thing, so...
    * Slope = Constant of Proportionality (Intro to Algebra) = Unit Rate = Constant Rate of Change
    * Slope-Intercept Form = Function Form = Linear Equation

Practice
---

1. Rewrite the equation in slope-intercept form.

    a. $-10x + y = -5$

    b. $\frac{1}{2}x - y = -4$

    c. $2.5x + y = 4.5$

2. Identify the equation that matches the graph.

    a. $y = \frac{3}{2}x - 3$

    b. $y = -3x + 2$

    c. $y = \frac{2}{3}x + 2$

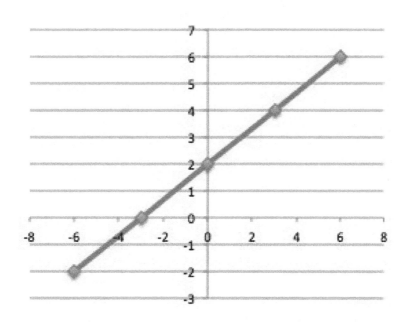

3. Find the slope and *y*-intercept of the equation, then graph the equation.

    a. $y = x + 6$

    b. $y = -\frac{1}{3}x - 3$

    c. $y = -4x + 2$

    d. $y = -2$

4. Rewrite the equation in slope-intercept form, then find the slope and *y*-intercept of the line.

 a. $y = 7 - x$

 b. $y - 3 = 5x$

 c. $y - \frac{5}{8}x = 0$

 d. $\frac{2}{3}x - y = 6$

 e. $\frac{1}{3}x + y = 3.5$

5. Write the equation of the graph in slope-intercept form.

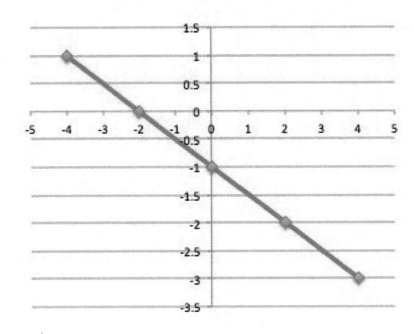

6. Use the point on the line and the slope of the line to find the *y*-intercept of the line, then write the equation of the line in slope-intercept form.

     a. (-1, -5), $m = 3$

     b. (3, 6), $m = -\frac{2}{3}$

7. Find the slope of the line and the *y*-intercept shown on the graph. Then write a linear equation that represents the graph using slope-intercept form. Use the points on the line (0, 2.5) and (2, 1).

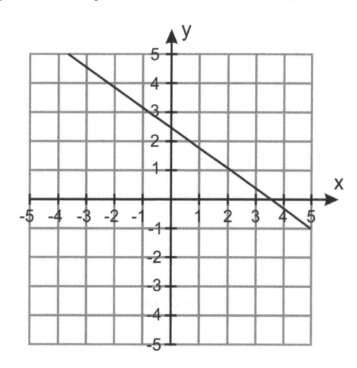

8. Find the slope of the line and the *y*-intercept shown on the graph. Then write a linear equation that represents the graph using slope-intercept form. Use the points on the line (-8, 0) and (8, 6).

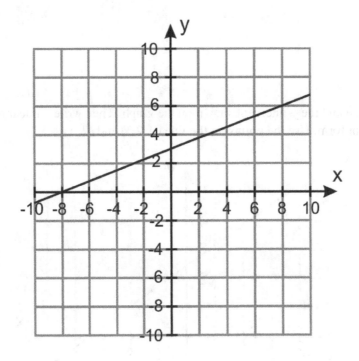

Bobcat Review

1.   Create a linear equation in slope-intercept form that contains the ordered points (2, 3) and (-2, -3) and the *y*-intercept is 0.

2. Solve for *m*: $6(m-1) = 3(\frac{1}{2}m - 5)$

3. Solve for *x*: $-\frac{1}{4}(3x + 11x) = -\frac{1}{2}(x + 6)$

Bobcat Stretch

1. A straight line passes through point (-10, -2) and has a slope of $-\frac{4}{5}$. Given this information, find the y-intercept and the equation of the line (written in slope-intercept form).

2. Identify the slope and y-intercept, then write the equation of the line.

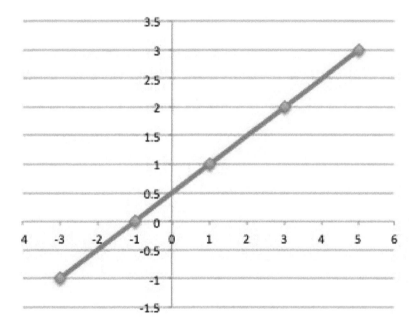

Further Review

For more videos and practice problems,

- click here to go to Khan Academy.
- search for "slope-intercept form" on Khan Academy (www.khanacademy.org).
- go to Khan Academy's Common Core page standard 8.F.A.3 or 8.F.B.4 (www.khanacademy.org/commonco re/grade-8-F).

Watch this video to further review finding the equation of the line given a point and a slope.

MEDIA
Click image to the left or use the URL below.
URL: https://www.ck12.org/flx/render/embeddedobject/114649

Answers

1. a. $y = 10x - 5$

   b. $y = \frac{1}{2}x + 4$

   c. $y = -2.5x + 4.5$

2. c

3. a. $m = 1$, y-intercept = 6

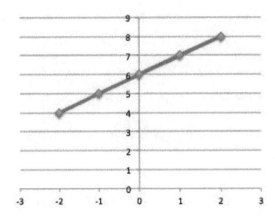

   b. $m = -\frac{1}{3}$, y-intercept = -3

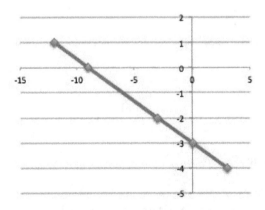

c. $m = -4$, y-intercept = 2

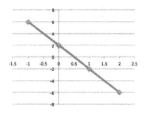

d. $m = 0$, y-intercept = -2

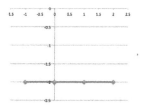

4. a. $y = -x + 7$, where m = -1 and y-intercept = 7

   b. $y = 5x + 3$, where m = 5 and y-intercept = 3

   c. $y = \frac{5}{8}x$, where $m = \frac{5}{8}$ and y-intercept = 0

   d. $y = \frac{2}{3}x - 6$, where $m = \frac{2}{3}$ and y-intercept = -6

   e. $y = -\frac{1}{3}x + 3.5$, where $m = -\frac{1}{3}$ and y-intercept = 3.5

5. $y = -\frac{1}{2}x - 1$

6. a. y-intercept = -2 and the equation of the line in slope-intercept form is $y = 3x - 2$.

   b. y-intercept = 8 and the equation of the line in slope-intercept form is $y = -\frac{2}{3}x + 8$.

7. $m = -\frac{3}{4}$, y-intercept = 2.5, and the equation is $y = -\frac{3}{4}x + 2.5$.

8. $m = \frac{3}{8}$, y-intercept = 3 (look at the scale if you answered 2.5), and the equation is $y = \frac{3}{8}x + 3$.

Bobcat Review

1. $y = \frac{3}{2}x$, the y-intercept is 0. Note: This is also a direct variation where $k = \frac{3}{2}$.

2. $m = -2$

3. $x = 1$

Bobcat Stretch

1. y-intercept is -10, so the equation of the line is $y = -\frac{4}{5}x - 10$

2. $y = \frac{1}{2}x + 0.5$

5.9 Interpretation of Linear Relationships

Graph a relationship and match simple graphs with situations. Identify if a graph is continuous or discrete.

By the end of this lesson, you should be able to define and give an example of the following vocabulary words:

- **Continuous graph** - graphs that are connected lines or curves.
- **Discrete graph** - a graph with distinct points only (no connections between the points).

Example 1

72 g of ice is heated up in a container. Graph this situation based on a description of each leg segment of the graph below. Classify the graph as continous or discrete.

Segment 1: The ice rises in temperature from -10.0 to 0.00 °C.

Segment 2: The ice melts at 0.00 °C, where the temperature DOES NOT CHANGE for awhile.

Segment 3: Once the ice is totally melted, the temperature begins to rise again and continues to go up until it reaches its normal boiling point of 100.0 °C.

Segment 4: The liquid water then boils at 100.0 °C and the temperature does not change.

Segment 5: Once the water completely changes to steam, the temperature begins to rise again. The steam rises in temperature from 100.0 to 120.0 °C.

Here's the graph that represents what happens to ice as it is heated up in a container.   This represents a continous graph as all the values in between the data points have meaning - the specific temperature at any given point in time.

A continous graph is represented by a line connecting the data points.

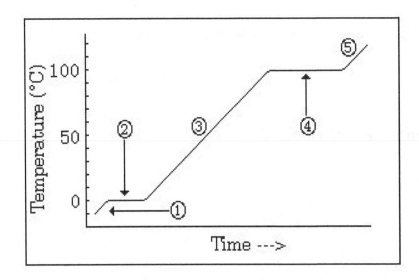

Example 2

Melanie earns $8.50 per hour washing cars, which is represented by the graph below. Classify this graph as continous or discrete. Explain your reasoning.

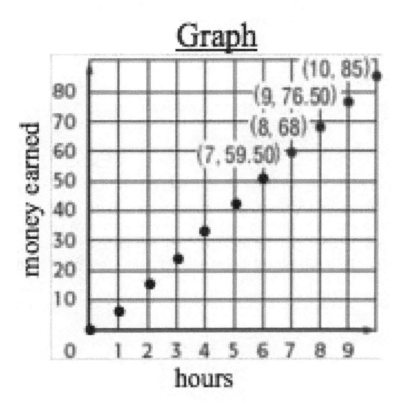

This is a discrete graph as Melanie probably will get paid for 15 minute or 30 minute increments, but not every minute or second that she worked.

In a discrete graph, only certain values work, which is why the data points are not connected by a line.

Tips & Tricks

- Discrete data is counted and can only take certain values.
    - For example, the number of students in a class (you can't have half a student).
    - It does not have any meaning between the data points.
    - The data points are not connected with a line.

- Continuous data can take any value (within a range).
    - For example, time in a race, temperature, a dog's weight, etc...
    - There is meaning between all the data points.
    - Any number makes sense (within the range), so the data points are connected with a line.

- Key word examples commonly used when describing or reading a description of a graph.
    - "Was constant" is represented by a horizontal line on a graph ($m = 0$).
    - "Stayed the same" is also represented by a horizontal line on a graph ($m = 0$).
    - "Rose steadily" is represented by a slanting upward line on a graph (m = positive).
    - "Dropped sharply" is represented by a line that <u>suddenly</u> slants downward on a graph (m = negative).
    - "Rapidly" is representing a steeper line than "steadily" (m = positive).

Practice

1. Choose the graph that best represents each situation.

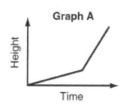 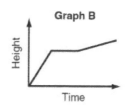 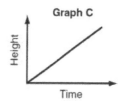

a. A tomato plant grows taller at a steady pace.

b. A tomato plant grows quickly at first, remains a constant height during a dry spell, then grows at a steady pace.

c. A tomato plant grows at a slow pace, then grows rapidly with more sun and water.

2. Don's hair grows steadily longer between haircuts.

a. Sketch a graph to show the length of Don's hair between two haircuts.

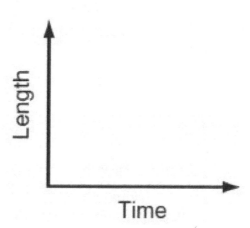

b. Classify this graph as discrete or continuous. Explain your reasoning.

3. True or False. Franklin has a $10 bus card. Each time he rides the bus, $2 is deducted from his card. It makes sense to draw a continuous graph to show how much Franklin has left on his bus card.

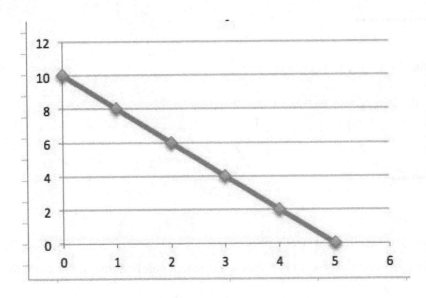

4. Lora has $15 to spend on movie rentals for the week. Each rental costs $3.

   a. Sketch a graph to show how much money she might spend on movies in a week

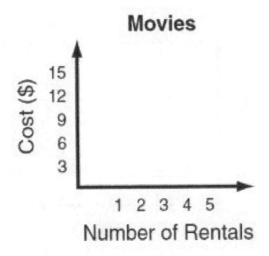

   b. Classify this graph as discrete or continuous. Explain your reasoning.

5. Write a possible situation for each graph below.

a.

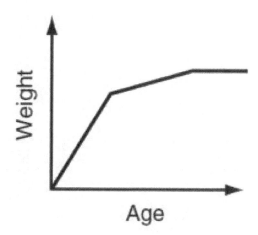

b.

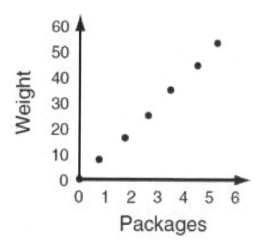

c.

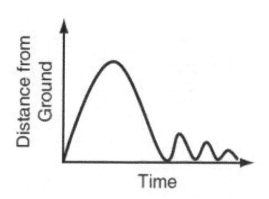

Bobcat Review

1. Determine if each relation is a function or not. Explain your reasoning.

    a. (3, -3), (4, -6), (2, 0), (3, 3)

    b.

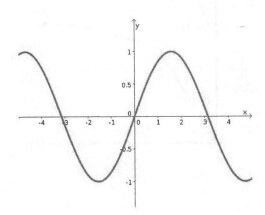

    c.

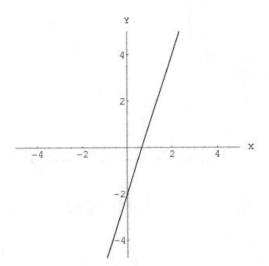

    d.

x	y
1.5	3
0.5	4.5
-0.5	6
0	5.25
1	3.75

Bobcat Stretch

1. Write a possible situation that is modeled by this graph.

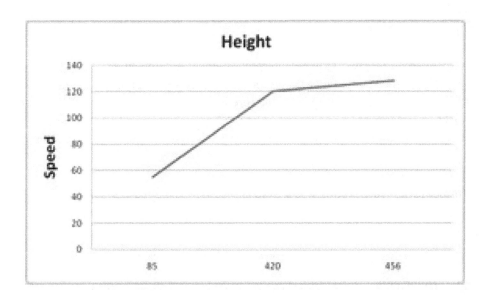

2. The value of a car depreciates at a steep constant rate for 2 years and then holds steady for a year due to a positive consumer report on the same model. Then, there is a shortage of used cars on the market and the value of the car raises slightly at a constant rate for 2 years. Sketch a graph that models this situation.

3. Lamar and his sister are riding a Ferris wheel at a state fair. Using their watches, they find that it takes 8 seconds for the Ferris wheel to make a complete revolution. At the bottom of the Ferris wheel they are 5 ft off the ground and at the top they are 45 ft off the ground. Sketch a graph that models their ride that lasted 40 seconds. Let the x-axis represent "time" (seconds) and the y-axis "Distance above ground" (feet).

Further Review

For more videos and practice problems,

- click here to go to Khan Academy to review interpreting linear relationships.
- click here to go to Khan Academy to review interpreting graphs of linear and nonlinear functions.
- search for "interpreting linear relationships" or "Interpreting graphs of linear and nonlinear functions" on Khan Academy (www.khanacademy.org)
- go to Khan Academy's Common Core page standard 8.F.B.5 (www.khanacademy.org/commoncore/grade-8-F)

Watch this video to further review interpreting linear graphs.

MEDIA
Click image to the left or use the URL below.
URL: https://www.ck12.org/flx/render/embeddedobject/115765

Answers

1. a. Graph C

    b. Graph B

    c. Graph A

2. a. The graph should show a straight line trending upwards (positive slope).

    b. It is a continuous graph showing a straight line.

3. False. A discrete graph should be used as there are no partial bus rides, so the values between the data points do not have meaning in this situation.

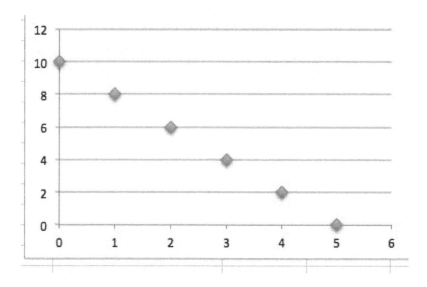

4. a. The graph should show data points trending upwards (positive slope).

   b. It is a discrete graph showing data points since she can't rent half a movie.

5. a. Various answers: A kitten gains weight quickly after birth, then more slowly, until it reaches its maximum weight.

   b. Various answers: Each package weighs 10 pounds. The box can hold up to 60 pounds.

   c. Various answers: An object is thrown up in the air; drops to the ground, and bounces 3 times.

Bobcat Review

1. a. Not a function because there is more than one output per input.

   b. Function because it passes the "vertical line test", which means there is only one output per input.

   c. Function because it passes the "vertical line test", which means there is only one output per input.

   d. Function because there is only one output per input.

Bobcat Stretch

1. a. Various answers: As the height of a roller coaster increases, the roller coaster goes faster. A roller coaster's speed increases at a steady rate as the height of the roller coaster increases from 85 ft to 420 ft tall. Then the speed still increases, but at a slower rate, from a height of 420 ft to 456 ft tall.

2. Various answers as long as the graph decreases, stays the same (horizontal line segment), and increases in the correct order shown below. The axes of the graph should also be labeled correctly.

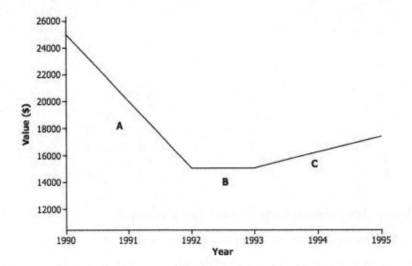

3.

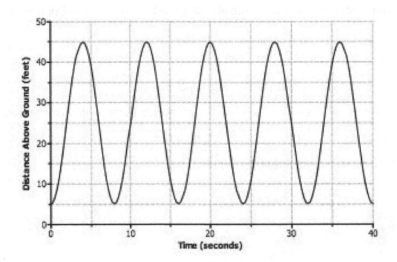

5.10 References

1. . http://www.wtamu.edu/academic/anns/mps/math/mathlab/int_algebra/int_alg_tut12_graph.htm .
2. . http://www.wtamu.edu/academic/anns/mps/math/mathlab/int_algebra/int_alg_tut12_graph.htm .
3. . http://www.wtamu.edu/academic/anns/mps/math/mathlab/int_algebra/int_alg_tut12_graph.htm .
4. . http://mathcentral.uregina.ca/QQ/database/QQ.09.06/alex3.html .
5. . http://madeeasymath.edublogs.org/tag/graph-of-horizontal-line/ .
6. . https://www.mathway.com/problemwidget.aspx?affiliateid=affil18092 .
7. . https://www.mathway.com/problemwidget.aspx?affiliateid=affil18092 .
8. . https://www.mathway.com/problemwidget.aspx?affiliateid=affil18092 .
9. . https://www.mathway.com/problemwidget.aspx?affiliateid=affil18092 .
10. . http://www.wtamu.edu/academic/anns/mps/math/mathlab/beg_algebra/beg_alg_tut22_int.htm .
11. . http://www.post-gazette.com/news/education/2009/09/01/Math-Quiz-Algebra/stories/200909010214 .
12. Stapel, Elizabeth. "The Meaning of Slope and y-Intercept in the Context of Word Problems." Purplemath. Available from http://www.purplemath.com/modules/slopyint.htm. Accessed 11 April 2014. .
13. . http://www.purplemath.com/modules/slopyint.htm .
14. . http://www.purplemath.com/modules/intrcept.htm .
15. . http://doversherborn.comcastbiz.net/highschool/academics/math/baroody/GeometryHonors/Class%20Notes/Chapter%204/Lesson4-6/Lesson4-6.html .
16. . http://www.mathwarehouse.com/algebra/linear_equation/slope-of-a-line.php .
17. . http://www.mathwarehouse.com/algebra/linear_equation/slope-of-a-line.php .
18. . http://www.mathwarehouse.com/algebra/linear_equation/slope-of-a-line.php .
19. . http://www.mathwarehouse.com/algebra/linear_equation/slope-of-a-line.php .
20. . http://doversherborn.comcastbiz.net/highschool/academics/math/baroody/GeometryHonors/Class%20Notes/Chapter%204/Lesson4-6/Lesson4-6.html .
21. . https://sites.google.com/site/geometry4sage20112012/home/resources/star-lessons/coordinate-geometry-ii .
22. . http://www.mathplanet.com/education/algebra-1/visualizing-linear-functions/the-slope-of-a-linear-function .
23. . http://illuminations.nctm.org/Lesson.aspx?id=2570 .
24. . Engage NY Module 4, Lesson 15, p192 .
25. Engage NY, Module 4, Lesson 15, p 194. .
26. Engage NY, Module 4, Lesson 15, p 194. .
27. Engage NY, Module 4, Lesson 17, p 250. .
28. . Engage NY Module 5, Lesson 1, p 10 .
29. . Engage NY Module 5, Lesson 2, p25 .
30. . Engage NY Module 5, Lesson 2, p27 .
31. . Engage NY Moduel 5, Lesson 3, p 34 .
32. . graphs using slope-intercept form (CK-12) .
33. Andrew Gloag Eve Rawley Anne Gloag. CK-12 Applications Using Linear Models .
34. Andrew Gloag Eve Rawley Anne Gloag. CK-12 Applications Using Linear Models .
35. . http://www.chemteam.info/Thermochem/Time-Temperature-Graph.html .
36. . http://www.ssms.scps.k12.fl.us/Portals/104/assets/pdf/Math%208th%20Grade/domain-range,%20discrete-continuous.pdf .
37. . Basic Algebra worksheet Interpretation of Linear Relationships .
38. . Basic Algebra worksheet: Interpretation of linear relations .
39. Graph of sin x by Duane Q. Nykamp is licensed under a Creative Commons Attribution-Noncommercial-ShareAlike 3.0 License. For permissions beyond the scope of this license, please contact us.. http://mathinsig

ht.org/image/graph_sin_x .

40. A line in two dimensions by Duane Q. Nykamp is licensed under a Creative Commons Attribution-Noncommercial-ShareAlike 3.0 License. For permissions beyond the scope of this license, please contact us.. http://mathinsig ht.org/image/line_in_2D .

41. Andrew Gloag Melissa Kramer Anne Gloag. CK-12 Problem Solving with Linear Models .

42. Engage NY, Module 6, Lesson 4 p 45. http://www.engageny.org/sites/default/files/resource/attachments/mat h-g8-m6-teacher-materials.pdf .

43. Engage NY, Module 6, Lesson 5, pg 57. http://www.engageny.org/sites/default/files/resource/attachments/mat h-g8-m6-teacher-materials.pdf .

CHAPTER **6**

Systems of Linear Equations

Chapter Outline

6.1 Solve Systems of Linear Equations by Graphing

Solve and identify solutions of systems of linear equations in two variables by graphing.

By the end of this lesson, you should be able to define and give an example of the following vocabulary words:

- **System of Linear Equations** - A set of two or more linear equations containing two or more varaibles.
- **Solution of a System of Linear Equations** - A solution with two variables in an ordered pair that satisfies each equation in the system.

Example 1

Solve the linear systems.

$$\begin{cases} x+y=-1 \\ -3x-2y=6 \end{cases}$$

Write each equation in slope-intercept form.

$$y=-x-1$$
$$y=-\frac{3}{2}x-3$$

Graph both equations on a coordinate plane.

\

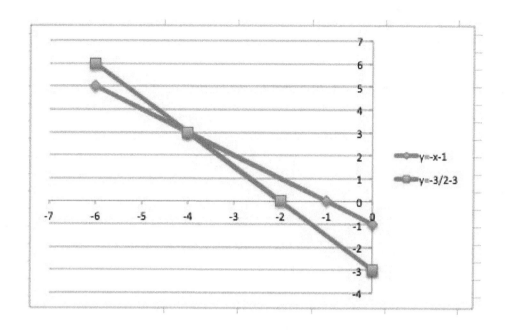

Estimate the point where the two lines intersect, which looks like point (-4, 3) on this graph.

Check your answer by substituting -4 for x and 3 for y in each of the equations.

$$-4 + 3 = -1$$
$$-3(-4) - 2(3) = 6$$

Both these equations are true, so **(-4, 3) is the solution** or intersecting point of this system of linear equations.

Tips & Tricks

- Rearrange equations to slope-intercept form before graphing.

- Sometimes it is difficult to tell exactly where two lines intersect on a graph, so it is a good idea to confirm your answer by substituting it into both equations.

- If an ordered pair is not the solution of the first equation, then there is no need to see if it is a solution of the second equation

Practice

1. Solve the linear system by graphing, then check the solution in both equations.

$$\begin{cases} y = -x + 4 \\ y = x - 2 \end{cases}$$

2. Solve the linear system by graphing, then check the solution in both equations.

$$\begin{cases} -2x + y = 1 \\ y = -x + 4 \end{cases}$$

3. Solve the linear system by graphing, then check the solution in both equations.

$$\begin{cases} y = -3x + 1 \\ 3x - y = -7 \end{cases}$$

4. True or False. This graph shows the solution for this system. Explain.

$$\begin{cases} y = -3x + 5 \\ y = 3x - 5 \end{cases}$$

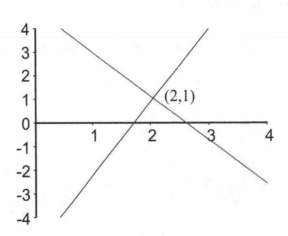

5. Solve the linear system by graphing, then check the solution in both equations.

$$\begin{cases} x = -2 \\ x + y = 4 \end{cases}$$

6. Solve the linear system by graphing, then check the solution in both equations.

$$\begin{cases} x - y = -2 \\ y = \frac{3}{5}x \end{cases}$$

7. Two trains leave the station going in the same direction. One train leaves two hours before the other. The first train's average speed is 65mph while the second train's average speed is 90mph. About how long will it take for the second train to catch up to the first? Estimate the solution by graphing the following linear system that models this situation.

$$\begin{cases} d = 90t \\ d = 65(t + 2) \end{cases}$$

Bobcat Review

1. Gretchen has a texting plan that costs $2.95 per month plus $0.05 per text. Write a function rule that models how much her texting plan costs per month.

2. The sum of two consecutive integers is 15. Write an equation to the model the situation and solve for the two consecutive integers.

3. Solve for x. $5(3 - 2x) = 7(-2x + 1)$

Bobcat Stretch

1. Solve the following system of linear equations graphically, then check your solution

$$\begin{cases} x - 2y - 2 = 0 \\ 3x + 4y = 16 \end{cases}$$

2. Solve the following system of linear equations by graphing, then check your solution.

$$\begin{cases} -3x + 4y = 20 \\ x - 2y = -8 \end{cases}$$

3. Solve the following system of linear equations by graphing, then check your solution.

$$\begin{cases} x + 3y = 4 \\ 5x - y = 4 \end{cases}$$

Further Review

For more practice problems and videos,

- click here to go to Khan Academy.
- search for "Graphing systems of equations" on Khan Academy (www.khanacademy.org).
- go to Khan Academy's Common Core page standard 8.EE.C.8a (www.khanacademy.org/commoncore/grade-8-EE).

Watch this video to further review solving systems graphically.

MEDIA
Click image to the left or use the URL below.
URL: https://www.ck12.org/flx/render/embeddedobject/114739

Answers

1. (3 ,1)

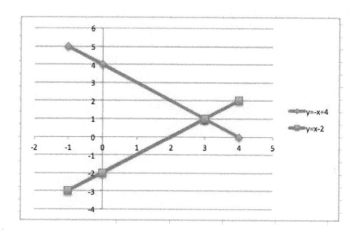

2. (1, 3)

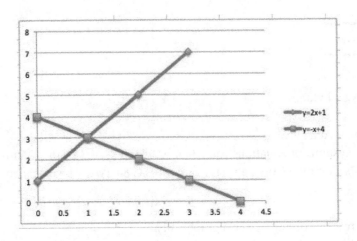

3. (-1, 4)

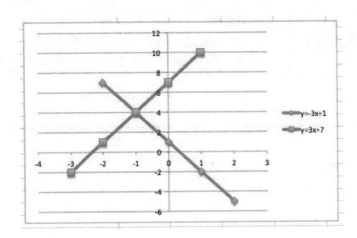

4. False, this graph does not show a solution for the following system. The solution (2, 1) works for the second equation, but not the first equation.

5. (-2, 6)

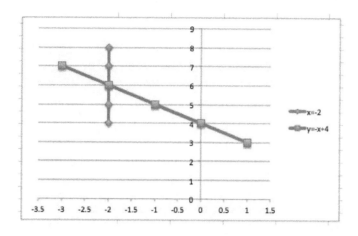

6. (-5, -3)

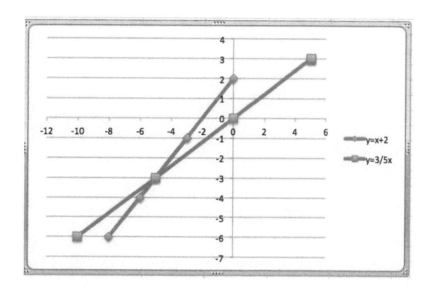

7. The lines intersect at about (5, 450), so the 2nd train will catch the first train about 5 hours later (450 miles down the track). (Note: in later lessons you'll learn how to find a more accurate solution using substitution. The actual solution is (5.2, 468), so the first train will catch the second train 5.2 hours later (468 miles down the track).

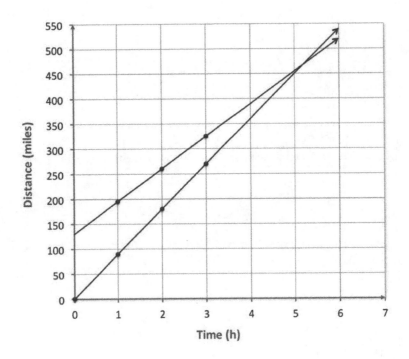

Bobcat Review

1. y = 0.05x + 2.95.

2. n + (n + 1) = 15, n = 7, so the two consecutive integers are 7 and 8.

3. x = -2

Bobcat Stretch

1. (4, 1)

Solution: Begin by writing each linear equation in slope -intercept form.

$$x - 2y - 2 = 0$$
$$x - x - 2y - 2 = 0 - x$$
$$-2y - 2 = -x$$
$$-2y - 2 + 2 = -x + 2$$
$$-2y = -x + 2$$
$$\frac{-2y}{-2} = \frac{-x}{-2} + \frac{2}{-2}$$

$$\boxed{y = \frac{1}{2}x - 1}$$ Equation One

$$3x + 4y = 16$$
$$3x - 3x + 4y = 16 - 3x$$
$$4y = 16 - 3x$$
$$\frac{4y}{4} = \frac{16}{4} - \frac{3x}{4}$$
$$y = 4 - \frac{3}{4}x$$

$$\boxed{y = -\frac{3}{4}x + 4}$$ Equation Two

Graph both equations on the same Cartesian plane.

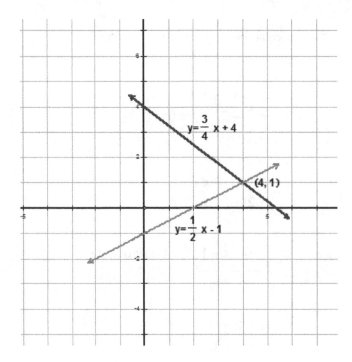

The lines intersect at the point (4, 1). The solution is an ordered pair that should satisfy both of the equations in the system.

Test (4, 1) in equation one:

$$x - 2y - 2 = 0 \qquad \text{Use the original equation}$$
$$(4) - 2(1) - 2 = 0 \qquad \text{Replace } x \text{ with 4 and replace } y \text{ with 1.}$$
$$4 - 2 - 2 = 0 \qquad \text{Perform the indicated operations and simplify the result.}$$
$$4 - 4 = 0$$
$$0 = 0 \qquad \text{Both sides of the equation are equal. The ordered pair } (4, 1) \text{ satisfies the equation.}$$

Test (4, 1) in equation two:

$$3x + 4y = 16 \qquad \text{Use the original equation}$$
$$3(4) + 4(1) = 16 \qquad \text{Replace } x \text{ with 4 and replace } y \text{ with 1.}$$
$$12 + 4 = 16 \qquad \text{Perform the indicated operations and simplify the result.}$$
$$16 = 16 \qquad \text{Both sides of the equation are equal. The ordered pair } (4, 1) \text{ satisfies the equation.}$$

2. (-4, 2)

$$\begin{cases} -3x + 4y = 20 \\ x - 2y = -8 \end{cases}$$

Begin by writing the equations in slope-intercept form.

$$-3x + 4y = 20$$
$$-3x + 3x + 4y = 20 + 3x$$
$$4y = 20 + 3x$$
$$\frac{4y}{4} = \frac{20}{4} + \frac{3x}{4}$$
$$y = 5 + \frac{3}{4}x$$
$$\boxed{y = \frac{3}{4}x + 5}$$

$$x - 2y = -8$$
$$x - x - 2y = -8 - x$$
$$-2y = -8 - x$$
$$\frac{-2y}{-2} = \frac{-8}{-2} - \frac{x}{-2}$$
$$y = 4 + \frac{1}{2}x$$
$$\boxed{y = \frac{1}{2}x + 4}$$

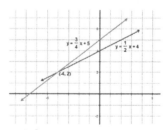

The lines intersect at the point (-4, 2). This ordered pair is the one solution for the system of linear equations.

3. (1, 1)

$$x + 3y = 4$$
$$x - x + 3y = -x + 4$$
$$3y = -x + 4$$
$$\frac{3y}{3} = \frac{-x}{3} + \frac{4}{3}$$
$$\boxed{y = \frac{-1}{3}x + \frac{4}{3}}$$

$$5x - y = 4$$
$$5x - 5x - y = -5x + 4$$
$$-y = -5x + 4$$
$$\frac{-y}{-1} = \frac{-5x}{-1} + \frac{4}{-1}$$
$$\boxed{y = 5x - 4}$$

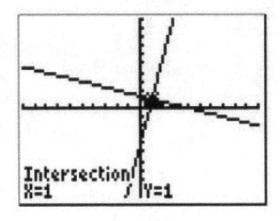

6.2 Solve Systems of Linear Equations by Substitution

Solve systems of linear equations in two variables by substitution.

Example 1

Solve the system of equations by using substitution.

$$\begin{cases} 3y = x - 2 \\ y - x = 4 \end{cases}$$

Rewrite one of the equations in terms of y (or slope-intercept form). In this case, the 2nd equation is easier to rewrite in terms of y.

$$y - x = 4$$

$$y \cancel{- x} = 4$$
$$\underline{\cancel{+ x} = +x} \qquad\qquad \text{Add } x \text{ to both sides of equation.}$$
$$y = 4 + x$$
$$y = x + 4 \qquad\qquad \text{Using the Commutative Property of Addition,}$$
$$\qquad\qquad\qquad\qquad \text{rewrite in Slope Intercept Form.}$$

If y is the same value in both equations and $y = x + 4$, then substitute $x + 4$ in the place of y in the first equation. This is why it's called the *substitution method*.

$$y - x = 4$$

and $\quad 3y = x - 2$ so substitute $3(x + 4) = x - 2$

$$y = \boxed{x + 4}$$

Now that there is only a single variable in the new equivalent equation, it is easy to solve for x.

$$3(x+4) = x-2$$
$$3x+12 = x-2$$
$$2x+12 = -2$$
$$2x = -14$$
$$x = -7$$

If $x = -7$, then substitute -7 for x in the first equation to solve for y.

$$y = x+4$$
$$y = -7+4$$
$$y = -3$$

The solution is (-7, -3).

Check your answer by substituting (-7, -3) in both equations.

$$3(-3) = (-7)-2$$
$$-9 = -9$$

$$-3-(-7) = 4$$
$$4 = 4$$

The solution works for both equations, so it is a solution of this system of equations.

Tips & Tricks

- Remember a system of equations refers to two or more equations at the same time, where the solution will be the ordered pair that works for both equations.
- A system of linear equations can be solved algebraically by the substitution method. In order to use this method, follow these steps:
  1. Solve one of the equations for one of the variables.
  2. Substitute that expression into the remaining equation. The result will be a linear equation, with one variable, that can be solved.
  3. Solve the remaining equation.
  4. Substitute the solution into the other equation to determine the value of the other variable.
  5. The solution to the system is the intersection point of the two equations and it represents the coordinates of the ordered pair.

- When you solve one equation for a variable, you must substitute the value (or expression) of that variable into the other original equation.

Practice

1. Solve the linear system by using substitution.

$$\begin{cases} y = 8 \\ 2y + 2x = 2 \end{cases}$$

2. Solve the linear system by using substitution.

$$\begin{cases} 2y + 8 = 12 \\ y + 2x = 20 \end{cases}$$

3. True or False. The solution for the following linear system is (-6, 15), which is found by substituting $y = 2x + 3$ for y in the second equation and solving for x. Explain your reasoning.

$$\begin{cases} 2x + y = 3 \\ 3x + 2y = 12 \end{cases}$$

4. Solve the linear system by using substitution.

$$\begin{cases} 2x + 3y = 6 \\ -4x + y = 2 \end{cases}$$

5. Solve the linear system by using substitution.

$$\begin{cases} x = 2y \\ x = 3y - 3 \end{cases}$$

6. Jason, who is a real computer whiz, decided to set up his own server and to sell space on his computer so students could have their own web pages on the Internet. He devised two plans. One Plan A charges a base fee of $25.00 plus $0.50 every month. His other plan, Plan B, has a base fee of $5.00 plus $1 per month. How many months will it take Plan B to make as much money as Plan A?

Write a system of equations to model the situation and solve the system of equations using the substitution method.

Bobcat Review

1. Identify if the following functions are linear or nonlinear. Explain your reasoning.

   a. $3x^2 + 2y = 18$

   b. $x + y = -2$

   c. $y = (2x + 4)^2$

   d. $y = \frac{x}{2}$

Bobcat Stretch

1. Solve the system of equations using substitution.

$$\begin{cases} 2y = x + 4 \\ y = 3x \end{cases}$$

2. Solve the system of equations using substitution.

$$\begin{cases} 4e + 2f = -2 \\ 2e - 3f = 1 \end{cases}$$

3. Solve the system of equations using substitution.

$$\begin{cases} x - y = 6 \\ 6x - y = 40 \end{cases}$$

Further Review

For more videos and practice problems,

- click here to go to Khan Academy.
- search for "Systems of equations with substitution" on Khan Academy (www.khanacademy.org).
- go to Khan Academy's Common Core page standard 8.EE.C.8. (www.khanacademy.org/commoncore/grade-8-EE).

Watch this video to further review solving systems of linear equations using substitution.

 **Multimedia**

MEDIA
Click image to the left or use the URL below.
URL: https://www.ck12.org/flx/render/embeddedobject/114743

Answers

1. (-7, 8)

2. (9, 2)

3. False. You must substitute y = -2x + 3 for y in the second equation, not y = 2x + 3.

4. $(0, 2)$

Solve the second equation for y :

$$-4x + y = 2 \qquad \qquad add\ 4x\ to\ both\ sides:$$
$$y = 2 + 4x$$

Substitute this expression into the first equation:

$$2x + 3(2 + 4x) = 6 \qquad distribute\ the\ 3:$$
$$2x + 6 + 12x = 6 \qquad collect\ like\ terms:$$
$$14x + 6 = 6 \qquad subtract\ 6\ from\ both\ sides:$$
$$14x = 0 \qquad and\ hence:$$
$$x = 0$$

Substitute back into our expression for y :

$$y = 2 + 4 \cdot 0 = 2$$

5. $(6, 3)$

6. It will take 40 months for Plan B to catch Plan A. At 40 months, the plans will have generated \$45 each. This is represented by the ordered pair (40, 45), where 40 represents time (x - months) and 45 represents cost (y - dollars).

Both plans deal with the cost of buying space from Jason's server. The cost involves a base fee and a monthly rate. The equations for the plans are:

- Plan A: $y = 0.50x + 25$
- Plan B: $y = 1x + 5$

where 'y' represents the **cost** and 'x' represents the **number of months.** Both equations are equal to 'y'. Therefore, the expression for y can be substituted for the y in the other equation.

$$\begin{cases} y = 0.50x + 25 \\ y = 1x + 5 \end{cases}$$

$$0.50x + 25 = 1x + 5$$
$$0.50x + 25 - 25 = 1x + 5 - 25$$
$$0.50x = 1x - 20$$
$$0.50x - 1x = 1x - 1x - 20$$
$$-0.50x = -20$$
$$\frac{-0.50x}{-0.50} = \frac{-20}{-0.50}$$
$$\frac{\cancel{-0.50}x}{\cancel{-0.50}} = \frac{\cancel{-20}^{40}}{\cancel{-0.50}}$$
$$\boxed{x = 40 \; months}$$

Since the equations were equal, the value for 'x' can be substituted into either of the original equations. The result will be the same.

$$y = 1x + 5$$
$$y = 1(40) + 5$$

$$y = 40 + 5$$
$$\boxed{y = 45 \; dollars}$$
$$\boxed{\text{Plan A} \cap \text{Plan B} @ (40, 45)}.$$

Bobcat Review

1.a. nonlinear - because one of the variables is squared.

  b. linear - All variables are only to the first power.

  c. nonlinear - because one of the variables is squared.

  d. linear - All variables are only to the first power.

Bobcat Stretch

1. $x = \frac{4}{5}, y = \frac{12}{5} = 2\frac{2}{5}$

2. $e = -\frac{1}{4}, f = -\frac{1}{2}$

3. $x = \frac{34}{5} = 6\frac{4}{5} = 6.8, y = \frac{4}{5} = 0.8$

6.3 Solve Systems of Linear Equations by Elimination - Addition

Solve systems of linear equations in two variables by elimination using addition.

Example 1

Solve the system $\begin{cases} 3x + 2y = 11 \\ 5x - 2y = 13 \end{cases}$.

These equations would take much more work to rewrite in slope-intercept form to graph, or to use the Substitution Property. This tells us to try to eliminate a variable.

Write the system so the like terms are aligned and add the equations together.

$$
\begin{array}{r}
3x + 2y = 11 \\
+ (5x - 2y) = 13 \\
\hline
8x + 0y = 24
\end{array}
$$

Looking at the $y-$variable, you can see the coefficients are 2 and -2. By adding these together, you get zero.

The resulting equation is $8x = 24$.

Solving for x, you get $x = 3$. To find the $y-$coordinate, choose *either equation*, and substitute the number 3 for the variable x.

$$
\begin{aligned}
3(3) + 2y &= 11 \\
9 + 2y &= 11 \\
2y &= 2 \\
y &= 1
\end{aligned}
$$

The point of intersection (or solution) of these two equations is (3, 1).

Tips & Tricks

- Use the elimination - addition method when you can easily eliminate one of the variables by adding the equations together (for example, look for variables with opposite coefficients).

Practice

---

1. What is the purpose of the elimination-addition method to solve a system? When is this method appropriate?

2. Solve $\begin{cases} 5x - 3y = -26 \\ x + 3y = 2 \end{cases}$.

3. True or False. The following system of equations should be solved using the elimination - addition method. Explain your reasoning.

$$\begin{cases} 5x - 3y = -14 \\ x - 3y = 2 \end{cases}$$

4. Solve $\begin{cases} 2x + 3y = -27 \\ 8x - 3y = -3 \end{cases}$.

5. Solve the system of equations by using the elimination - substitute method.

$$\begin{cases} 3y - 4x = -33 \\ 5x - 3y = 40.5 \end{cases}$$

6. The sum of two numbers is 361 and the difference between the two numbers is 173.

Write a system of linear equations and solve for the two numbers using the elimination - addition method.

7. Solve the system of equations by using the elimination - addition method.

$$\begin{cases} 3x + 4y = 2.5 \\ 5x - 4y = 25.5 \end{cases}$$

Bobcat Review

1. A botanist watched the growth of a lily. At 3 weeks, the lily was 4 inches tall. Four weeks later, the lily was 20 inches tall. Assuming this relationship is linear:

> a. Write an equation to show the growth pattern of this plant.

> b. How tall was the lily at the 5-week mark?

Bobcat Stretch

1. Andrew is paddling his canoe down a fast-moving river. Paddling downstream he travels at 7 miles per hour, relative to the river bank. Paddling upstream, he moves slower, traveling at 1.5 miles per hour. If he paddles equally hard in both directions, calculate, in miles per hour, the speed of the river and the speed Andrew would travel in still (or calm) water. (Hint: Use x to represent the speed Andrew paddles and y to represent the speed of the river.)

Further Review

For more videos and practice problems,

- click here to go to Khan Academy.
- search for "Systems of equations with simple elimination" on Khan Academy (www.khanacademy.org).
- go to Khan Academy's Common Core page standard 8.EE.C.8 (www.khanacademy.org/commoncore/grade-8-EE)

Watch this video to further review the elimination - addition method.

MEDIA
Click image to the left or use the URL below.
URL: https://www.ck12.org/flx/render/embeddedobject/114747

Answers

1. When the system of equations would take much more work to rewrite in slope-intercept form to graph, or to use the Substitution Property. In this case, see if you can eliminate a variable by adding the equations together to easily solve for one of the variables.

2. (-4, 2)

3. False, there are no variables you can cancel out by addition (5x + x = 6x), (-3y + -3y = -6y).

4. (-3, -7)

5. (7.5, -1)

6. $\begin{cases} x+y = 361 \\ x-y = 173 \end{cases}$ $x = 267, y = 94$

7. (3.5, -2)

Bobcat Review

1. a. y = 4x - 8 (Use points (3, 4) and (7, 20) to calculate the slope to derive the linear equation).

   b. At 5 weeks the lily is 12 inches tall (y = 4 (5) - 8). This would be represented by point (5, 12).

Bobcat Stretch

1. The speed of the river is 2.75 mph. In still water, Andrew would paddle 4.25 mph in all directions.

We have two unknowns to solve for, so we will call the speed that Andrew paddles at x, and the speed of the river y. When traveling downstream, Andrew's speed is boosted by the river current, so his total speed is the canoe speed plus the speed of the river $(x+y)$. Upstream, his speed is hindered by the speed of the river. His speed upstream is $(x-y)$.

$$\begin{aligned} \text{Downstream Equation} && x+y &= 7 \\ \text{Upstream Equation} && x-y &= 1.5 \end{aligned}$$

$$\begin{cases} x+y = 7 \\ x-y = 1.5 \end{cases}$$

Notice y and $-y$ are additive inverses. If you add them together, their sum equals zero. Therefore, by adding the two equations together, the variable y will cancel, leaving you to solve for the remaining variable, x.

$$\begin{aligned} x+y &= 7 \\ + (x-y) &= 1.5 \\ \hline 2x+0y &= 8.5 \\ 2x &= 8.5 \end{aligned}$$

Therefore, $x = 4.25$; Andrew is paddling 4.25 *miles/hour*. To find the speed of the river, substitute your known value into either equation and solve.

$$\begin{aligned} 4.25 - y &= 1.5 \\ -y &= -2.75 \\ y &= 2.75 \end{aligned}$$

The stream's current is moving at a rate of 2.75 *miles/hour*.

6.4 Solve Systems of Linear Equations by Elimination - Subtraction

Solve systems of linear equations in two variables by elimination using subtraction.

Example 1

Solve the system $\begin{cases} 5s + 2t = 6 \\ 9s + 2t = 22 \end{cases}$.

Since these equations are both written in standard form, and both have the term $2t$ in them, use the elimination by subtraction method. This will cause the t terms to cancel out and leave only one variable, s, which will be easy to isolate.

$$5s + 2t = 6$$
$$- \ (9s + 2t = 22)$$
$$\overline{-4s + 0t = -16}$$
$$-4s = -16$$
$$s = 4$$

$$5(4) + 2t = 6$$
$$20 + 2t = 6$$
$$2t = -14$$
$$t = -7$$

The solution is $(4, -7)$.

Tips & Tricks

- The purpose of the **elimination method** to solve a system is to cancel, or eliminate, a variable by either adding or subtracting the two equations. This method works well if both equations are in standard form (Ax + By = C, where A, B, and C are rational numbers).

- Make sure you line up like variables with like variables when adding or subtracting systems of equations.

Practice

1. Solve $\begin{cases} 5x - 3y = -14 \\ x - 3y = 2 \end{cases}$.

2. Solve $\begin{cases} -x - 6y = -18 \\ x - 6y = -6 \end{cases}$.

3. True or False. The following system of equations should be solved by using the elimination - subtraction method. Explain your reasoning.

$$\begin{cases} 3x + 4y = 2.5 \\ 5x - 4y = 25.5 \end{cases}$$

4. Solve the system of equations by using the elimination - subtraction method.

$$\begin{cases} -3y - 4x = -7 \\ 5x - 3y = -25 \end{cases}$$

5. If one apple plus one banana costs $1.25 and one apple plus two bananas costs $2.00, how much does it cost for one banana? One apple? Write and solve a system of equations to answer the questions.

6. Solve the system.

$$\begin{cases} 2x + y = 2 \\ -3x + y = -18 \end{cases}$$

7. Solve the system.

$$\begin{cases} 2x + 3y = 3 \\ -y = -2x + 23 \end{cases}$$

8. Solve the system.

$$\begin{cases} 6x + 3y = -3 \\ 3y = -7x + 1 \end{cases}$$

Bobcat Review

1. The sum of two numbers is 15 and their difference is 3. Find the two numbers.

2. Given $\begin{cases} y = 3x - 5 \\ y = -2x + 5 \end{cases}$,

    a. Solve the system by graphing.

    b. Solve the system by substitution.

Bobcat Stretch

1. Nadia and Peter visit the candy store. Nadia buys three candy bars and four fruit roll-ups for $2.84. Peter also buys three candy bars, but he can afford only one fruit roll-up. His purchase costs $1.79. What is the cost of each candy bar and each fruit roll-up?

2. Paul has a part-time job selling computers at a local electronics store. He earns a fixed hourly wage, but he can earn a bonus by selling warranties for the computers he sells. He works 20 hours per week. In his first week, he sold eight warranties and earned $220. In his second week, he managed to sell 13 warranties and earned $280. What is Paul's hourly rate and how much extra does he get for selling each warranty?

3. A plumber and a builder were employed to fit a new bath, each working a different number of hours. The plumber earns $35 per hour and the builder earns $28 per hour. Together they were paid $330.75, but the plumber earned $106.75 more than the builder. How many hours did each work?

Further Review

For more videos and practice problems,

- click here to go to Khan Academy.
- search for "Systems of equations with elimination" on Khan Academy (www.khanacademy.org).
- go to Khan Academy's Common Core page standard 8.EE.C.8 or 8.EE.C.8b (www.khanacademy.org/commoncore/gr 8-EE).

Watch this video to further review solving systems of equations by elimination.

MEDIA
Click image to the left or use the URL below.
URL: https://www.ck12.org/flx/render/embeddedobject/114865

Answers

1. (-4, -2)

2. (6, 2)

3. False, the elimination - addition method should be used to cancel out the opposite terms.

4. (-2, 5)

5. A banana costs $0.75 and an apple costs $0.50.

Begin by defining the variables of the situation. Let $a =$ *the number of apples* and $b =$ *the number of bananas*. By translating each purchase into an equation, you get the following system:

$$\begin{cases} a+b = 1.25 \\ a+2b = 2.00 \end{cases}$$

.

You could rewrite the first equation and use the Substitution Property here, but because both equations are in standard form, you can also use the elimination method.

Notice that each equation has the value $1a$. If you were to subtract these equations, what would happen?

$$\begin{aligned} a+b &= 1.25 \\ -(a+2b &= 2.00) \\ \hline -b &= -0.75 \\ b &= 0.75 \end{aligned}$$

Therefore, one banana costs $0.75, or 75 cents. By subtracting the two equations, we were able to **eliminate** a variable and solve for the one remaining.

How much is one apple? Use the first equation and the Substitution Property.

$$\begin{aligned} a+0.75 &= 1.25 \\ a &= 0.50 \rightarrow \textit{one apple costs } 50 \textit{ cents} \end{aligned}$$

6. (4, -6)

7. (9, -5)

8. (4, -9)

Bobcat Review

1. (9, 6)

2. a. (2, 1)

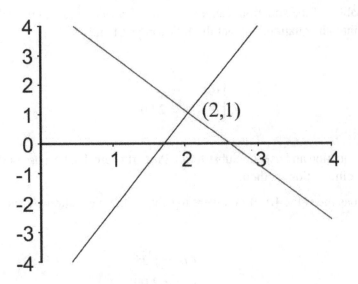

b. (2, 1)

$-2x + 5 = 3x - 5$, $10 = 5x$, $x = 2$.

Bobcat Stretch

1. A candy bar costs $0.48 and the fruit roll-ups costs $0.35.

2. He earned $6.20 an hour and $12 per warranty sold.

3. The plumber worked 6.25 hours and the builder worked 4 hours. Did you catch to use the elimination - addition method on this one?

6.5 Special Systems of Linear Equations

Solve special systems of linear equations in two variables. Classify systems of linear equations and determine the number of solutions.

By the end of this lesson, you should be able to define and give an example of the following vocabulary words:

- **Consistent** - a system of equations with at least one solution.
    - **Independent**- a consistent system with exactly one solution, where the graph shows two lines with different slopes intersecting at only one point.
    - **Dependent** - a consistent system with infinite solutions, where the graph is of the same for both lines (coincident lines with same slope and y-intercept).
- **Inconsistent** - a system of equations that has no solution, where the graph shows two parallel lines that have the same slope, but different y-intercepts.

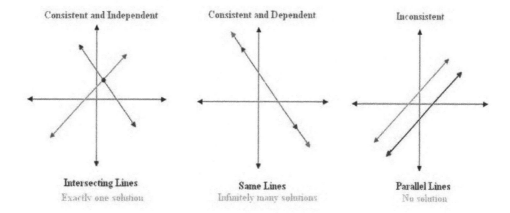

Consistent and Independent	Consistent and Dependent	Inconsistent
Intersecting Lines	**Same Lines**	**Parallel Lines**
Exactly one solution	Infinitely many solutions	No solution

Example 1

Solve the following system of equations. Identify the system as consistent or inconsistent and dependent or independent.

$$\begin{cases} 10x - 3y = 3 \\ 2x + y = 9 \end{cases}$$

Let's solve this system using the substitution method.

Solve the second equation for y :

$$2x + y = 9 \Rightarrow y = -2x + 9$$

Substitute that expression for y in the first equation:

$$10x - 3y = 3$$
$$10x - 3(-2x + 9) = 3$$
$$10x + 6x - 27 = 3$$
$$16x = 30$$
$$x = \frac{30}{16} = \frac{15}{8}$$

Substitute the value of x back into the second equation and solve for y :

$$2x + y = 9 \Rightarrow y = -2x + 9 \Rightarrow y = -2 \cdot \frac{15}{8} + 9 \Rightarrow y = \frac{21}{4}$$

The solution to the system is $\left(\frac{15}{8}, \frac{21}{4} \right)$. The system is consistent and independent since it has only one solution. This means the graph of this system will show 2 lines intersecting at one point , $\left(\frac{15}{8}, \frac{21}{4} \right)$, on the graph (different slope and y-intercept).

Example 2

Solve the following system of equations. Identify the system as consistent or inconsistent and dependent or independent.

$$\begin{cases} y = 3x - 4 \\ 9x - 3y = 1 \end{cases}$$

Substitute the expression for y in the second equation:

$$9x - 3(3x - 4) = 1$$
$$9x - 9x + 12 = 1$$
$$12 \neq 1$$

This is a false statement, so the system is inconsistent because it does not have a solution. This means the graph of this system will show two parallel lines that have the same slope, but different y-intercepts, so they never intersect.

Example 3

Solve the following system of equations. Identify the system as consistent or inconsistent and dependent or independent.

$$\begin{cases} 3x + y = 9 \\ 6x + 2y = 18 \end{cases}$$

Solve the second equation for y:

$$y = -3x + 9$$

Substitute the expression for y in the second equation:

$$6x + 2(-3x + 9) = 18$$
$$6x - 6x + 18 = 18$$
$$18 = 18$$

This is a true statement that is always true, so the system is consistent and dependent. If you look at the equations closer, you see that the second one is twice the first equation, so they both graph the same line (coincidental lines with the same slope and y-intercept).

Tips & Tricks

- A **consistent and independent system** will always give exactly one solution.
    - Graph of intersecting lines that have a different slope and y-intercept, the point where the lines cross is the solution of the system.

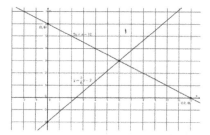

- A **consistent and dependent system** will yield a statement that is *always true* (like $9 = 9$).
    - An infinite number of solutions does not mean that *any* ordered pair (x, y) satisfies the system of equations. Only ordered pairs that solve the equation in the system (either one of the equations) are also solutions to the system. There are infinitely many of these solutions to the system because there are infinitely many points on any one line.
    - Graph of coincidental lines (the same lines) that have the same slope and y-intercept.

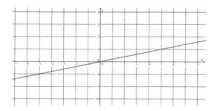

- An **inconsistent system** will yield a statement that is *always false* (like $0 = 13$).
    - Graph of parallel lines that have the same slope, but different y-intercept.

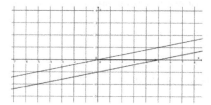

Practice

1. Solve the system $\begin{cases} 3x - 4y = 13 \\ y = -3x - 7 \end{cases}$ using substitution and classify the system as consistent or inconsistent and dependent or independent.

2. Solve the system $\begin{cases} 3x + 2y = 4 \\ -2x + 2y = 24 \end{cases}$ using elimination and classify the system as consistent or inconsistent and dependent or independent.

3. True or False. The following system is a Consistent and Independent system. Explain your reasoning.

$$\begin{cases} 3x - 2y = 4 \\ 9x - 6y = 1 \end{cases}$$

4. Solve the system $\begin{cases} 4x + y = 3 \\ 12x + 3y = 9 \end{cases}$ and classify the system as consistent or inconsistent and dependent or independent.

5. Derek scored 30 points in the basketball game he played and not once did he go to the free throw line, so he only scored a combination of 2-point shots and 3-point shots. If Derek made five more 2-point shots than the number of 3-point shots, then how many of each shot did he make?

  a. Write a system of equations to model this situation.

  b. Solve the system using graphing.

  c. Check the solution algebraically.

  d. Classify if the solution is Consistent or Inconsistent and Independent or Dependent.

6. Solve the system $\begin{cases} 4x - 5y = 20 \\ y = \frac{4}{5}x - 2 \end{cases}$ and classify the system as consistent or inconsistent and dependent or independent.

7. Answer each question true or false about graphs & solutions of linear systems. Explain your reasoning.

    a. Parallel lines have the same slope.

    b. Some linear systems do not have a solution.

    c. Parallel lines have infinite solutions.

    d. Perpendicular lines have one solution.

    e. Lines with an infinite number of solutions are not coincidental.

8. Given $\begin{cases} y = \frac{1}{8}x - 3 \\ y = \frac{1}{8}x + \frac{3}{4} \end{cases}$, classify the system as consistent or inconsistent and dependent or independent without solving (just by inspecting the two equations). Explain your reasoning.

9. Given $\begin{cases} -y = x \\ -9y = 9x \end{cases}$, classify the system as consistent or inconsistent and dependent or independent without solving (just by inspecting the two equations). Explain your reasoning.

Bobcat Review

1. A movie theater charges $4.50 for children and $8.00 for adults.

    a. On a certain day, 1200 people enter the theater and $8375 is collected. How many children and how many adults attended?

    b. At the same theater, a 16-ounce soda costs $3 and a 32-ounce soda costs $5. If the theater sells 12,480 ounces of soda for $2100, how many people bought soda? (**Note:** Be careful in setting up this problem!)

Bobcat Stretch

1. Write you own system that meets the following requirements.

    a. Write a system which is consistent and independent.

    b. Write a system which is consistent and dependent.

    c. Write a system which is inconsistent.

    d. Write a system where the solution is (-1, 2), one line is vertical or horizontal and the second is neither.

2. Sandy and Charlie walk at constant speeds. Given the following data, answer the following questions.

Number of Minutes (x)	Miles Walked (y)
0	0
5	1
10	2
15	3
20	4
25	5

Number of Minutes (x)	Miles Walked (y)
0	$\dfrac{8}{15}$
5	$\dfrac{18}{15} = 1\dfrac{3}{15} = 1\dfrac{1}{5}$
10	$\dfrac{28}{15} = 1\dfrac{13}{15}$
15	$\dfrac{38}{15} = 2\dfrac{8}{15}$
20	$\dfrac{48}{15} = 3\dfrac{3}{15} = 3\dfrac{1}{5}$
25	$\dfrac{58}{15} = 3\dfrac{13}{15}$

    a. Sandy walked 1 miles in 5 minutes and Charlie walked $3\frac{1}{5}$ miles in 20 minutes. Identify the table of values that represents Sally's walks? Charlie's walks?

    b. Write the system of equations tha models this data.

    c. Sandy walks from their school to home in 15 minutes and Charlie walks the same distance in 10 minutes. Charlie starts 4 minutes after Sandy left the school. Can Charlie catch up to Sandy before she gets home? The distance between the school and the station is 2 miles. Use a graph to explain your reasoning.

3. Solve $\begin{cases} 0.05x + 0.25y = 6 \\ x + y = 24 \end{cases}$, classify the system as consistent or inconsistent and dependent or independent.
Explain your reasoning.

Further Review

For more videos and practice problems,

- click here to go to Khan Academy.
- search for "Solutions to systems of equations" on Khan Academy (www.khanacademy.org).

Watch this video to further review solutions to linear equations with one variable.

 **Multimedia**

MEDIA
Click image to the left or use the URL below.
URL: https://www.ck12.org/flx/render/embeddedobject/115026

Answers

1. (-1, -4), the system is a consistent and independent system because it has only one solution.

2. (-4, 8), the system is a consistent and independent system because it has only one solution.

3. False, it is a inconsistent system because it has no solution, which is represented by parallel lines (same slope, different y-intercepts). $y = \frac{3}{2}x - 2$ and $y = \frac{3}{2}x - \frac{1}{6}$

4. $9 = 9$, so the system is consistent and dependent because it is always true.

Solve the first equation for y :

$$4x + y = 3 \Rightarrow y = -4x + 3$$

Substitute this expression for y in the second equation:

$$12x + 3y = 9$$
$$12x + 3(-4x + 3) = 9$$
$$12x - 12x + 9 = 9$$
$$9 = 9$$

This statement is always true. A second glance at the system in this example reveals that the second equation is three times the first equation, so the two lines are identical. The system has an infinite number of solutions because they are really the same equation and trace out the same line.

For example, (1, -1) is a solution to the system in this example, and so is (-1, 7). Each of them fits both the equations because both equations are really the same equation. But (3, 5) doesn't fit either equation and is not a solution to the system.

In fact, for every $x-$ value there is just one $y-$ value that fits both equations, and for every $y-$value there is exactly one $x-$ value—just as there is for a single line.

5. a. x = # of 2 point shots, y = # of 3 points shots

$$\begin{cases} 2x + 3y = 30 \\ x = 5 + y \end{cases}$$

b. The lines intersect at point (9, 4), which is the solution. Derek made nine 2-pointers and four 3-pointers for a total of 30 points.

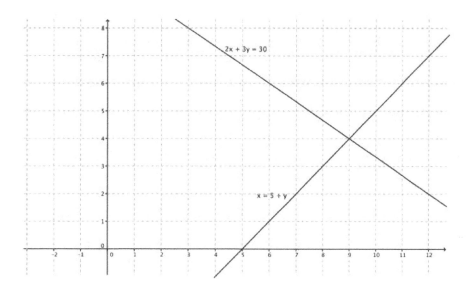

c.

$$2(9) + 3(4) = 30$$
$$18 + 12 = 30$$
$$30 = 30$$
$$9 = 4 + 5$$
$$9 = 9$$

d. Since this system has only one solution, then it is a Consistent and Independent system.

6. $10 \neq 20$, so the system is inconsistent since it doesn't have a solution. This means the graph of the system shows 2 parallel lines that have the same slope, but different y-intercept.

7. a. True

b. True

c. False - they have no solutions.

d. True

e. False

8. The system is inconsistent since both equations have the same slope $\frac{1}{8}$, but different y-intercepts -3 and $\frac{3}{4}$. The lines are parallel, so they will never intersect.

9. There are infinitely many solutions as these equations have the same graph, so the system is consistent and dependent.

Bobcat Review

1. a. (850, 350), so 850 adult tickets were sold and 350 children tickets were sold. $\begin{cases} 4.50x + 8y = 8375 \\ x + y = 1200 \end{cases}$, where x = child tickets and y = adult tickets.

   b. 300 16-oz sodas were sold and 240 32-oz sodas were sold. $\begin{cases} 16x + 32y = 12480 \\ 3x + 5y = 2100 \end{cases}$, where x = # of 16 oz sodas sold and y = # of 32 oz sodas sold.

Bobcat Stretch

1. Good Luck! An infinite amount of answers are acceptable as long as they meet the requirements. Hint - look at the systems that meet the requirements in the examples above to help you write your own system.

2. a. Sandy's walk is represented by the first table and Charlie's is represented by the second.

   b. Sandy = $y = \frac{1}{5}x$ and Charlie = $y = \frac{2}{15}x + \frac{8}{15}$, so the system is $\begin{cases} y = \frac{1}{5}x \\ y = \frac{2}{15}x + \frac{8}{15} \end{cases}$

   c. It looks like the lines intersection at a point between 1.5 and 2 miles; therefore, the answer is yes, Charlie can catch up to Sandy. (10, 1.8)

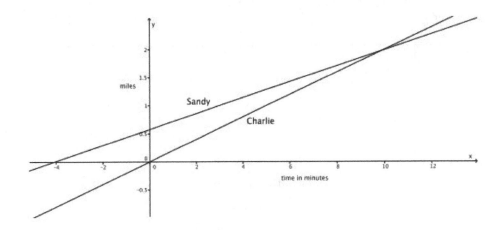

3. (0, 24), so the system is consistent and independent since there is only one solution.

6.6 References

1. . CK-12 Solving Linear Systems by Graphing .
2. Jen Krenshaw. CK-12 Graphing Linear Equations .
3. Jen Krenshaw. CK-12 Graphs of Linear Systems .
4. . CK-12 Graphs of Linear Systems .
5. Jen Krenshaw. CK-12 Graphing Linear Solutions .
6. . CK-12 Graphs of a Linear System .
7. . CK-12 Graphs of Linear Equations .
8. Brenda Meery and Kaitlyn Spong. CK-12 Substitution Method for Systems of Equations .
9. Jen Krenshaw. Solving Linear Systems by Substitution CK-12 .
10. Andrew Gloag Melissa Kramer Anne Gloag . CK-12 Linear Systems with Addition or Subtraction .
11. Andrew Gloag, Melissa Kramer, Anne Gloag. CK-12 Linear Systems with Addition or Subtraction .
12. Lori Jordan, Kate Dirga. CK-12 Linear systems with addition or subtraction .
13. Andrew Gloag Eve Rawley Anne Gloag. Graphs of Linear Equations CK-12 .
14. . Engage NY Module 4, Lesson 25, pg 38 .
15. . Engage NY Module 4, Lesson 24, p365 .
16. . Engage NY Module 4, Lesson 24, p364 .
17. . Engage NY Module 4, Lesson 24, p362 .
18. Andrew Gloag Eve Rawley Anne Gloag. CK-12 Applications of Linear Systems .
19. . Engage NY Module 4, Lesson 24, p367 .
20. . Engage NY Module 4, Lesson 24, p363 .